Virgil and *The Tempest*

Virgil and *The Tempest*

THE POLITICS OF IMITATION

Donna B. Hamilton

Ohio State University Press
COLUMBUS

An earlier version of "Imitation and *The Tempest*" appeared in *Style* 23, no. 3 (Fall 1989). Used by permission.

Copyright © 1990 by the Ohio State University Press.

All rights reserved.

Library of Congress Cataloging-in-Publication Data

Hamilton, Donna B.
  Virgil and *The Tempest* : the politics of imitation / Donna B. Hamilton.
    p. cm.
  Includes bibliographical references.
  ISBN: 978-0-8142-5322-9
  1. Shakespeare, William, 1564–1616. Tempest. 2. Shakespeare, William, 1564–1616—Political and social views. 3. English drama—Roman influences. 4. Virgil—Influence—Shakespeare. 5. Imitation (in literature) 6. Politics in literature. 7. Virgil. Aeneis. I. Title.
PR2833.H34   1990
822.3′3—dc20   89-77752
                                                              CIP

∞ The paper in this book meets the guidelines
for permanence and durability of the Committee
on Production Guidelines for Book Longevity
of the Council on Library Resources.

9 8 7 6 5 4 3 2 1

For Gary

CONTENTS

PREFACE ix

ACKNOWLEDGMENTS xv

NOTE ON TEXTS AND EDITIONS xvi

Introduction 3

Part 1
Imitation and Occasion

Imitation and *The Tempest* 11

Occasion and *The Tempest* 32

Part 2
The Tempest as Masque and Romance

Three Spectacles 67

The Education of Ferdinand and the Dialectic of Bondage and Freedom 92

Part 3
Prospero and the Best State of the Commonwealth

The Virgilian Patterns in Prospero 106

Occasional Patterns in Ariel and Caliban 110

The Giving of Mercy and the Suspension of Power 122

Discasement and Reunion 129

Epilogue   133

ABBREVIATIONS USED IN NOTES   139

NOTES   141

INDEX   179

PREFACE

IN *THE TEMPEST*, Shakespeare situates his writing between two authorities, the poet Virgil and the monarch James I, each the possessor of a set of symbols and idioms that Shakespeare reappropriates for himself. In the process, he pays homage to their respective eminences and, at the same time, brings them into dialogic relation with each other, changing their language to suit his own purposes. In the case of Virgil, this means rewriting the *Aeneid* to suit a new time, a new situation; in the case of James, it means repeating the king's language about rule in a manner which also changes that language.

It is well to keep in mind from the outset that the use of Virgilian idioms in the national literature and for the language of national politics was, in Shakespeare's time, a thoroughly naturalized practice. In one of his glosses in *The Haddington Masque*, Ben Jonson wrote that "*Aeneas*, the sonne of *Venus*, *Virgil* makes through-out the most exquisit patterne of *Pietie, Justice, Prudence*, and all other Princely vertues, with whom (in way of that excellence) I conferre my Soveraigne."[1] A few years earlier, Jonson had also presented James as the new Augustus in the triumphal arches that he designed for the coronation procession, a presentation that displayed the king as a peacebringer, unifier, providential ruler, and renewer of golden times.[2]

The Virgilian idiom was used to dignify, but also to evaluate, any number of national projects. When William Strachey, writing in *A True Reportory of the Wrack* (dated July 15, 1610), described the first voyage of Captain Newport down the James River toward the Virginia coast, he glorified the venture by comparing Newport's arrival to that of Aeneas in Italy: "At length, after much and weary search (with their Barge coasting still before, as Virgill writeth Aeneas did, arriving in the region of Italy called Latium, upon the banks of the River Tyber) in the Country of a Werowance . . .

within the faire River of Paspiheigh, which wee have called the Kings River . . . they had sight of an extended plaine." On that site, "half an Acre, or so much as Queene Dido might buy of King Hyarbas," they raised their fortress and called it "in honour of his Majesties name, James Towne."[3] Likewise, Sir John Davies, writing home in the same year to celebrate the progress of plantation in Ireland, quoted the lines from the *Aeneid* that describe the building of the walls of Carthage.[4] But in contrast, Roger Owen, also writing in 1610, used the classical precedent to express the fear that they might be reliving a part of the story which it was not necessary or wise to repeat. Concerned over the growing dissension and bitterness of the debates in the House of Commons, he framed his objections by remarking that what they were quarreling over "is not worth the destruction of Troy."[5] Clearly, the language of Virgil was found readily appropriable for any number of contemporary political issues and perspectives.

Shakespeare's reappropriation of this discourse in *The Tempest* is so inclusive, however, as to warrant our describing it as complete repossession; for in the play, he reworks the chiefly contested issues of national politics by rewriting some major sections of the *Aeneid*. Such an act of writing, with all its implications, might be approached as a manifestation of Kenneth Burke's idea that "the organization of a work can be considered with relation to a 'key' symbol of authority." According to Burke, "The work is a ritual whereby the poet takes inventory with reference to the acceptance or rejection of this authority."[6] Yet, in *The Tempest*, where the authority is bipolar—Virgil and James—the writing involves a simultaneous response to both an ancient poetic text and a contemporary political context, and thus also demonstrates a command of both sets of authoritative symbols.

In the following pages, I shall argue that Shakespeare's involvement in the Virgilian idiom surpasses that of allusion and echo, and that his investment in Virgil's text is so great as to constitute a formal and rigorous rhetorical imitation of the major narrative kernels of *Aeneid* 1–6. Moreover, Shakespeare's management of the Virgilian idiom is matched by an equally thorough encompassment of the contemporary discourse about monarchy—a discourse that, especially in 1610, took the form of debate as king and Parliament argued about the limits of royal power, and thus the respective merits of absolutism and constitutionalism. Shakespeare, then, is involved both in demonstrating his mastery of the master poetic discourse and in responding to the master discourses of high politics.

Part 1 of this book deals, respectively, with the means by which the discourses at issue have a presence in the play. First, I outline a theory of rhetorical imitation that incorporates the prescribed Renaissance methods for rewriting a single precursor text. This section shows why *imitatio* is more descriptive of Shakespeare's craftsmanship than saying that the *Aeneid* is his "source," and it explains some of the various systems by which the play imitates the *Aeneid*. I assume that my claim about how deeply indebted *The Tempest* is to the *Aeneid* both requires and justifies an extended description and discussion of imitation theory. Second, I consider three contemporary political issues—the situation of the royal children, the 1610 parliamentary debates on the royal prerogative, and the colonization projects in Virginia and Ireland—and how they might be said to have some bearing on the play. Although all three are important, I argue for the centrality of the debates on the royal prerogative, which grew out of James's request for a financial settlement and focused on the issues of how much power a king should have, when his power might be said to have become unreasonable and transcendent, and when it could be described as having become so great that its effect was to reduce his subjects to slaves.

I argue that, in the rehandling of these discourses, Shakespeare constructed an argument for constitutionalism, the ideology most directly in competition with absolutism. His rhetorical strategies involve representing the importance of the monarch's godlike and fatherlike roles, along with representations of the "necessary" powers of the monarch; but these validations are accompanied by equally strong ones of the constitutional principles of consent and reciprocity. Although the latter, in relation to the king's position, comprise an oppositional stance, Shakespeare casts the argument in epideictic form, a choice consonant with the use of Virgil and also with the idiom of the contemporary masque. The result is an incorporation of the most highly regarded traditions and forms of praise into a play that offers instruction and advocates a course of action consistent with what James's critics wanted the king to do. In other words, the play presents the constitutionalist argument in a comely manner that is, in itself, an exemplary illustration of how to argue with the king without accusing him or otherwise diminishing his dignity.

Part 2 offers a detailed discussion of Shakespeare's rewriting of the *Aeneid* as that project is represented in the play's three scenes of spectacle—the harpy banquet scene, the betrothal masque, and the glistering apparel episode—and in the part of Ferdinand from 1.2 to 5.1. A great deal of attention is paid here to *what* in Virgil is now *where* in *The Tempest*, but generalizations about the direction in which Shakespeare is transforming Virgil are also central to the discussion. My main point is that in many cases the rewriting of the Virgilian text (often the reversal of it) results in a presentation of the heroic that praises reciprocity, along with discipline, austerity, retrenchment, and limit. The play demonstrates the value of limit by displaying royal figures—a duke, a king, a son—in a variety of circumstances whereby they subject themselves to discipline, regret that they once usurped power, and decide to relinquish it. The play also retells the story of Dido and Aeneas through the story of Ferdinand and Miranda, a version of the ancient story in which lust is replaced by a disciplined and reciprocating love relationship.

Part 3 concentrates on Prospero, on the combination of Virgilian patterns that Shakespeare used in constructing this character, and on the issues and language of the political debates of 1610, which Prospero, especially in his relations with Ariel and Caliban, replicates. In Prospero's displays of magic—now punishing the wicked, now threatening the faithful—exist symbolic representations of how power can manifest itself. These scenes suggest how much good a great power can accomplish, but also the circumstances under which a powerful figure may choose to diminish his power. Shakespeare presents this last idea by using a "bridging device," that is, a "symbolic structure whereby one 'transcends' a conflict in one way or another."⁷ By writing so that his own relinquishment of his life in the theater can serve as an available parallel, and by having directly claimed and defined his own authority all through the play by his partnership with Virgil, at the end of the play Shakespeare is in a position to offer a representation of what the king's response on this issue should be: he, too, should give up some of his magic.

Many books have been and could be written about *The Tempest*. The one I have chosen to write is not about Shakespeare and a literary tradition—Virgilian, romance, or any other. Rather, this book is deeply committed to the practice of historicizing the literary text and constructing "specific and localized contexts"⁸ that can suggest the rhetorical situation within which that text was produced. I assume that to pursue such a methodology expands the possibilities for describing *The Tempest*, as well as for circumventing some of the limits that seeing it as a transcendent, universal work impose upon it. This commitment to a historical method also entails treating the *Aeneid* as a "warehouse of society's resources and tools"⁹—that is, it entails understanding the *Aeneid* as a text that many writers and speakers in Shakespeare's time found useful, and for different purposes. Be this as it may, I also assume that Shakespeare was interested in defining and securing his place as an artist in his society. Thus, while this book considers the *politics* of imitation, it also takes into account (even relishes) the *craft* of imitation, by attending closely to the details of both Shakespeare's text and Virgil's. Finally, I assume throughout that Shakespeare's own politics here, as elsewhere, involved a response to the conflicts among the dominant ideologies of his time, that he frequently took positions in relationship to those conflicts, and that his plays can be seen as participatory events in their historical present.

ACKNOWLEDGMENTS

THIS PROJECT LEAVES ME in the debt of many people, but of three in particular who gave me more information, correction, patience, and friendship than I could have hoped for; they are Marion Trousdale, Gary Hamilton, and Annabel Patterson. Members of the staff at the Folger Shakespeare Library were always helpful. Jeanne Fahnestock made a valuable contribution late in the day; and Leah Marcus, Maynard Mack, Jr., and Leopold Damrosch, Jr., at earlier stages. Manju Suri and the office staff in the English department at the University of Maryland gave expert and generous assistance on numerous occasions. Peter Givler and Alex Holzman of the Ohio State University Press were scrupulous editors. Theresa Coletti, Marie Ferington, and Anita Virkus were the finest of personal friends.

For the pleasure they have shown in seeing this project come to completion, I thank especially my mother, Ellen Bechtel, my sister, Alice Ann Gordon, my son, Nathan Hamilton, and my daughter, Nicole Hamilton.

TEXTS AND EDITIONS

References to *The Tempest* are to Frank Kermode, ed., *The Tempest*, Arden Shakespeare (London: Methuen, 1954). References to the *Aeneid* are to Virgil, *Works*, trans. H. Rushton Fairclough, rev. ed. (London: W. Heinemann, 1940).

Virgil
and
*The
Tempest*

INTRODUCTION

THE TEMPEST IS ONE of three plays by Shakespeare (the others being *Love's Labour's Lost* and *A Midsummer Night's Dream*) for which it is generally agreed that information about "sources" is lacking. In the case of *The Tempest*, as well as the other plays, there is no known text with a narrative line that compellingly matches the plot constructed by Shakespeare. Nevertheless, over the years a growing consensus has arisen that there are significant and undeniable links between the *Aeneid* and *The Tempest*, even that the *Aeneid* had an important defining effect on the composition of the play. Attempts to describe that effect, however, have remained problematic.

How inconclusive have been the efforts to draw parallels between the narrative lines of these two works is best illustrated by some examples. J. M. Nosworthy concluded that Shakespeare's plot takes its direction from the storm–shipwreck–new love sequence in the *Aeneid*, but only for the first two scenes. Jan Kott, on the other hand, argued that the play follows the pattern of the Dido and Aeneas narrative until midway through act 4. And Colin Still saw the entire play as relying on the *Aeneid*; but rather than considering the Dido and Aeneas love story the chief shaping influence, he gave precedence to Aeneas's journey to the Underworld. Put another way, Nosworthy and Kott found that *Aeneid* 1–4 are crucial (through to differing degrees); Still, that *Aeneid* 6 is crucial.[1] It is hard to imagine such divergence as this in any traditional source study. Having lost, by general consensus, the option of considering the two works as only casually related, we are left to conclude that, for this play at least, the method by which we assess the impact of a precursor text on a Shakespeare play needs revision. We need a method that can accommodate the repetitions, analogies, allusions, citations, and echoes that Nosworthy, Kott, Still, Gary Schmidgall, John Pitcher, Barbara Bono, Robert Miola, Robert Wiltenburg, Peter Hulme, Stephen Orgel, and others have found or emphasized,[2] as well as the seeming contradictions in their various conclusions.

I shall argue that we can use what we know about the theory and practice of rhetorical imitation (*imitatio*) to reconsider the question of the relatedness of these two works.[3] This study pursues that relationship by considering *The Tempest* as a work that is a formal imitation of the first six books of the *Aeneid*, both in its larger patterns of theme and structure and in its smaller details of vocabulary and syntax. Many steps must be taken before one can feel comfortable either posing or granting that such a strong and deep connection exists between these two texts, and not everyone will be persuaded of the kind of genealogical link I am proposing; so much depends, not merely on noticing the connections that are easy to see, but also on finding that, in Shakespeare's play, the *Aeneid* has been dismantled, reversed, and rewritten. The fundamental obstacle to pursuing such a notion, therefore, is not simply the expectation that a narrative link will be relatively obvious (as Shakespeare's use of Sidney in *King Lear* is obvious), but involves the nature of imitation itself. For imitation, a method of composition taught in grammar school, was a practice founded on methods for changing (that is, for disassembling, rearranging, and redistributing) the precursor text, as well as for concealing those changes; it is a common rule in treatises on imitation that what the imitator is doing should not be made too evident.

Among the various conditions which can make recognition possible is simply the patience for "quiet meditation" that Petrarch said was necessary if one was to discover the deep similarities between texts that imitation produces.[4] Another condition, one easier to come by, is sufficient understanding of the methods used in imitation. A reader who would recognize an act of imitation must understand the existing possibilities whereby a precursor text can make a reappearance in a new text. For without that understanding, often the codes that make recognition possible cannot even be seen. When that understanding is available, however, one can reach the point where it is possible to find, in the very act of concealing, the systems that promote revealing.

In "The Life of Ariosto" that Sir John Harington included in his translation of *Orlando furioso*, he remarked that Ariosto privileged Boiardo for imitation because Boiardo was so familiar at the time: "he chose *Boyardo* upon whose work he would ground . . . because he said *Boyardos* worke was fresh in everie mans minde."[5] One implication here is, as Michael Riffaterre might express it, that the text "is constructed in such a way that it can control its own decoding,"[6] and that the author who uses a very familiar system (as indeed the *Aeneid* also was very familiar), even when his use of it is extraordinarily clever and obscure, offers his audience or reader the opportunity to see that from which the text has been made. Here, as everywhere, the fact that something is hidden does not mean that it is lost. The issue is one that Riffaterre addresses in formulating his theories of text production. For him, the concealment that occurs in a literary work often exists as a means of calling attention to the genetics of a text and therefore to its artistic ideas. I would suggest that we may be able to say of *The Tempest* what he says about some of the French texts he has studied: it is a work that "conceals only in order to reveal," and it "veils" its art, "but it also points to where it is hidden and how it can be revealed."[7]

This study is concerned with the conditions under which the play text was produced, that is, written. So far these conditions have been identified as including the procedures for imitative writing and also the choice of Virgil's text as the material for this particular imitative act. But another point to consider is the question of belatedness, of writing "after" another.[8] While this issue can be expressed in the distinctly Bloomian form of focusing on the need of the poetic "son" for self-authentication, it can also be taken in another direction, as Thomas Greene does in his study of imitative texts. For Greene, consideration of the issue of belatedness takes the form of speculating on how the poet perceived the relationship between the historicity of the precursor text and his own historical moment.

In Greene's formulation of the problem, the imitative writer's "dialogue with the past" always risked being incomplete by virtue of the "historical breaches" that ultimately could not be mended.[9] But one of the results of having so to contend with the past was that the imitator developed a more acute sense of the concrete moment in which he himself was writing, a sense that, in turn, also "shook [the] absolute status" of the precursor text "by calling attention to the specific circumstances of its production." "The radicality," Greene continues, "is present a fortiori in the humanist imagination which asserts a limited but shaping power of the imagination over the passage of history."[10]

Greene's attention to the historical is consistent with the assumption that a text made over for another time cannot, by definition, be an ahistorical, disinterested, freestanding aesthetic production; it cannot be a culturally innocent text. In addition to the impossibility of a writer ever transcending the cultural and ideological *mentalité* in which he has been constructed, this point about historicity also involves other issues, including that of the responsiveness or "addressivity"[11] of all writing. Even as we say that all writing is intertextual and "utterance is filled with *dialogic overtones*,"[12] we can also add that in all writing, the writer or speaker is involved in an act of communication which requires him to formulate a concept of his audience.[13] In the case of imitative writing, where the writing will partly be a response to a precursor text, the characteristics of that response will be affected by the interests and characteristics of the audience to whom the writer now speaks.[14] They will also be affected by the position or set of positions—in relation to the precursor and to the audience and their stances on various issues—which the poet wishes to take.

In the process, it can be assumed that what the imitative poet selects from and responds to in the precursor will always relate to the values of the society in which he himself lives, but also that his recasting of the precursor will be governed by and supportive of his own ideological position, whether that position is supportive of the dominant ideology or critical of it. The transforming of old art for a new time thus becomes an act of ideological intervention. And the production of a new text modeled on an old one exists, in itself, as a historical event.[15]

What form this intervention will take depends to a large extent on the genre that is being imitated as well as the genre in which the new work is cast. In the cases of epic, of Renaissance imitations of Virgil, and of other forms of heroic poetry, the specific form of writing is epideictic,[16] a discourse of praise that involves articulation of a society's commonly held values. But while epideictic does indeed praise, it also always presents itself as praise even when the object of the writing includes significant evaluative and interventionist strategies.

During the reign of James I, the epideictic function was performed on a regular basis by the court masque,[17] a genre richly constructed from classical materials. The occasional nature of the masque, along with its epideictic rhetorical stance, provided a means not only for approving but also for criticizing the court,[18] and not only by way of the antimasque. For example, in *Oberon*, performed on January 1, 1611, Ben Jonson produced a masque that would praise, even flatter, Prince Henry and the entire Jacobean court. But instead of using as the vehicle for this praise Henry's preferred form of representation as a warrior and conqueror, Jonson presented the prince in *Oberon* as a figure of love. In assigning Henry this role, a part which Henry himself danced, Jonson privileged a value different from those represented by war and conquest and thus offered the prince an alternative to the policies and interests that he had favored.[19]

In this example, as elsewhere, what presented itself as praise could also possess the force of correction, even reprimand. Thus the range and method of epideictic are very broad, and remain so even when the rhetorical stance is strictly that of praise with no shifting to epideictic's alternative, blame. For a later reader to gain access to what the further implications of any such praise might have been, it is necessary to have some knowledge of the rhetorical situation[20] to which the writing was a response.

Only when that knowledge is available can one be aware of the element of persuasion and argument in epideictic. Praise functions as encouragement and support for politics already undertaken or as an argument for the alternatives. When Jonson compared James to Augustus in the triumphal arches that he designed for the occasion of James's coronation, he was supporting the image of James that James himself favored.[21] That same level of support is also evident in the prefatory material to the *Workes* (1616) of James, where the bishop of Winchester, James Montagu, represented the king as the Prince of Peace, one who had restored the peace of Augustus.[22]

There are other instances, however, in which praise has an obviously corrective thrust. For example, in one of the correspondences of Salisbury to James during the Parliament of 1610, the lord treasurer, distraught that James had not yet achieved a financial settlement with Parliament, urged the king to keep better records of expenditure: "it is for your Majesty to do as the Roman emperor did, who when public treasure was much exhausted, called forthwith for the book which he termed the book of remembrance."[23] With this admonition, Salisbury managed to praise James, even as he criticized him, merely by associating him with an ideal image of Augustus. Like Jonson's representation of Henry as a figure of love, Salisbury's response to James invoked an ideal in order to urge a different course of action. Many examples do not offer their criticism as directly as this one, but the element of persuasion and argument is nonetheless strong.[24]

In 1610-11, the rhetorical situation within which Shakespeare was writing *The Tempest* was characterized by considerable public controversy over values. King and Parliament, locked in a dispute over the king's financial settlement, had been arguing the opposed values of constitutionalism and absolutism. Also under way was a great national effort for the colonization of both Virginia and Ireland, an effort that excited nationalistic feelings of pride, offered new opportunities to many for power and wealth, but also provided situations in which there were quite overwhelming possibilities for failure in the face of enormous conflicts over the relationship of rule and subjection. In placing himself between Virgil and the contemporary moment, Shakespeare also situated his imitation generically within the conventions of romance and masque, contemporary versions of the heroic that promoted epideictic strategies. In this context, he presented a narrative of travel, rule, love, and education that praised the values of order, discipline, and reciprocity.

Although these values may seem to a later time to be as transcendent as Jonson's attention to love in *Oberon*, articulated at this moment in time, these values can also be understood as presenting a commentary on contemporary issues, and most particularly an anti-absolutist argument for limited monarchy. Shakespeare's method of arguing is to bring to the fore an uncontested value, the method which Chaim Perelman and L. Olbrechts-Tyteca highlight in their discussion of the persuasive role of epideictic: "the argumentation in epidictic [sic] discourse sets out to increase the intensity of adherence to certain values, which might not be contested when considered on their own but may nevertheless not prevail against other values that might come into conflict with them."[25] In privileging discipline and reciprocity in the context of granting the value of rule and order, Shakespeare articulates generally held values of the time which could never have been contested on their own, but which were in danger of not prevailing against the value that was coming in conflict with them—namely, the value of absolute rule. In featuring the value of discipline and reciprocity in a context that does not pit these values against others (for example, the value of making a ruler more powerful), the play proceeds, not by focusing on a conflict, but as though the values it espouses were beyond question. In fact, the chief proponent of discipline and limit in the play is Prospero, the established authority.

My point, then, is at least twofold. First, in the Renaissance an imitation of Virgil was always ideologically oriented, and newly so for its own historical time. Second, while use of epideictic would in itself be part of the requirement for heroic poetry, epideictic also offered poets and dramatists committed to commenting on ideological conflict the means by which to do so. It offered them a noncontroversialist rhetorical stance, and one that was as politically proper as it was politically shrewd. For to speak through epideictic was, ultimately, to speak by indirection.[26] As Puttenham had explained:

> in negotiating with Princes we ought to seeke their favour by humilitie & not by sternnesse, nor to trafficke with them by way of indent or condition, but frankly and by manner of submission to their wils, for Princes may be lead but not driven, nor they are to be vanquisht by allegation, but must be suffred to have the victorie and be relented unto: nor they are not to be chalenged for right or justice, for that is a maner of accusation.[27]

Writing from the point of view of giving explicit instructions in decorum, that is, in "comelynesse" and "decencie,"[28] Puttenham left it to the reader to infer that "decencie"—which often proceeds from and thrives on forms of indirection—provided a way of speaking that secured one's safety with no sacrifice to personal integrity, to ethical function, or even to clarity.

Because imitation, like other forms of writing, is more accessible when it is located historically, any consideration of the procedures of imitation must be accompanied by a consideration of the scene of writing. In the following section, I shall first discuss the theory of *imitatio*, along with some examples of how one can see that theory operating in *The Tempest*. Next, there is a discussion of the political topics, languages, and arguments of 1610-11 that seem to have made the strongest impact on the process of contemporizing the Virgilian idiom for *The Tempest*.

PART 1
Imitation and Occasion

IMITATION AND *THE TEMPEST*

Defigurations of the Text

"IMITATION" IN THE RENAISSANCE meant making something new from the art of another artist. This assumption about poetic composition is implicit in Ben Jonson's definition of imitation; the imitative poet, he wrote, was "to draw forth out of the best, and choisest flowers, with the Bee, and turne all into Honey, worke it into one relish, and savour."[1] And it is also the assumption articulated by Petrarch, who, in writing to Boccaccio about the problem of imitating Virgil, used not the familiar bee but a filial metaphor, which was also common to ancient and Renaissance discussions of imitation:

> A proper imitator should take care that what he writes resembles the original without reproducing it. The resemblance should not be that of a portrait to the sitter—in that case the closer the likeness is the better—but it should be the resemblance of a son to his father. Therein is often the great divergence in particular features, but there is a certain suggestion, what our painters call an "air," most noticeable in the face and eyes, which makes the resemblance. As soon as we see the son, he recalls the father to us although if we should measure every feature we should find them all different. But there is a mysterious something there that has this power. Thus we writers must look to it that with a basis of similarity there should be many dissimilarities. And the similarity should be planted so deep that it can only be extricated by quiet meditation.[2]

To compare the new work to its model as one would compare son to father is to suggest how much the two works hold deeply in common; the new work unmistakably bears the essence of the other. But it is equally important that there should be radical dissimilarities between the two. Just as the son is indisputably an individual entirely separate from his father, so the dissimilarities between the parent work and the imitation are so many that the new work stands securely on its own.

In placing the emphasis on the differences between the model and the new work, Petrarch followed the lead of one of his forerunners in the art of imitation, Seneca. In his well-known Epistle 84, Seneca answered his own question of whether or not the model would be obvious: "I think that sometimes it is impossible for it to be seen who is being imitated, if the copy is a true one; for a true copy stamps its own form upon all the features which it has drawn from what we may call the original" (84.9). For both Seneca and Petrarch, then, the poet's object was to change the model so that the genealogical lines disappeared from sight and the parent work became hidden. If Petrarch differed from Seneca, it was in his consideration of the ability to notice resemblances. While Seneca held out the possibility that recognition might never occur, Petrarch assumed that "a certain suggestion," "an air" would be glimpsed. But his emphasis, at the same time, on the "quiet meditation" needed for recognition implicitly acknowledged that recognition was not always easy.

It is not hard to see that these notions about how texts relate to each other apply in a general way to the relationship between *The Tempest* and the *Aeneid*. The two works are profoundly different from each other, but there is still an "air," easily and frequently sensed, of the *Aeneid* in *The Tempest*: the storm-shipwreck-new love sequence ensures that. But to go further than making statements that sound as though we might just as well use the terms "influence" and "analogue" to describe the relationship of these two texts, and to reach the point where we can see *The Tempest* as a formal imitation of the *Aeneid*, we must also go further with our understanding of what the object of imitation is. Imitation is not merely building echoes of one work into another or taking the work of another writer and dressing it up for one's own purposes. It involves the poet in the finest subtleties of another's work, its art

Imitation and Occasion   13

and workmanship; in fact, it is the art that is often a primary object of imitation.

This point was forcibly made by Johannes Sturm in *Nobilitas liberata*, published in Germany in 1549 and in English translation in 1570 under the title *A Ritch Storehouse or Treasure for Nobilitye and Gentlemen*. Called "perhaps the most suggestive document in English that we have on the practice of imitation,"[3] *A Ritch Storehouse* contains Sturm's instructions to his students on how to write well.

Sturm took the standard Renaissance position that good writing came from imitating other good writing. Although his subject was writing compositions for classroom exercises rather than writing poetry, he proceeded with the same assumptions about models and newness that we have just noted in the statements of Jonson, Petrarch, and Seneca. For models Sturm directed his students to the best authors; if they were to learn to imitate, then they had to follow Virgil, and this included learning how Virgil had imitated Theocritus and Homer. But what makes Sturm's book especially helpful for understanding what an act of imitation involved is the emphasis he placed, first, on the process of reading and analyzing the text to be imitated and, second, on the alternative methods available for changing that text into something new.

When Sturm took up the subject of reading, he distinguished the reading one did in preparation for imitation from the reading one did to acquire "knowledge and understanding." The chief distinction was that reading in preparation for imitation required more time and painstaking care; it required "a pawse or stay" (H7) because the object of the reading was to discover "the Arte or workmanship" (E3) that had gone into the text being studied. The students who would become these more pausing and observant readers were encouraged to notice what the text consisted of and how it had been put together. To that end, Sturm instructed them to attend to the arrangement of its various parts; they were to observe "the order and placing of things" (D5^v), an exercise that made them pay attention to beginning, middle, and end. They were also to analyze the "handling" (D5^v). Handling included what was treated briefly, what at length, and what was repeated; it also referred to the "kindes of wordes and formes of sentences" (D5ᵛ). Sturm elaborated this last point later in his discussion when he explained that "handeling . . . conteyneth as well the ornaments and figures of speach, as the polishing of sentences and reasons, as also the framing, knitting and numerousnesse both of members and whole Periodes, with the varietie of all those things compared togither" (F8-F8ᵛ).

To aid further the process of observation and analysis, Sturm recommended that students perform three different kinds of noting—that is, three different methods of representing on paper the text being studied. One method was "when we write out whole places," that is, take one segment of a text and copy it down word for word. In the second, which Sturm called "abridgements," "we gather the summe of the same places in fewe words." But it is the third kind of noting that alerts us to the fact that Sturm was urging his students to a higher order of thinking than what these first two methods alone might suggest. Sturm wanted to teach them to conceptualize a text and articulate its art; thus he recommended that they cast the patterns they perceived into linear shapes: "drawe out every part in figures." Explaining that this exercise had also been done in Greece and Italy, Sturm first called these drawings "figurative draughts," but later, considering that making figurations was what the author himself did, he suggested the drawings might better be called "defigurations" (D8). The concept of defiguration reflects in yet another way how a precursor text could be conceived of as art and design, a requisite step if the imitator were to be able to proceed from "defiguration" to "figuration." Both of these terms are so rich in their connotations that we shall do well to fetch them from the *Ritch Storehouse* for our own critical purposes.

When Sturm left the topic of reading and analyzing behind to take up that of composition, his emphasis throughout was on hiding. To write was to conceal. "For he ought to be a hider of his Arte, which would be a good Imitator" (G4), Sturm explained; "an Imitator must hide all similitude and likeness" (G5ᵛ). Thus he advised that "we must first endevour that our doing may appeare unlike the patterne" (G4ᵛ) and suggested that it might be necessary to get a teacher to help with this step, "to shewe us how we may hide and cover lyke thinges by unlike using and handling" (G4). Being such a teacher himself, Sturm directed his students to try various techniques, such as "addition, ablation, alteration, and chaunging: wherein is contained, conjunction, figuration, commutation, and transformation, both of wordes and sentences, of members, and periodes" (G5ᵛ). Sturm clarified this list by giving definitions of each term and illustrations.

His longest example was the familiar comparison of Virgil's first lines in the *Aeneid* to the Homeric lines that he therein imitates: "For as Homer sheweth the wrath and furie of *Achylles*, so Vergill painteth out Aeneas with more words and speciall tokens: so that in the persons there is varietie and in the handling there is likenesse." As Sturm proceeded with this example, he cited lines only from Virgil, for it would have been superfluous to have to write down for these students the corresponding lines from Homer. They would have known what he was referring to when he observed "what distinction of Genders, numbers, vowels or voyces is there," or that this "doth differ from the invocation of Homer by order and placing," or that "Vergil hath separated the proposition from that invocation, and hath changed the persons and matters, and hath recited more plentie of things which is proper to addition" (H3).

So self-assured was Sturm with this type of analysis that it comes as somewhat of a surprise to find him acknowledging that people might deny the intricate relatedness between texts. He introduced this point while considering one of Virgil's imitations of Theocritus: "But some will say, he useth not the same polishing of his sentence, nor the same wordes that Theocritus doth," and, again, "But peradventure some man will denie that this was done by imitation seeing the thinges be not all one in both writers" (H1ᵛ). Sturm countered these objections, as we might expect, by emphasizing the large degree of difference that there had to be between the old text and the new one: "Imitation is not in things that be all one, but in things that be like, and that which is like, must be, not the same, but another thing" (H1ᵛ). And he explained, moreover, that the imitator strove to make it impossible for "unskillfull persons" to perceive all of his art: "he would have it known whome he imitateth, although he would not have it spyed, how and after what sort he doth it."

We should notice in this last remark both what was given and what was taken away. The imitator wished to be both a concealer and a revealer, Sturm suggested.[4] If the copy was a true one, by Seneca's standards, then the use of the precursor text would be concealed. But if his art was to be discovered, and so appreciated, then he had to do some revealing too. This meant, among other things, that he might decide to advertise that to which he was indebted and yet do so in such a way as not to remove the pleasure of the reader in discovering the artistry that the concealment itself promoted.

For mature poets setting out to copy an ancient text, the following of step-by-step instructions like those of Sturm would not always have been necessary. They would already have learned these habits of composition years earlier and also acquired through long acquaintance and frequent rereading a knowledge of classical texts that far surpassed what a school child might have. Such surely was the case for Petrarch, who spoke of knowing the classical texts so well as to have completely ingested them, intellectually and spiritually:

> I have read Virgil, Horace, Livy, Cicero, not once but a thousand times, not hastily but in repose, and I have pondered them with all the powers of my mind. I ate in the morning what I would digest in the evening; I swallowed as a boy what I would ruminate upon as a man. These writings I have so thoroughly absorbed and fixed, not only in my memory but in my very marrow, these have become so much a part of myself, that even though I should never read them again they would cling in my spirit, deep-rooted in its inmost recesses.[5]

Jonson alluded to knowledge of a similar kind when he remarked on the challenge it had been to annotate *The Masque of Queenes* (1609) for Prince Henry: "it hath prov'd a worke of some difficulty to mee to retrive the particular *authorities* . . . to those things, which I writt out of fulnesse and memory of my former readings."[6] Greene, thinking about what permits imitation of a high order to occur and guided by Petrarch's remarks about his knowledge of texts, ascribes the capacity to imitate to this very "intimacy of conversation with the ancient text, a habitual interiorization of its letter and essence," "a kind of assimilation [that] must occur if the modern text is truly to recall its paternal model imprecisely but unmistakably."[7]

While we do not have Shakespeare's personal letters, as we have some of Petrarch's, or prefaces and marginal glosses, as we have from Jonson, we do know that Shakespeare was well grounded in the many classical texts that had wide currency in the Renaissance and also that he would have had the same access to the techniques of and assumptions about imitation that his contemporaries had. As far as his specific knowledge of Virgil goes, we know that most of Shakespeare's explicit allusions to Virgil in the canon as a whole are to material in the first six books of the *Aeneid*, and that of these most are references to the story of Troy's fall, the love story of Dido and Aeneas, and the visit to the underworld. We may draw more than one conclusion from this information. What it suggested to T. W. Baldwin is that Shakespeare, like many people in his day, knew the first half of the *Aeneid* better than he knew the last half.[8] That may be so. But the reuse of the same patterns over and over for different purposes also suggests something about how the patterns available in Virgil, and especially in the first six books, had become part of the permanent but moveable furniture of Shakespeare's mind, intimately interiorized to the point where they were endlessly available for rearrangement and changing in one work after another throughout his entire oeuvre. Frequently, Shakespeare's reuse of Virgil is as simple as an obvious allusion; but very often it is more complex. And occasionally, the Virgilian patterns become the chief means by which Shakespeare accomplishes a large and complex figuration.

Perhaps the most simple and obvious reference to Virgil in all of Shakespeare occurs in *The Tempest* in the conversation in act 2, scene 1, where the name Dido or Widow Dido[9] is repeated six times. Also at this point, Gonzalo makes some statements about equivalencies: "This Tunis, sir, was Carthage . . . I assure you, Carthage." It is possible to dismiss this entire conversation as idle chatter, or even as another example of the miscellaneous quality of some Renaissance citation of classical details. It is also possible to wonder, as Frank Kermode did,[10] whether the allusions are there to reveal anything. Two lines especially—"You make me study of that" and "What impossible matter can he make easy next?"—offer encouragement to anyone who is inclined to feel that the unusual specificity in the lines is in itself a signal to pay attention to them. What that specificity does refer to, I am arguing, is a complicated use of Virgil that Shakespeare, utilizing the procedures of imitation, has concealed. In order to gain access to this use, we need to pay further attention to the methods and principles whereby things can be hidden.

Variation and Reversal

Upon finishing Sturm's book, his students were presumably prepared for the task of writing something. As we have seen, this process would involve first reading and analyzing a text and then setting out to vary it. Varying being the handmaiden of imitation, the students could replace syntactical units of one design with those of another design, one word or image with another, and units of one length with those of another length. Something that had come at the beginning now could come in the middle or at the end, and one rhetorical device could stand where a different one had stood; tone, occasion, context, order, and style all could change. And, again, if the art were good, if the copy were true, the originating work would be obscured, at least from the superficial view.

When Sturm chose illustrations to show his students how to arrive at such results, they were inevitably short ones. Even though he knew how Virgil's whole work had been imprinted with Homer's, he illustrated that use and others with one or two sentences or a few lines of verse. The changes on which he focused are comparable in size and degree, we might say, to that of changing and rearranging the furniture in the smallest room of a house. What is moved is not moved very far; what is added, even though it fits in perfectly, can be found because, the room being small, there are not many places to look. Moreover, the observer who would understand all the changes can stand at the door and see the entire room all at once.

Imitation and Occasion   19

In comparison to what is required when one analyzes a few lines or a single passage, analyzing the imitative techniques in a longer work is not only a bigger task but also a different one. There is not only more to do, more places to look, but when the object of imitation is long, the art of imitation has involved larger and different features of structure than can be contained in a few lines. A longer work contains all the smaller structures of vocabulary and syntax. But there are also the larger structures within which the smaller ones are contained, and which are superimposed upon, bridge, or bind them together.

In the following pages, I shall suggest what the range of imitative techniques consist of in *The Tempest*. We shall look at some instances of imitation that give recurrence to smaller segments in Virgil and also illustrate various degrees of hiding and changing. We shall consider, too, how Shakespeare has organized his imitation and, in the process, structured his whole play, using some of the larger structures of character, action, and meaning in the *Aeneid* for these ends. These structures, moreover, are not simply those which a modern reader might deduce from the *Aeneid*, but are also those defined by a long tradition of allegorical interpretation with which Shakespeare and his contemporaries were familiar.

A logical place to start is where Shakespeare did, namely, with the tempest that begins the play. The first stage direction reads, "A tempestuous noise of thunder and lightning" (*Tempest*, s.d. 1.1), and the action opens on a ship and its passengers about to be wrecked in a storm. Were Sturm doing this analysis, he would no doubt have first remarked that Shakespeare begins where Virgil begins. But here it is not Virgil's first phrases that Shakespeare copies, as Virgil began by copying Homer's first phrases, but Virgil's first *action*, his "tempestas" (*Aen.* 1.53, 377), that shipwrecks Aeneas at Carthage. Shakespeare does, of course, move us a bit further into the middle of things by beginning at a point where the storm is already in full force. And he adjusts the ominous and despairing tone of Virgil's opening to something more suitable to comedy. The words near the end of the scene that seal this generic identity is the phrase "we split," repeated five times; a phrase that tells an audience which knows other stories where ships split that all will be well, for occupants of ships that split are typically reunited, and in sound body.

Still, the occurrence of a tempest at the beginning of the play is a more complicated matter for a discussion of imitation than it might first appear to be. One could say that Shakespeare, by beginning in the same way Virgil began, is being quite open and direct about the work which is the parent of his new play. The reuse of the same action in the same place allows his text to be "ostentatiously diachronic," to make an "explicit adoption"[11] of Virgil's text. What complicates the truth of this statement is that Virgil's tempest had, over the centuries, been reused by writer after writer until it had passed into the literary language as topos, convention—even as cliché.[12] No literate audience experiencing this first scene and inclined to relate it to earlier works would think only of the *Aeneid* as a precedent. It would be possible to argue, then, that by beginning *The Tempest* with a tempest Shakespeare was being explicit about nothing; in itself, the tempest contains no information whatsoever about the genetics of this work. It may not even be Virgil's storm: "the fact that the same descriptive system appears in two texts does not prove influence; nor does it prove that any such influence, if real, is of significance."[13] The only thing that can make the opening seem to be a compellingly significant, though changed, copy of Virgil's opening, is our awareness that the *Aeneid* is a constant presence in the rest of the play.

Provided such presence can be established, one option we have in assessing the technique of imitation represented in the tempest is to consider that the familiarity of Virgil's storm as a topos allows Shakespeare to imitate that topos frankly without his ostentatious reuse calling attention to itself as imitation. By being so overt, he is, on the one hand, revealing his art; he offers information that authorizes us to scrutinize his procedure for still more connections to Virgil. But because what he offers is so obvious, so conventional, it is equally effective at deflecting that attention, even concealing his art. Only after the play has been searched for other traces of Virgil is it possible to see that the tempest at the beginning, far from being merely conventional, is virtually necessary.

Imitation and Occasion   21

Another imitative technique Shakespeare uses is that of translation, the technique that played such an important part in the development of the sixteenth-century lyric and sonnet. When Shakespeare translates Virgil for a word or phrase in *The Tempest*, a metamorphosis occurs simply in the act of changing languages. But however much is changed, translation provides a way of citing the parent work that is sometimes more specific, sometimes more traceable, than what is exemplified by a topos. Moreover, translation provides a means whereby the old text can actually be inserted into the new one, providing the materials out of which the new text is made. The new text thus becomes the container and the bearer of the old.

One of the best-known uses of Virgil in *The Tempest*, one that editors have always accurately glossed, happens to be also an example of translation. In the second scene of the play, where Ferdinand first sees Miranda, Shakespeare has him utter the phrase that Aeneas speaks when he sees his mother disguised as a huntress at Carthage: "o dea certe" (*Aen.* 1.328) becomes "Most sure the goddess" (1.2.424). What distinguishes this translation from some others in the play is that it is a verbatim translation of a famous phrase and appears in a context (a man seeing an extraordinary woman) that prompts reader or audience recognition. Like the tempest in the first scene, this line is an obvious repetition that need cause no stir; it can be, and often has been, taken as merely an incidental allusion by a poet who works eclectically and whose poetry is often randomly intertextual. Nevertheless, both the topos and the translation remain in the text as encoded points of entry for anyone who would recognize that Shakespeare is somehow being newly and truly serious about the relationship of the whole play to the *Aeneid*.

In other instances, however, Shakespeare's use of Virgil's topoi and language is obscure. A changed context and a dismantling of phrases can make the use of Virgil almost disappear from sight. An example of this more hidden use, and one that combines the technique of imitating a topos with that of imitating by translating, occurs in that florid speech by the otherwise nearly speechless Francisco (at 3.3.40 he has three more words), who describes Ferdinand swimming to shore. In response to Alonso's lament that his son has been drowned, Francisco offers the opinion that Ferdinand must still be alive; certainly when Francisco saw the prince swimming in the sea, he had appeared strong enough to make it to shore:

> Sir, he may live:
> I saw him beat the surges under him,
> And ride upon their backs; he trod the water,
> Whose enmity he flung aside, and breasted
> The surge most swoln that met him; his bold head
> 'Bove the contentious waves he kept, and oared
> Himself with his good arms in lusty stroke
> To th'shore, that o'er his wave-worn basis bowed,
> As stooping to relieve him: I not doubt
> He came alive to land.
>
> (2.1.109–18)

Within the large general pattern of the journey-storm-wreck sequence that occurs early in both the *Aeneid* and *The Tempest*, this description of Ferdinand's coming to shore may seem broadly analogous to Virgil's description of the Trojans swimming from their ships to the Carthaginian shores. But the specific details of the speech about Ferdinand originate elsewhere in the *Aeneid*, namely, in the passage in the midst of the famed Laocoön episode in which two snakes swim to shore and, after attacking the son of the priest Laocoön, wind themselves around the waist and throat of Laocoön himself.

Here is the comparable passage from Virgil:

> and lo! from Tenedos, over the peaceful depths—I shudder as I tell the tale—a pair of serpents with endless coils are breasting the sea and side by side making for the shore. Their bosoms rise amid the surge, and their crests, blood-red, overtop the waves; the rest of them skims the main behind and their huge backs curve in many a fold.

> ecce autem gemini a Tenedo tranquilla per alta
> (horresco referens) immensis orbibus angues
> incumbunt pelago pariterque ad litora tendunt:
> pectora quorum inter fluctus arrecta iubaeque

sang' ,neae superant undas; pars cetera pontum
po\1e legit sinuatque immensa volumine terga.
(2.203-8)

In constructing the passage that describes Ferdinand, Shakespeare appropriates for his own use several of the key verbs, nouns, and images that Virgil used for the snakes, and with a degree of exactness that leaves no doubt about their origin. Both Virgil and Shakespeare emphasize the power of the swimmers by describing them as high in the water. Virgil pictures the snakes as "breasting [*incumbunt*][14] the sea"; their "bosoms rise amid the surge [*fluctus*], and overtop [*superant*] the waves." Shakespeare follows Virgil when he writes that Ferdinand has been seen to "beat the surges under him," has "trod the water," and having "breasted the surge" has kept "his bold head / 'Bove the . . . waves."

But although Shakespeare retains all of these details from Virgil, he also changes many things. First of all, he makes an alteration in the persons and in the number, as Sturm would say; he changes two serpents into one man. He also changes the nature of these swimmers: in Virgil, the serpents come as a death-bringing menace and ill omen; in Shakespeare, that menace is eliminated and replaced by a Ferdinand who comes as a heroic victor. To this end, Shakespeare remakes the huge backs (*terga*) of the snakes into the "backs" of the surges that Ferdinand rides. And he exchanges the association of the serpents with threat and slaughter for Ferdinand's strong ability to battle with the sea, to defeat the "enmity" of the water and "the contentious waves." In fact, so welcome is the healing and mediating power that resides in Ferdinand that the shore seems to stretch out to help him reach it, "the shore, that o'er his wave-worn basis bowed, / As stooping to relieve him."

One of the most important points about Shakespeare's imitation here has still not been made and has to do with the fact that the Laocoön passage occurs in a different place in Virgil from where Virgil's tempest and the narration of Aeneas and his men swimming to shore occur. Were we to assume that Shakespeare's use of Virgil depended upon the matching of corresponding parts of narrative lines, then we might anticipate that the only place in Virgil's text where we might find something that corresponds to Ferdinand's swimming is in *Aeneid* 1, where the action of the storm and shipwreck yields to the action of swimming. But because Shakespeare is imitating Virgil, not using him as a source for plot, he responds to his text by varying it. What this means, as always, is that a detail that one poet used in one place may be used somewhere else by another. It also means that things that were not in the same place before may now be in the same place. Varying causes separation of some things, conflation of others. And while this method may obstruct recognition of the connections between Shakespeare's text and Virgil's, it confirms a sense of what Shakespeare is doing. He is not borrowing a plot; he is imitating, and this requires handling Virgil's text discontinuously.

It should also be apparent from what has been said so far that, in this example of varying, one important characteristic of the imitation is that here Shakespeare alters Virgil to the point of reversal. Shakespeare may repeat Virgil's words, but the changes he makes in context result in his being able to use Virgil's text for effects and for matter that are opposite to those it originally possessed. This use of Virgil, it should also be noted, differs decidedly from what we see in the "o dea certe" line, as well as from the use of a tempest for an opening.

All three of the examples of imitating Virgil noted so far—the tempest, "o dea certe," and the Laocoön passage—together offer a chance to ask how much of Virgil would have to recur in any studied imitation of the *Aeneid*. Although even the first six books of the *Aeneid* hold virtually an infinite number of things that could be imitated, it may be taken for granted that anyone considering a rigorous imitation of them would be obliged to copy many of the most well-known things, from some of the very famous lines ("o dea certe" and "Italiam non sponte sequor," perhaps) to many of the most famous narrative kernels. Sturm acknowledged this requirement when he wrote about what one might choose to imitate from Cicero; he recommended going first to the sections of Cicero "which have either some necessarie, or some notable place in them. I call that necessarie that is almost ever to be used" (E7^v). The Laocoön episode qualifies as one such "place" in the *Aeneid*; likewise, in *Aeneid* 1 so do the tempest and the reaction of Aeneas to being shipwrecked, in *Aeneid* 2 the Trojan horse conspiracy, in *Aeneid* 4 the cave episode at Carthage, and, from the underworld episodes of *Aeneid* 6, both hell and Elysium, both the Sibyl and Anchises, both the joyous prophecies and the lamentation.

It can, of course, be argued that all of these notable "places," on which thousands of readers and hundreds of commentators had previously focused attention, do in fact reappear in *The Tempest*, and that they do so by way of the different systems used to organize the imitation. One of the most obvious of these is the use of the Dido and Aeneas love story as the model for the love story of Ferdinand and Miranda, a pattern that is present from the moment of their first meeting in act 1 all the way through the game of chess in act 5. But Shakespeare alters, even reverses, the model so that the Virgilian patterns this time tell a story of true love, not lust, and of right choice rather than delay and diversion.

A somewhat less obvious use of Virgil is that which produces the series of conspiracy plots: Prospero's expulsion from Milan, Antonio and Sebastian's plot to overthrow Alonso, and Caliban's to overthrow Prospero. Shakespeare patterns all three episodes on Virgil's tale of how the Greeks conquered Troy: all three involve victims who will be threatened or attacked while they sleep. In these instances, the sack of Troy not only presents an event out of which the action for a play can be made (as the love-test Leir gave his daughters in the old play suggested an action for a new one) but functions also as a cultural premise. Although this premise may be variously stated, it includes the notion that to attack a sleeping city is to attack order and civility, and thus it also shows that, however strong any society is, it is not strong absolutely. These ideas are so embedded in the traditional readings of Virgil's story of Troy's fall that Shakespeare can transfer them to his own new work simply by transplanting the narrative kernel that represents them. Significantly, the Virgilian narrative of the fall of Troy is not treated in *The Tempest* simply as a memory of a past event but is represented by Shakespeare as a circumstance that is alarmingly recurrent, essentially repeatable.

In a third system of organization, Shakespeare again employs this method of repetition but applies it to character instead of action. Here I refer to the use he makes of Aeneas as the basic model for nearly all of the male characters in the play, not only Prospero and Ferdinand but also Alonso, Gonzalo, and Caliban. The differences among these characters are a result of rhetorical varying; in the case of Caliban, Shakespeare reverses the pattern and parodies it until Caliban becomes an anti-Aeneas figure. In other instances, he either combines more than one pattern to make a new construct, or he disassembles the parts of a pattern. An example of the latter is his redistributing, among several different characters, the mixed reactions that Aeneas had upon arriving in Carthage. In response to the storm and shipwreck they have experienced, Gonzalo offers comfort to others, Antonio and Sebastian complain, Alonso falls into despair, and Ferdinand, whom Shakespeare sets above the others, feels a calm settle over him. Even as the story of Troy includes a set of ideas that can be transferred to a play by copying the pattern of Troy, so does the figure of Aeneas. All of these details help us to understand why Nosworthy and Kott could define so differently *how* the *Aeneid* is in *The Tempest*; it truly *is* in there in more ways than one (and often simultaneously).

Imitation and Allegory

In considering the theory and practice of Renaissance imitation as it is applicable to Shakespeare's art, we need to return to Sturm once more to address more directly the issue of what it is "the duetie of an Imitator" to imitate (G4), what things are "worthy of imitation" (G3^v). On this subject Sturm made two points that are especially relevant to *The Tempest*. The first, though long in implication, can be quickly stated. According to Sturm, "what is worthy of imitation" was "whatsoever is worthy of prayse" (G3^v); this remark grasps the commitment of epideictic as well as the commitment to favor the best poets for one's imitations. A second point Sturm made was that it was the duty of the imitator to include in his imitation not only what was apparent but also "what is secret, and is not expressed" (G4); he was to imitate the "hidden and secret poyntes," which included "sometime a further meaning than is expressed in wordes" (G3^v).

This point is crucial to a study of imitations of Virgil because of the tradition, well known in the Renaissance, that the *Aeneid* was a text that contained, as both Thomas Phaer and Richard Stanyhurst acknowledged in the prefaces to their translations of it, "many misticall secretes," many "hidden secrets." Spenser made a like acknowledgment in his "Letter of the Authors" when he declared that he was following the practices of Homer and Virgil by presenting the virtues "clowdily enwrapped in Allegorical devises."[15]

What these writers were referring to was the medieval and Renaissance tradition of reading Virgil's text allegorically, a tradition which, as it evolved, treated the allegorical meanings as a constitutive part of Virgil's text, and as having been intended by Virgil, not added by his interpreters. Thus the *Aeneid* text we read today is, in a very particular sense, not the text as Renaissance readers knew it. To them, the *Aeneid* besides being all of Virgil's text, was also all of the philosophical meanings that they understood to be in it and that they could read in the various commentaries on Virgil.

This perception that Virgil's text was both open and secret gave rise to various systems of reading that operated simultaneously for any reader. On the one hand, the story of Aeneas was said to comprise the adventures of an exemplary public hero. In *The Defence of Poesie*, Sir Philip Sidney referred implicitly to this system when he recommended Aeneas as the model for virtuous action: "Only let Aeneas be worn in the tablet of your memory."[16] Such a reading is humanistic and educational in its orientation; it considers the adventures and trials of the hero to be the means to a public end, the founding of a new civilization. As William Webbe remarked in *Discourse of English Poetrie*, "Under the person of Aeneas [Virgil] expresseth the valoure of a worthy Captaine and Valiaunt Governour."[17] This reading of Aeneas as an ideal public figure was also what lay behind Tasso's conclusion that, of all the noble actions that a poet composing heroic poetry had ever devised, "the noblest action of all is the coming of Aeneas to Italy."[18] This way of reading Virgil's text is pertinent to a consideration of *The Tempest* because it illuminates, by confirming, our sense of the play as deeply political and as deeply and importantly tied to the epideictic tradition.

But knowledge of a system wherein the *Aeneid* is read allegorically is also helpful because it furnishes a widely disseminated example of how Virgil's text could be conceptualized, conceptualization being the mental operation on which successful imitation so often depended. Although there is much variety as one moves from one commentator to another—Fulgentius in the fifth century, Bernardus Silvestris in the Middle Ages, and Cristoforo Landino in the fifteenth century[19]—it is possible to make a few careful generalizations about this tradition of reading the hidden or secret story in Virgil. Generally it is true that the commentary was discursive and philosophical in content, that it espoused Platonic doctrine and assumed Virgil was a Platonist,[20] and that it addressed itself primarily to the first six books of the *Aeneid*, the same books that are the object of Shakespeare's imitation. Also, the commentators read these six books as a maturation process of one sort or another. In the case of Fulgentius and Bernardus, the progress related by Virgil in six books was that of the six ages of man, the progress from infancy to the wisdom of old age. Landino, however, read it as the journey of the soul toward wisdom. It will be assumed as we proceed that Shakespeare would have worked with, or would have possessed eclectic knowledge of, these differing but still highly complementary readings—as indeed surely did many readers of his time, who were used to seeing the *Aeneid* printed in an edition that surrounded Virgil's text with an enormous critical and glossarial apparatus. But whatever eclecticism might have existed for Shakespeare or his contemporaries, and however much all these commentaries overlap, the reading that found in the *Aeneid* an allegory of the soul, rather than the ages of man, is always the one more relevant to the art of *The Tempest*.

In considering how Shakespeare might have used or been affected by this commentary tradition, we do well to recall the instructions in conceptualization that Sturm gave his students when he described for them methods of defiguration. When he instructed them to represent the text through line drawings, he was trying to get them to perceive the form of the text as an abstraction, and then to represent their perceptions in a nontextual way. What the commentary tradition offered Shakespeare that was similar to Sturm's method was, first of all, a set of ideas, and so abstractions, to which the text of Virgil was understood to refer. Even as Sturm's defiguration drawings were suggested by a text but not constructed from pieces of that text, so too the body of meanings in the commentary tradition was not textualized by Virgil but by his followers, in the texts they wrote about his text. Virgil's text might have given rise to those meanings, but it did not itself express them.[21] To the extent that it is possible to talk about the *Aeneid* as providing a sequentially ordered pattern of events that corresponds to a sequence in *The Tempest*, we shall do better to look for the correspondences in the sequence of philosophical and ethical states of being that the commentary describes than in a plot outline of the *Aeneid* itself. For what Shakespeare seems to have done in *The Tempest* was to use that sequence—the organized discourse of this commentary tradition that tells of an educational process—as one organizing principle for composition. In other words, for the purposes of the imitation, Shakespeare has treated the commentary tradition as a continuous text and Virgil's literal narrative as a discontinuous one. And if both the commentary tradition and the *Aeneid* were utilized in the composing of Shakespeare's play, it is, then, possible to use both of them to trace the transformations that he wrought on both. Before we can be more specific, it is necessary to set down a brief summary of Landino's method of reading Virgil.

Called by modern critics "the prince of Virgilian allegorists" and "the most impressive and influential of the fifteenth-century Virgil scholars,"[22] Landino included his commentary on Virgil's first six books in the *Camaldolese Disputations*, first printed in 1480. Subsequently, these views were summarized, along with those of his predecessors, in many of the Renaissance editions of the *Aeneid* that printed commentary in the margins and in introductory notes and essays.[23] To produce his reading of the soul's progress toward perfection, Landino did not follow the chronology of Virgil's narrative (as had Fulgentius and Bernardus) but the chronology of Aeneas's actions, and so discussed the books of the *Aeneid* in the order 2, 3, 1, 4, 5, 6.[24] Thus, Landino saw in *Aeneid* 2 and the story of the Trojan War a representation of the soul's efforts to subdue the passions. The departure from Troy and the subsequent adventures in *Aeneid* 2 and 3 figured the spirit's initial resistance to the passions and its new tendency toward virtue. The progress of the soul is continually threatened by recurrent disruptions of appetite which throw it off course, the most significant of which is represented for Landino by the arrival of Aeneas at Carthage and his experiences with Dido (*Aeneid* 1 and 4). But finally, in *Aeneid* 6, the narrative of Aeneas's arrival in Italy and journey to the underworld, the soul comes to rest in an intellectual experience that unites it with truth.

Landino's commentary is very detailed, but a summary of it reveals the importance he attributed to the Carthage experience and to the arrival at Italy in *Aeneid* 6 as representative of two poles between which the soul, struggling toward goodness, must move. Gavin Douglas, whose translation of the *Aeneid* was well known in sixteenth-century England and was used by both Henry Howard, Earl of Surrey, and Thomas Phaer for their own translations,[25] showed in his marginalia that he too understood the significance that Carthage and *Aeneid* 6 had in Landino's system. Of the several references to Landino in Douglas's glosses, the most detailed treatment occurs at the point in the translation where Aeneas arrives in Carthage, at which point Douglas summarized Landino by stating the significance of Carthage in terms of the ultimate goal: "Eneas purposis to Italy, his land of promyssion." Here is this gloss in its entirety:

> Cristoferus Landynus, that writis moraly apon Virgill, says thus: Eneas purposis to Italy, his land of promyssion; that is to say, a iust perfyte man entendis to mast soueran bonte and gudnes, quhilk as witnessyth Plato, is situate in contemplation of godly thyngis or dyvyn warkis. His onmeysabill ennymy Iuno, that is frenzeit queyn of realmys, entendis to dryve him from Italle to Cartage; that is, Avesion, or concupissence to ryng or haf warldly honouris, wald draw him fra contemplation to the actyve lyve; quhilk, quhen scho falis by hir self, tretis scho with Eolus, the neddyr part of raison, quhilk sendis the storm of mony warldly consalis in the iust manis mynd. Bot, quhoubeyt the mynd lang flowis and delitis heirintyll, fynaly by the fre wyll and raison predomynent, that is ondirstand, by Neptun, the storm is cessit, and, as follois in the nyxt c., arryvit in sond havin, quhilk is tran-

quilite of consciens; and fynaly Venus, in the vi c. following, schawis Ene his feris recouerit again, quhilk is, fervent lufe and cherite schawis the iust man his swete meditationys and feruour of deuotion, quham he tynt by warldly curis, restorit to hym again, and all his schippis obot on, be quham I ondyrstand the tyme lost.[26]

As important as this gloss is, and suggestive as it is of Landino's influence in England, we know from reading Douglas's accompanying translation that such a reading was for him only half the story. The translation itself is a heavily politicized one, emphasizing not the story of private life that could be read allegorically in the *Aeneid*, but the story of public life that Virgil's narrative tells, Aeneas's founding of a new civilization. *Aeneid 6* has great importance for both, as the arrival in Italy is the occasion on which the goals toward which both stories strive come to fulfillment. What can be found in Douglas that is not apparent in Landino, then, is the more common tradition of reading Virgil as telling at the same time at least two stories, one a public tale of political commitment and one an allegorical treatment of an intensely private struggle. As Bernardus said, "we treat Virgil both as poet and as philosopher," one who observed a method of "twofold teaching" (p. 3).

One way of explaining how Shakespeare responded to this tradition in his own imitation is to say that he invented a way of telling these two stories as one. He structured the central political action of the play—Prospero's plot to regain his dukedom—so that it incorporates a series of educational journeys.[27] By the end of the play we have the sense that all the characters have been on progresses, as Gonzalo indeed suggests when he remarks that among all that has been found "in one voyage" is "all of us ourselves / When no man was his own." Admittedly, some (Prospero, for example) started before others, and some do not progress as far as others. Caliban, for example, does not get much beyond "Carthage." There is, as well, the more particularly enacted educational progress of Ferdinand, whom Prospero disciplines, tests, and finally rewards. This story of moral progresses is virtually the same as the story of the soul's journey that Landino read in Virgil. It is, moreover, the continuous "text" that Shakespeare transfers to *The*

Tempest from the medieval and Renaissance Virgilian tradition, where he uses *it* (not the chronology of Virgil's narrative) as the framework within which, and on which, to construct the intricate details of his imitation. Because this story is essentially philosophical and moral in content, a discourse in every sense of the word "commonplace," it conceivably can be told in or with any number or variety of specific plot structures and narrative kernels. In this instance, however, and with this discursive chronology in place, Shakespeare is able to move freely about in the text of the *Aeneid*, disassembling that literal narrative and rearranging its bits and pieces as it suits him in order to invent the new speeches and new actions for the play he is writing.

While Shakespeare's management of the Virgilian text attests to an expert craftsmanship, it also confirms Greene's sense that one effect of imitation is that it "shook [the] absolute status" of the precursor text "by calling attention to the specific circumstances of its production."[28] Grasping some features of Shakespeare's disruption of the *Aeneid*, Kott thought that it signaled a rejection of Virgil.[29] Another possibility is that the rewriting was gauged so that the imitation would better suit new circumstances of production. Although Shakespeare changed Virgil, he also worked a change on contemporary authoritative symbols, an intervention that amounts to a disruption of more than one kind of absolutism.

OCCASION AND *THE TEMPEST*

Imitation and Occasion

Although the art of *imitatio* involved a writer's turning to the past, it also required that the new writing take the author's own age into account. Thomas Greene recounts how the remaking of Homer involved Virgil in a Romanizing of Greek art:

> Virgil deals with the Homeric shadow . . . by transmuting each minor form through context into something new and Roman. Thus his fable of transitivity was orchestrated everywhere by a transitive technique that demonstrated the fact of preserva-

tion but also the fact of transmutation. This special historical character of Virgil's poem makes it the central and supreme expression of Roman civilization.[1]

A similar act of rewriting is what makes *The Tempest* so deeply resonant of its own historical time; like Virgil, Shakespeare transmutes minor forms through context into something contemporary. His medium is rhetorical structures; his set of referents, as is appropriate for an imitation of Virgil, is national politics—the royal children, the contemporary debate on monarchy, and the projects for colonization. The resulting transitive and mediating maneuvers legitimate both the imitation and his engagement of contested issues. High politics are as necessary to an imitation of Virgil as is the imitation of key narrative kernels.

The high politics in the *Aeneid* most obviously concern the story of Aeneas's founding of Rome and the accompanying celebration of the reign of Augustus. Renaissance imitations of Virgil typically repeat this combination. They tell stories of heroes involved in grand quests and public undertakings along with praising a contemporary ruler. In *Orlando furioso*, Ariosto celebrated his patrons by making Ruggiero the founder of the Este line. Tasso, who dedicated *Gerusalemme liberata* to Alfonso II, duke of Ferrara, made Alfonso's ancestor, Rinaldo, a central hero and had his work prophesy the glorious deeds of Rinaldo's descendants. Spenser, who dedicated *The Faerie Queene* to Queen Elizabeth I, had Arthur read the history of Britain while Guyon read the history of Faeryland, and, later, in Merlin's prophecy about the progeny of Britomart and Arthegall, foretold the coming of the reign of Elizabeth. In these works, as in *The Tempest*, the most immediately accessible referential aspects are laudatory. The degree to which the works also evaluate the contemporary situation is more difficult to estimate, but evaluation is nonetheless routinely felt to be present, and also to be a feature of the best imitative writing.[2] An analogous situation exists for readers of the *Aeneid*.

As is the case with some of the works written in imitation of Virgil's epic, the most easily recognizable political elements—the ⁀plicit prophecies, in books 1, 6, and 8, of the glories of Augustus and Actium and the golden age to come—strongly support the idea that Virgil's stance toward his ruler was an enthusiastically celebratory one. And indeed, precisely for this reason, these elements constitute an aspect of the work that has been somewhat troubling to Virgil's critics and admirers throughout the centuries. Ariosto, for example, complained that "Augustus Caesar was not such a saint, / As Virgill maketh him by his description," and Thomas Hobbes pondered, in his "Answer . . . to Sir William Davenant's *Preface before Gondibert*," whether Virgil's attention to Augustus was anything more than flattery, a question that stirred considerable interest in some of the writers of Alexander Pope's generation as well.[3] Yet despite the extravagance of the praise conveyed in Virgil's prophecies, there are, nevertheless, elements in the epic that tend to complicate this version of the relationship between the poet and his ruler. Only if one concentrates exclusively on the overt references to Augustus and his age can one accept without qualification the notion that, as Boccaccio put it, Virgil's purpose was to extol Augustus and his family as he exalted "the glory of the name of Rome."[4]

One can easily lose the sense that Virgil's attitude toward Augustus was that of single-minded praise when one considers—in the context of Virgil's "historical present"—some of the implications of the story he tells. The central complication, of course, is that Virgil's poem is not *about* Augustus and Actium, but about an ancient hero from the distant past. Yet it focuses on a plot that had a particular relevance in the aftermath of Actium, the activities involved in bringing two "peoples" together. And if one attempts to approach that story as an Augustan plot—as many readers have felt compelled to do—one's assessment of the politics of the *Aeneid* inevitably becomes more problematic. Two of the most notoriously complex aspects of the work, the outcome of the Dido-Aeneas affair and the final scene of the work, Aeneas's killing of Turnus, can help us illustrate some dimensions of the interpretive issues. In both of these incidents resides the problem of the Aeneas-Augustus relationship, especially as it centers around Aeneas's callousness.

The Dido-Aeneas affair is a place in the *Aeneid* where discussions of Virgil's indebtedness to his predecessors often expand to include patterns available in the poet's historical present, the most

Imitation and Occasion   35

famous of which is the love affair between Mark Antony and Cleopatra.[5] And needless to say, one's conclusions will vary according to the historical pattern about which one is thinking. Like Antony, Aeneas is waylaid by a foreign queen, and his entanglement with her threatens the future glory of Rome, even as Antony's similar involvement presumably did. With this historical pattern in mind, the most noteworthy aspect of Virgil's episode is the way he changes the outcome so that Aeneas abandons Dido, choosing for himself the greater destiny which is Rome. To the extent that Aeneas shadows Augustus throughout the poem, a shadowing that Dryden and many other readers have insisted upon,[6] Aeneas's rejection of Dido in favor of Rome might suggest the triumph of Octavius (Augustus) over Eastern luxury and decadence at Actium. Or it could support Dryden's conjecture that the story is a subtle justification for "the divorce which not long before had passed between the Emperor and Scribonica."[7] Any connections drawn between Aeneas's choices and Augustus's actions are bound to complicate the theory that the poem is a celebration of Virgil's emperor, however. For Dido is not an entirely unsympathetic character, as the reactions of centuries of readers testify.[8] Her charges of cruelty and coldness linger in our minds and return to us as we consider Aeneas's final ruthless actions in book 12.

The final action of Virgil's work features a proud warrior, without a sword and begging for pity, being refused mercy by Aeneas and, out of revenge for the death of Pallas, killed. The death of Turnus is the culmination of the war between the Latins and the Trojans, a combat that has, by this point in the text, been identified as a tragic civil war in which good people have been wasted on both sides. In other words, it has become a dramatic image of what Virgil's contemporaries have recently lived through. Earlier in book 12, in Jupiter and Juno's discussion of this war, we are reminded that one way of dealing with a war between two peoples who should be one is to compromise, a path Juno is finally willing to take. Providing a poignant contrast to that compromise is the bloody revenge that Aeneas insists on taking against Turnus at the end of this book.

One consequence of this ending is that it opens up the text in such a way that, in the words of Michael Putnum, it can "negate any romantic notion of the *Aeneid* as an ideal vision of the greatness of Augustan Rome."[9] While there will always be those who will be able to find justification for Aeneas's action by arguing, with Giraldi Cinthio, that "it seemed contrary to justice to let a wicked man live,"[10] the circumstances under which Turnus is killed make it less easy to regard Aeneas as "a model for Augustus, or more unfortunate still, a glorification of the accomplishments of Rome through his character and life."[11] The very least that must be said about Virgil's ending is that it is handled in such a way as to allow into his work precisely those views of Augustus to which his opponents were most committed—namely, that his coming to and holding of power were products of his cruelty to his enemies and his needless slaughter of them.[12] In other words, Virgil devised an ending that had the capacity to unsay what the prophecies had earlier said.

A last point about Virgil's ending that lies at the heart of the general problem we are considering is that Aeneas's final brutal act is an important imitative moment in the work. For this climactic moment, Virgil reproduced the action at the center of the *Iliad*, the wrathful Achilles' slaughter of the noble Hector. It is possible to explain this episode as one more instance in which Virgil's modeling on the Greek epic calls attention to himself as a rejuvenator of the best ancient art. However, in the context of the discussion of how Virgil addresses his contemporary world, another option presents itself—namely, that Virgil imitated this particular aspect of Homer at this particular place in his text as a way of commenting on the nature of the action he was portraying. Recalling the image of a pitiless Achilles hardly promotes the sense of a triumphant ushering in of a glorious future; rather, it epitomizes the tragedy that a brutal war has produced. As such, this imitative moment exists not only as rejuvenated old art but as a potential device for making a political statement that calls into question the validity of the unambiguously celebratory statements made earlier in the text.

At issue in *The Tempest* is the extent to which Shakespeare's reworkings of Virgilian structures may be said to be simultaneous reworkings of certain aspects of the contemporary culture. As with the *Aeneid*, the most accessible referential aspects of *The Tempest* are the idioms of congratulation and mystification. The contemporary representation of James I as a philosopher-ruler and patriarch, the flattering representation of royal children, and the idealizing court masque were all part of the rhetoric in which King James and his contemporaries confirmed his authority and associated it with the national identity. Despite the clarity with which these materials recur in the play, what makes it impossible to read them as unambiguous repetitions of court ideology has to do both with the nature of the conflicts that the play narrates and with the nature of the political conflicts contemporary with the play. There may be no exact correlation between what is inside the play and what is outside of it, but the conceptual similarities that do recur are sufficient to allow the voices of opposition, competition, and conflict to be recalled, if not actually heard. The topic of royal children, inside the play and outside it, can illustrate the point rather quickly, even as it reminds us of the link between the play and the *Aeneid*.

One parallel between the plots of the *Aeneid* and *The Tempest* and the story that was being lived out at the court of King James involves the education of princes. Throughout the *Aeneid* the idea persists that the hope for the future resides in the children, and thus also in their being properly prepared, an emphasis that Virgil locates most importantly in the story of Anchises' teaching of Aeneas in *Aeneid* 6 and in the frequent reminders to him that he must look to the needs of his son. Likewise, Prospero, a father and ruler, takes Ferdinand in hand as soon as he gets to the island and uses the time he spends there to prepare him for marriage and rule. Expressed in typical romance form through a series of trials, the progress of this moral education repeats the same sequence that the Virgilian allegorists described.

The attention King James devoted to the education of Prince Henry was, of course, part of his own self-image as one whose contribution to England's destiny would be distinct and distinguished. In Henry and his other children, James had something to offer England that had not been available from any other monarch, without serious complications, since Henry VII. His providing

Henry a humanist education, his plans for a lavish investiture, and his establishing for Henry the court at St. James Palace were all consonant with the effort to display himself and the prince as guarantors of the nation's future, and thus to authenticate his own worth to the nation.

The spiritedness with which the English people responded to this offer attests to its success. Interest in Henry ran especially high in 1610, the year of his investiture as Prince of Wales. *Londons Love*, a pageant organized by London officials to celebrate the investiture,[13] generated so much enthusiasm that the Speaker of the House of Commons dismissed the House; the "Drums and Fifes were so loud," as the "Lord Mayor and Citizens of *London* in the Liveries of their several Companies" waited for Prince Henry to proceed from Richmond down the Thames and to Whitehall (*Commons Journals*, p. 434). Other evidence of the nation's participation in the mystification of Henry exists in the records showing whose sons were sent to him to learn the ways of a courtier, in the masques written to celebrate him, and in the artists who sought his patronage and dedicated their works to him.[14] George Chapman, one poet who secured that patronage, dedicated his translations of Homer to Henry, including the partial translation of the *Iliad* made in 1609 followed by the completed translation in 1611. As Graham Parry remarks, "Not surprisingly, the prefatory material attributes to the sponsor of the translation the full range of Homeric virtues and grandeur."[15]

In associating Henry with classical ideals, Chapman was following what had become a typical way to refer to him. Jonson's *Oberon*, performed at court on January 1, 1611, and featuring Henry dancing the title role, proclaimed: "He is above your reach. . . . He is the matter of vertue. . . . He is a god, o'er kings; yet stoupes he then / To teach them by the sweetnesse of his sway. . . . 'Tis he, that stays the time from turning old / And keeps the age up in a head of gold" (ll. 338–51). This same style marked the sermon preached in the College of Westminster the day before the prince's investiture as Prince of Wales. The chosen text—"*Create in mee a new heart,*" Psalms 51:10—was used to praise a perfection seemingly already realized: "such a young *Ptol-*

omey for studies and Libraries; such a young Alexander for affecting martialisme and chivalrie, such a young Josiah for religion & piety."[16]

Consistent with this image of potential greatness was the proposal of Henry as a unifier of dissenting groups, as even the above examples have suggested. During 1610, when James and Parliament were quarreling over finances, the king and his supporters repeatedly invoked the need to finance Henry—both the investiture and St. James Palace—as one reason to increase the king's supply. In Henry the concerns of the entire nation could be united, as James explained: "As for him I say no more; the sight of himselfe here speakes for him" (McIlwain, p. 319). Even the choice of Parliament as the location of the investiture was implicated in this effort. Held there on June 4, 1610, "in open Parliament, bothe Howses sitting together,"[17] this event in itself became one more way for James to ingratiate himself with a Parliament whose support he needed if he was to settle his problems of supply.[18] Here and elsewhere the effort to create a stable and unambiguous image of the prince was a means of countering national unrest and suppressing the effects of social and political tensions. So successful was the effort that even historians have responded slowly to evidence suggesting that Henry was also a source of conflict.

Despite James's rhetoric about the unequivocal value of his son, there was considerable concern that the cost of Prince Henry's court would be exorbitant and thus an exacerbation of the nation's already serious financial problems.[19] With spending habits like those of his father, the prince could offer little assurance that the worst fears were ill-founded. In 1611, he even admitted that "he was 'like enough to prove an unthrift,' " a likelihood that has provoked from Pauline Croft the wry remark that "Henry's premature death in 1612, although a political blow, was nevertheless a financial relief to the crown, and the significance of the four-year break between 1612 and prince Charles' majority in 1616 should not be underestimated as a monetary factor of some significance."[20]

In *The Tempest*, Shakespeare rhetorically portrays the young prince as an exemplary figure. Like the idealized Henry and the ideal pattern for education that many read into the story of Aeneas,

Ferdinand evolves steadily toward perfection. Moreover, also like the idealized Henry, he becomes the means in the play through which various factions move toward relationship and reciprocity. Prospero instructs the son of Alonso, his erstwhile enemy, betroths his own daughter to that son, and then gives him back to Alonso as a reward for repentance. Despite these features, the element in Ferdinand's role that resonates with current affairs is the strong emphasis upon exercises in discipline and self-control in Prospero's education of him, an emphasis that registers contemporary anxieties, especially about the expansion of royal power and excessive royal expenditures.

Thus, the play can as easily be read as a complicated response to a real-life situation as a reworking of the Virgilian pre-text. In the latter case, quite striking are the changes wrought on Virgil by refashioning Ferdinand as a chaste Aeneas. To effect that change, Shakespeare guided the imitation in a direction involving simplification rather than complication of the structures that he adopted from Virgil. Unlike Aeneas, Ferdinand is not a conflicted figure. In his portrayal of Ferdinand, Shakespeare flattened Virgil, weakening the tensions that dominate the parent work. This method surprises us, so accustomed are we to finding that Shakespeare made his sources more intricate than they originally were.

Another way of understanding the implications of this compositional strategy, and one that makes sense particularly when read in the context of James's court, is that the presentation of Ferdinand as an ideal is a rhetorical choice that created options for the author. It furnished him with a "*charitable* attitude"[21] with which to confront some contemporary issues that were full of conflict and that, in the view of court critics, required correction. The play's presentation of a prince might well remind one of Henry, yet Ferdinand's characteristics are not only the characteristics that Henry possessed but those his critics wished he had. Thus the flattening and weakening of the Virgilian tensions cooperate with this style of instruction and criticism.

A different handling of royal children is evident in the case of Ferdinand's sister, Claribel. In this instance, the anxieties about royal policy are presented quite directly, and by means of a different rhetorical technique. Shakespeare casts the presentation of the court party's response to the wedding of Claribel, Alonso's other child, in the style of vituperation or blame, epideictic's alternative to praise. The story of Claribel, whom Antonio and Sebastian describe as having been married to the wrong person, someone who lives too far away, is, of course, homologous to the marriage negotiations for Prince Henry and Lady Elizabeth.[22] Speculation and advice about how James would or should use the marriages of his children to effect political allegiances had been continuous since his accession. Some felt that if Elizabeth were married to a Protestant (the most favored being the Palatine prince from Germany whom she eventually did marry), then Henry should be married to a Catholic (a Spanish infanta or the daughter of Henry IV of France), a plan that this committed Protestant prince eschewed. Another option was to marry both children to the Catholic offspring of the duke of Savoy. In the several months immediately preceding the November 1, 1611, performance of *The Tempest*, negotiations for all these possibilities were in progress. The ambassador of the duke of Savoy arrived in England on March 23, 1611,[23] and was still pressing his suit on November 29, 1611.[24] Meanwhile negotiations were continuing with both France and Spain, the latter of which (in October 1611) withdrew the offer of the first infanta for Henry and offered the second instead, much to the consternation of the king.[25]

Sir Walter Raleigh wrote two letters to James on the subject of the marriages, declaring against the Savoyan suits.[26] His letters record how the contemporary argument against these suits was structured. The similarity between the structure of that argument and the manner in which Shakespeare states the case against Claribel's marriage is striking.

Raleigh's central argument was that to marry the Savoyans would be to increase the risk of Spanish, and so Catholic, treachery against England: "Savoy and Spain are inseparable, and . . . Savoy dare not offend the pope nor the emperor" (p. 237; cf. pp. 239, 241, and passim). Besides, Savoy, he noted, was too far away: "Our kings of England . . . have no business over the Alps" (p. 234), and such a marriage for Princess Elizabeth would necessitate that she "be removed far from her nearest blood . . . into a country far estranged from our nation as any part of Christendom" (p. 235). Raleigh and others preferred that Elizabeth marry Frederick of Germany and that Henry either marry the French Catholic princess or bide his time, "keep his own ground for a while. . . . While he is yet free, all have hope" (p. 250).

In *The Tempest* the complaints about Claribel's marriage parallel these contemporary anxieties about James's arranging proper marriages for his children—a structure that is supported also by a Virgilian context. Claribel has been married in Tunis, and Tunis, Gonzalo explains, "was Carthage." Immediately afterward, in a conversation among Alonso, Antonio, and Sebastian, Alonso laments and his comrades reproach him with the fact that he had married Claribel to someone too far away: "You were kneel'd to, and importun'd otherwise, / By all of us" (2.1.124–25). The marriage itself may have been a "sweet" (2.1.69) wedding, but now that the child remains physically removed from her own land—"So far . . . removed / I ne'er again shall see her" (2.1.106–7), so far away that now she "is banish'd from your eye" (2.1.122)—her absence signifies to her father and countrymen the precariousness and unpredictability of their own future, a future that might have been better secured had the marriage been to someone else.[27]

In addition to the complaint about distance, there is also a more specific reprimand for choosing the wrong nation. Sebastian complains that the king did not marry Claribel to a European, was not willing to "bless our Europe with your daughter" (2.1.120). Instead of following counsel, Sebastian complains, Alonso decided to "loose her to an African" (2.1.121), Africa being as alien a land to an Italian as a Catholic marriage would have seemed "alien" to the proponents of Protestant matches for James's children.[28] In producing this argument about mistaken political marriage, the play supports the faction that was urging against Savoy and thus associates blame with anyone who takes another position.

Because the discourse of this contemporary issue recurs in the play in generalized, metaphoric, and analogic rhetorical structures (there are no overt topical allusions to track down, nothing more specific than the reference to Europe), it can disappear from sight

Imitation and Occasion 43

once the controversy and the language that created it are no longer current. This capacity for disappearance, characteristic of any discourse, also suggests how a work can become newly contemporary, as would have been the case when *The Tempest* was played for the betrothal festivities of Princess Elizabeth in 1613.[29] So universalized can the play's images appear to be that the play, performed at a later date for an exceedingly context-rich occasion, could take on the concreteness of this new situation. Like all other drama that is newly "authenticated" by a new audience "in terms of live contemporary issues," *The Tempest*, too, exists as an "abstract . . . blueprint,"[30] the referentiality of which always depends on what an audience knows and thinks about.

Be that as it may, the handling of the story of Ferdinand's education and of the attitudes toward Claribel's marriage suggests some of the ways in which the play textualizes the contemporary culture. It does not report or replay what has been going on, but it does tell analogous stories, repeat in similar circumstances familiar arguments, and make points in ways that signal acceptance of some cultural values and rejection of others.[31] In all of these instances, the play—its stories and its languages—is a set of responses to current situations, just as any speech act is a response both to language and situation.[32] It is "a rejoinder in a given dialogue," "shot through with dialogized overtones . . . [and] calculated nuances on all fundamental voices and tones of this heteroglossia." Moreover, as a response, it is written with the working assumption that, even as it is a response so will there be response to it: "All rhetorical forms, monologic in their compositional structure, are oriented toward the listener and his answer."[33] If these statements are always true, they are more immediately true whenever the rhetorical form is oral and in front of an audience.

Like Ferdinand and Claribel, Prospero is also a response to Virgil through contemporary situations. In his roles as father and magus ruler, Prospero participates in the most mystifying terms of royal ideological representation.[34] But where he exercises control over other characters, the implications of his actions are more ambiguous. In part, that ambiguity and complexity result from the exceedingly wide range of patterns from Virgil that Shakespeare used to create him, including Aeneas, the gods, Priam, and, in one instance, Ovid's Medea. Another indication of this complexity lies in the various ways that the part of Prospero (especially in relation to Ariel and Caliban) reconstitutes the political languages of high politics, especially the languages of monarchy and colonization.

The Limits of Royal Power

The topic of royal children illustrates the method that will be used throughout this study of *The Tempest* to identify and suggest the range of the play's referentiality. Central to the method is attention not only to what was happening at the time of its writing, but also to the language in which the arguments about what was happening were cast. In the case of the children, laudatory materials dominate the extant documents. But when it comes to the debates on royal power, a detailed record of the nature and degree of conflict is available. These highly polemical documents record the characteristic features of the opposing arguments, information that is indispensable for estimating the response the play registers.

By 1611, the year of *The Tempest*, the discussion in England about how much power a king should have had been going on for at least three hundred years.[35] During the reign of Elizabeth, the topic elicited frequent and vigorous debate. In the early years of the reign of James, and especially during the parliamentary session of 1610, these debates resumed, and for more than one reason. The English had been, from the start, suspicious and fearful of this Scot sitting on England's throne; James had been injudiciously and repetitively articulate about his own notions that a king's power was absolute, and the agendas he set for his first Parliament, which ran in three sessions from 1604 to 1610, gave the king and the Commons what we can see in retrospect to have been a best possible context for expressing fear and contending for power. Those agendas featured the king's plan for uniting England and Scotland and his request that the sovereign be given more suitable financing—clearly the two most important issues of the first years of the reign.[36] Both topics were brought up in 1604 during the first session of Parliament. By the end of the second session, which ran from 1606 to

1607, the king's project for the union had, in effect, been defeated. During the third and final session of this Parliament—which met for twelve months (February 9, 1610, to February 9, 1611)—the focus of debate was the project for a financial settlement, a project that was also destined to fail.

James's summoning Parliament in 1610 for the purpose of settling the matter of supply was, in itself, an entirely reasonable move.[37] At the outset of his reign, Parliament had allotted the king a generous financial grant, partly in celebration of his accession, but then in subsequent years it had taken no further action on supply, distracted as it had been by the Gunpowder Plot and the issue of the union of England and Scotland. As a result, by 1610 the court was in a state of financial emergency, a crisis brought about not merely by the king's extravagance but by the fact that the Crown's income from patrimonial property, wardships, knights' service, and purveyances was no longer adequate to the court's needs. This fiscal situation had been inherited from Elizabeth, who had taken extreme measures in her later years to acquire adequate financing,[38] and James could not leave the matter unsettled any longer. But when he requested supply, the Commons responded not with money but with arguments.

As the 1610 session opened, the specific issue that engaged the opposition was the matter of the customs the Crown levied on imported and exported goods. Traditionally, the English monarch had levied such impositions for the regulatory purpose of protecting English merchants from foreign competition. Desperate for revenue, James and Salisbury had recently increased the impositions beyond what was needed for regulation, thereby altering the function that impositions had served in the past. Although their action was legal, and certainly in conformity with the 1606 court decision in Bates's Case,[39] some in the Commons interpreted the move as an extension of the royal prerogative. What the Commons feared was not the custom of imposing in and for itself, but the action of increasing the impositions without consulting Parliament. The fear bred by this action—that the king was inclined to overextend his power—was increased all the more by his next move, the proposal that the system for supply be changed to one of a guaranteed revenue. While most modern historians agree that this proposal, the Great Contract, was a good plan, one that would have benefited the people as much as the king, some in Parliament feared that once the proposal was passed the king would no longer need to summon Parliament, a situation that would eliminate their voice in government. Others, who supported the king, thought that the Great Contract would actually reduce the royal prerogative.

In the earlier 1606–07 session, devoted to a large extent to the Union, the focus of debate had been on how the relationship between England and Scotland might be defined, a topic which produced a discourse concerned with issues of equality, preference, and benefit.[40] In the later session of 1610, an identifiably different discourse predominated. Devoted almost entirely to the question of the king's finances, this session developed a discourse—a lexicon and a set of arguments—that kept the debates focused on the relationship between king and subject. If the subjects were to supply the king, the Commons wanted to know what he would give them in return. What did each owe to each? Or, put somewhat differently, what were the limits of the king's power?

King James typically defended his position by arguing that he had the right to all the power he already was exercising and all that he planned to exercise, a position he articulated by comparing kings to gods, to fathers, and to the head of a body: "In the Scriptures Kings are called Gods, and so their power after a certain relation compared to the Divine power. Kings are also compared to Fathers of families; for a King is trewly *Parens patriae*, the politique father of his people. And lastly, Kings are compared to the head of this Microcosme of the body of a man."[41] He gave this speech to Parliament in March as part of his strategy to contain and divert the opposition[42] raised by his policies. While James had his supporters in Parliament, those who opposed him cast their arguments in the oppositional language that had been dignified in England by generations of use.[43] They said that a king who exercised a transcendent power was one who deprived his subjects of liberty, threw them into bondage, and treated them as slaves.

So important were these debates considered at the time that

documents from this Parliament were given unusually wide distribution. The speech of James just cited was printed at least four times in 1610.[44] Pauline Croft has covered other details of this subject with just the thoroughness we need at this point: "Numerous copies were circulated of Salisbury's speech of 15 February, which opened the discussions on the great contract, and his speech of 10 July defending impositions was also widely copied . . . the terms of the great contract as concluded in July 1610 were discussed in every county as members returned home with instructions from the Commons to sound out their neighbours' opinions. [William] Hakewill's remarkable attack on the legality of the new impositions, and the list of the Commons' grievances presented at the end of the fourth session, were also circulated. . . . Perhaps most striking of all was the appearance in 1611 of a hitherto unprecedented collection of printed parliamentary material, aiming to defend the proceedings of the house of Commons over the great contract. This volume claimed to have been printed abroad, to avoid the censorship of the privy council."[45]

Also notable in this record of what was printed is John Chamberlain's expression of anxiety about what *might* be printed. In a letter of May 24, 1610, he reported that James's March speech, which "strained so high and made so transcendent" the royal prerogative, had "bred generally much discomfort"—so much discomfort, in fact, that there was now the "wish that this speach might never come in print."[46] Finally, two important speeches of the opposition—those by Hakewill and Whitelocke—were to be printed in 1641, a detail that further corroborates our sense of the clarity and fullness with which these earlier documents were understood to have articulated the issues at hand.[47]

Taken together, these details suggest the importance of this session of Parliament, the contemporary interest in high politics,[48] the availability of news, and, especially important to this study of *The Tempest*, the contemporary availability of the language in which these events were discussed. The discourse that developed to argue the relationship between king and subject was not a private language but one produced in the public arena of court and

Commons and then distributed for public knowledge. Once in circulation, it was available for any number of different projects or discursive practices.

It would be possible to formulate in different ways just how *The Tempest* relates to this context, how it manages to "draw the real into its own texture."[49] The thesis to be pursued here is that the political discourse, especially of 1610, is re-presented by Shakespeare in fictional constructs that imitate the language—that is, the metaphors, idioms, and rhetoric[50] that James was using to represent his identity (the king as god, father, head of a microcosm)—as well as the rhetorical structures that the opposition parliamentarians were using to represent the identity they felt they would acquire as subjects to such a king (the subject in bondage and servitude). Prospero, a ruler with magical and thus transcendent powers, stands in homologous relationship to King James and his concerns about his rights to a certain amount of power and to be served (and supplied) properly. Ariel and Caliban, who are in bondage and who continually express their longing for freedom, are homologous to the metaphors, idioms, and rhetoric used in the Commons to express the subjects' right to liberty and freedom, their right to present grievances or to "complain," and their fears of "restraint" and loss of property.

To the extent that different attitudes toward rule and subjection find expression in *The Tempest*, the play authenticates and validates both sides in the debate while at the same time producing an argument for constitutionalism. *The Tempest*, then, does not only mystify the court of the current political scene; it also dignifies public debate and demystifies absolutist claims and strategies—all of which deepens the significance of the play's repetitions of a classical text that was understood as a mirror of the time and also the importance of the presentation of such a play on the Jacobean stage. We may not know how *The Tempest* was received, but we can estimate the possible applicability of plays in general, a subject Andrew Gurr has addressed: "The fictional presentation of affairs of state, in a city devoted to the art and trade of 'application,' is probably a sharper guide to popular and even governing modes of thought about politics and society in Shakespeare's time than is the case today. The fictions of the state were certainly not so marginal to the affairs of state, because imaginative thought had few other outlets, and none with the coerciveness of the minds of men in company."[51]

The best context in which to examine the relationship of this play to its time is that which takes the most complete account of what was happening in politics in the year prior to the play's first performance. An especially important source, therefore, are the parliamentary records of 1610–11. As one would expect, many of the details of the debates they record involve the recitation of numerical figures and historical precedents as the Commons sought to arrive at a solution to the problem. More relevant to *The Tempest*, however, is the language aimed, not at arriving at a solution, but at laying out the theoretical issues of rule and rights that this fiscal situation brought into focus. Just as Ariel seeks Prospero's assurance that in exchange for tasks performed Prospero will grant him freedom, so the Commons wanted the king to know that they expected something in return for their willingness to grant supply.

This point was made powerfully at the very outset of the session, when the Commons responded to the king's request for supply not by talking about it, but by requesting a conference with the Lords, at which they demanded to know, " 'What the King will give to his subjects?' *Quid mihi dabis?*" (Gardiner, p. 13). Before they would supply the king, they wanted to know which grievances he would satisfy. As Henry Montague told the Lords, the Lords might have special knowledge of royal powers, the "*arcana imperii,*" but the Commons knew much about "*vota populi*" (Gardiner, p. 14).

This insistence that the king express a willingness to satisfy grievances was but one strategy developed by the opposition for arguing that the king's use of impositions seemed to be an abuse of the royal prerogative. Other strategies involved rhetoric that would, for them, satisfactorily define and characterize the kind of power that James was exercising, or seemed to want to exercise. Especially notable in these arguments is the fact that the opposition appropriated for its own use the language of natural law, language that in so many other instances had been used to defend absolute rule.[52] Henry Martin argued that the king's imposing showed "an arbitrary, irregular, unlymited, and transcendent power" (Gardiner, p. 88). Later, Martin's emphasis on notions of arbitrariness and irregularity was replicated in John Hoskyns's explanation that a royal power that has no limits "is contrary to reason" (Gardiner, p. 76), and again, in a remark from the discussion in April 1610, that "To stretch prerogative so as to extend beyond measur" is something that "nature it selfe speakes against" (Gardiner, p. 152).

Significantly, those in the Commons who were arguing against the king explained that the danger in such immeasure and irregularity was that it could result in a loss of liberty so serious as to amount to a change of status for the people. Thomas Beaumont expressed the "Fear, that our whole Liberty be swallowed up" (*Commons Journals*, p. 430), and Adam Blackwood feared that "we [would be] all Slaves" (*Commons Journals*, p. 399). The more precise definition of how the status could change came from Whitelocke, who warned that if they allowed the king to set up a system whereby he could get all the money he wanted "without our consent," they would in effect be changing their status from that of subjects—people who had rights before the law and could plead and intreat to the king—to that of tenants, and "tenants at his will" (*Learned and Necessary Argument*, B3ᵛ). They would find themselves in a position, in other words, whereby the king could, if he would, appropriate the subjects' goods. And this alteration was of such consequence, explained Whitelocke, that it "subverteth the fundamentall Law of the Realme, and induceth a new forme of state and government" (B4ᵛ).

Of the documents produced by the Commons during these debates, two of the most important were the Petition of Right and the Petition of Temporal Grievances, both of which were printed at the time. The former (not to be confused with the more famous Petition of Right of 1628) was entered in Parliament on May 23, 1610, and then delivered to the king.[53] The main thrust of this petition is the Commons's insistence that there be no infringement of "the ancient and fundamental right of the liberty of the Parliament" to debate freely the king's use of his prerogative, for only if this right is protected is it "possible for the subject either to know or to maintain his right and property to his own lands and goods."[54]

The Petition of Temporal Grievances (accompanied by a Petition of Ecclesiastical Grievances) was presented to the king at Whitehall on July 7, 1610. In attendance at this presentation were the Privy Council and twenty members of the House of Commons.[55] In this document, the Commons reminded the king that there was nothing more "precious" to them than "to be guided and governed by the certain rule of the law, which giveth both to the head and members that which of right belongeth to them."[56] As even these examples show, both the Petition of Right and this later document contain language that emphasizes that the king was subject to restraint. A notion of restraint did not mean that the king was not absolute, but, as Whitelocke had earlier insisted, it did mean that the absolute power of the king, the "*Suprema Potestas*," did not exist in the king by himself, but in "the King in Parliament" (*Learned and Necessary Argument*, C).

The rhetoric that King James and his supporters developed to counter these arguments focused on the issue of the legality of the impositions and on the need to protect the king's prerogative. Arguing the legality of supply, Francis Bacon explained that "the question is not whether the King may alter the law by his prerogative but whether the King have not such a prerogative by law."[57] Choosing the Great Contract rather than the impositions as the focus of his contribution to the discussion, Sir Julius Caesar argued against the Contract on the grounds that it would diminish the royal prerogative.[58] And that diminution would, in turn, lead to the king's losing control of the people, for it would "free" them "from the King's greatest lawfull power" (Gardiner, p. 175). Anxious that Parliament find a way to supply the king other than by way of the Contract's guaranteed income, he explained that "to strengthen the King is to preserve the state" (Gardiner, p. 176).

Like the arguments of the Commons, the arguments of Bacon and Caesar emphasized the implications of any actions they now might take. Those implications were also the concern of King James, whose power and policies were the focus of all the discussion. It is, then, of particular interest to notice what he had to say on these matters. In his first speech to this Parliament, on March 21, 1610, he included the placating remark that "Kings wil be glad to bound themselves within the limits of their Lawes" (McIlwain, p. 309), and, in a statement quite similar to the one Whitelocke would make later in the year, he even explained, "For the King with his Parliament here are absolute (as I understand) in making or forming of any sort of Lawes" (McIlwain, p. 311).[59] Obviously, James was in part anxious to dilute the Commons's impression that he was a maverick foreigner out to disrupt the English way of doing things. He took the position that the king was not like a god who "spake by Oracles, and wrought by Miracles," but rather he became *"Lex Loquens"* (McIlwain, p. 309).

However willing James was to acknowledge the importance of law and the ways in which a king is not a god, he nevertheless used this comparison to express that quintessential nature of the king's position: "The State of MONARCHIE is the supremest thing upon earth: For Kings are not onely GODS Lieutenants upon earth, and sit upon GODS throne, but even by GOD himselfe they are called Gods." Kings resemble gods in many ways; even as gods "create, or destroy, make or unmake," so do kings "make and unmake their subjects" and have power "of life, and of death" over them. In fact, kings can "make of their subjects like men at the Chesse" (McIlwain, pp. 307–8). In these metaphors, James was developing language that Salisbury, the Lord Treasurer, would imitate when he referred to the king as the *"primum mobile"* (Gardiner, p. 52), and that Bacon would use when explaining that it was the nature of a king to be the *"principale agens"* (Gardiner, p. 67). James hoped, of course, that this language of agency could be translated into trust. To that end, he assured the Commons that he would not abuse his power and that he had no intention of saying one thing in public and then contradicting it in private: "Kings Actions (even in the secretest places) are as the actions of those that are set upon the Stages, or on the tops of houses" (McIlwain, p. 310).[60]

On the specific issue of supply, James had two especially important things to say. First, he stated flatly that subjects owed him supply, a position that, in itself, no one would deny.[61] In exacting payments, James said, the king only took that which the subject was bound to give. His second point, and the one that eventually triggered the Commons to issue their Petition of Right, was that, because supply was his right, the Commons was not to dispute the matter. On this issue, James scolded, the Commons was to restrain itself; the Commons was to be quiet. Thus the reasoning rhetoric of explanation, reassurance, and definition joined the language of threat; the power of gods was not to be questioned.

The outcome of this year-long debate was that James finally silenced Parliament by dissolving it before any resolution had been reached, an event which some historians have in retrospect thought may have been "a turning point in the financial and constitutional history of the early seventeenth century."[62] Ideally, some would say, Parliament's role was not to make the king's task impossible (even as the king's was not to prevent Parliament from meeting) but to "produce union between crown and people."[63] As Bacon would tell James in 1612, a Parliament had two purposes, "the one for the supply of your estate; the other for the better knitting of the hearts of your subjects unto your Majesty . . . for both which, Parliaments have been and are the ancient and honorable remedy" (Spedding, p. 280). Early in 1611, that remedy seemed not to be available. Having dissolved Parliament, the king would not call it again until 1614, when it would meet for only two months.

In *The Tempest* the central metaphors of the debates of 1610 are literalized in a fiction that reproduces the structures of the opposing arguments. As a magus, Prospero is like a god, a first mover; he makes and unmakes all the situations on the island. He also takes it for granted that Ariel and Caliban should serve him (supply him), that they should be punished if they complain, perhaps even silenced. The position of each of them in relation to Prospero is not, of course, the same: Ariel serves an apprenticeship; Caliban has been made a prisoner. At times Ariel seems to reflect the king's faithful followers, at others, he exhibits the formally obsequious behavior that even a distraught Commons would use when confronting the king. Likewise, Caliban images the displanted native of Virginia or Ireland, but also the English fear of being made "slaves" in their own land. Whatever the case, together these characters represent the issues of service and supply, restraint and complaint from different angles, which, in combination and in juxtaposition, present a complex and provocative picture of the issues of reciprocity as they were being debated at this time. Depending on one's perspective, supplying the king could be understood, or experienced, either as that which was paid in return for freedom or as that which represented the loss of freedom. To serve Prospero is to give him his due and secure for oneself the promise of a good life in the future; to serve Prospero is also to add to his power.

If *The Tempest* plays off the dialogic nature of the topic at hand, it also credits constitutionalism as the standard which, of necessity, had to be activated if the dialogue was to reach a harmonious closure. A commonwealth can thrive only when there is both sovereignty and liberty. The king's mysterious and secret powers (the *arcana imperii*) and the voice of the people (the *vota populi*) must somehow be made to coexist. Restraint on both king and people is the only means through which each acquires more freedom and power. Displaced into the love plot in *The Tempest*, this idea recurs in Miranda's pledge to be Ferdinand's servant and in his rejoinder that he will be her husband "with heart as willing / As bondage e'er of freedom" (3.1.88–89). Likewise, Prospero, who appears at one point "*on the top (invisible)*," and has the power to do anything he wishes to the people on the island, decides at the end to surrender his magic, an action that curbs his power. Thus the play legitimizes the king's position while at the same time exerting pressure on it by legitimizing the position of the opposition. While "order," then, is a value the play espouses and, like the masques, a value to which it refers in the actual world, the play nevertheless acknowledges the stance, taken by many, that it was royal authority, not the Commons, that was growing disorderly.

That stance had been expressed so strongly that it was remarked in a conference of the House of Lords that anyone who could put questions to a ruler as the Commons had "did either look for a Tiberius or Sejanus" (Gardiner, p. 121).[64] That such a remark could be voiced at this time makes Shakespeare's choice of a Virgilian text as his precursor for this play all the more interesting. Like James, Augustus had the reputation of being a peace-bringer. But he also had been called a tyrant, one who had destroyed Rome's

Imitation and Occasion   55

mixed government and deprived the people of their liberties, the tradition to which Ariosto referred when he remarked that Augustus "was not such a saint" as Virgil had made him. It was this aspect of Augustus that caused some readers to question Virgil's integrity in writing poetry to celebrate him. For Shakespeare ostentatiously to play off the central Jacobean idioms for royal power in a work that engages Virgil's central text is also for him to participate in this dialogue concerning the poet's right relationship to the ruler. Shakespeare honors and celebrates James by representing the monarch's godlike, fatherlike role, but he also shows concern for the just use of that role.

Colonization

The context of the parliamentary debates on the limits of royal power enlivens as well as qualifies the important work that has been done on *The Tempest* as a colonization play. For the most part, recent interest in this topic has focused either on how periods later than *The Tempest* appropriated the play for their own colonizing—or, more often, decolonizing—projects,[65] or on the presence in the play of a Renaissance discourse of colonization.[66] Central to these discussions are the means by which the play establishes a dialectic on issues of exploitation and legitimation. As in the debates on the limits of royal power, at issue in colonization were questions about rule and subjection, who had the right to how much power over whom.

It is important to my argument to establish that, in the sixteenth and seventeenth centuries, the discourses of English monarchy and constitutionalism and the discourse of colonization were linked. More specifically, there was a great deal of lexical and metaphoric crossover between the language of rule and the language of colonization. Each discourse provided idioms and metaphors for the other; likewise, each could appropriate the rhetoric and structures of argument that were developed in the other. For example, in 1610 King James used the language of colonization for one of his defenses of royal power. Comparing kings to gods, fathers, heads, and also colonizers, James insisted that "Kings had their first originall from them, who planted and spread themselves in *Colonies* through the world" (McIlwain, p. 308). Here King James used the idea of colonization to buttress his argument that nothing must be allowed to diminish the power of kings because that power was the origin and ensured the continuance of civilization. As colonization rhetoric was appropriated by the king to defend his power, so did both defenders and detractors of colonization mine the commonplaces about rule to bolster their positions.

The documents from the Virginia project illustrate this point from several angles. In the sermons and treatises written to defend and promote the project, writers addressed the issue of whether or not England had the legal right to take the land of another people. Anxious to answer those who had charged that England had no such right, the author of *A True Declaration of the Estate of the Colonie in Virginia, With a confutation of such scandalous reports as have tended to the disgrace of so worthy an enterprise* (London, 1610) devoted the first section of his treatise to the issue of whether or not plantation was "lawfull." Among his many defenses is an argument from historical precedent: "why that should bee lawfull for *France*, which is (in us) unlawfull: that which to *Rome* was possible, (to us) is impossible: that which to others is honourable, and profitable, (in us) should bee traduced, as in commodious, base, and contemptible." There is also an argument that some of the property the English had acquired had not been taken but purchased: "*Paspehay*, one of their Kings, sold unto us for copper, land to inherit and inhabite."[67] Earlier, Robert Gray, in *A Good Speed to Virginia* (London, 1609), addressing this issue of "right or warrant"[68] and appropriating for his own argument the notion that rights to property cannot be violated, had explained that, because the natives "have no particular proprietie in any part or parcell of that Countrey, but only a generall recidencie" (C_3^v-C_4), it was unnecessary to apply the same legal or constitutionalist standard to this situation: "there is not *meum & tuum* amongst them: so that if the whole lande should bee taken from them, there is not a man that can complaine of any particular wrong done unto him" (C_4).

But discourses about the right to rule over another were not confined to discussions about whether or not England had the right to dominate the native American population. This rhetoric was also present, and in the most complex ways, in the documents that established the organization of the Virginia Company and prescribed the governance of the Jamestown colony. After suffering great losses in its earliest years, in 1609 the Virginia Company undertook a project for reorganization, an initial step of which was to secure from James a second charter (issued May 23, 1609). Insofar as a central aim of this charter, drafted by the constitutionalist Edwin Sandys, was to shift control of the company away from James and disperse it among the organizers of the company, it stands as one more document from the period that attests to an anti-absolutist project.[69] At the same time, however, this document changed the form of government in the colony from that of a president who reported to a council to that of a governor who was given "absolute power and aucthority to correct, punishe, pardon, governe and rule."[70] In addition, the institution of martial law was soon to follow.[71]

When William Strachey, who helped codify the laws for the colony, returned to England in 1611, he brought with him the completed manuscript of these laws. Published in January 1612, *Lawes Divine, Morall and Martiall, etc.* served in part to assure those who wanted to invest in Virginia that their own interests were being protected. The use of martial law did not, however, meet with universal approval. While it could also be argued that severe discipline was required to maintain order in this isolated and vulnerable community, still, both contemporary and modern commentary have characterized these laws as "draconian."[72] In 1612, *The New Life of Virginea* would advise that the "dutie towards your Colonie [is to] let them live as free English men, under the government of just and equall lawes, and not as slaves after the will and lust of any superiour."[73] And in 1624, the report from the colony would recall that, when Sir Thomas Dale arrived in May 1611, "He immediately published most tyrannous and cruel laws sent over by Sir Thos. Smythe."[74]

While this mix of detail can be variously interpreted and accounted for, in itself it provides an example both of the ideological complexities of the situation and of how this situation displays the problems of subjection from different angles. Equally to the point for this study is that the overlapping features among the discourses of absolutism, constitutionalism, and colonization, especially as these features can be identified as present in *The Tempest*, make it impossible to separate them, and thus their contexts, from each other in the play. Or, put positively, the indistinguishability of these discourses in *The Tempest* is a central feature of its metaphoric and parodic structures, which depend on the ability of the metaphors of rule and rights to blend with and collapse into the metaphors of colonization. Each enhances the others and suggests the implications of the others.[75] The "*picturing function*" of these metaphors "make[s] discourse appear."[76]

In addition, this coincidence suggests both the impossibility of and the distortion involved in distinguishing the play's participation in the language of colonization as a discourse relevant only to the colonization of the New World, the plantation context that most English and American scholars have privileged for this play. The colonization of Ireland was also contemporary with the play[77] and was routinely acknowledged at the time as analogous to the colonization of the New World.[78] Moreover, the discourse about the plantation of Ireland is older and much more developed, certainly in regard to issues of rule. (England's formal project to take over Ireland had been in process since the 1560s.)

To recognize this point raises more than one issue, including the problem of setting limits when one engages in the task of historicizing a literary text. In any study of intertextuality, often it is impossible to limit consideration to a single progenitor, or even to a set number of progenitors, because others are so much like the one at issue or have themselves been crossed by the same progenitors. In this case, the problem seems to be especially acute, however. For if one eliminates the Irish context, one has eliminated both the older discourse and also the discourse that fully elaborates the link between colonization and constitutionalism.[79] The central reason for pursuing the Irish colonial discourse for the study of *The Tempest* is, then, precisely the fact that one of its principal constituents is constitutional language.[80] In addition to clarifying for the modern reader the points of contact between a colonial and a constitutional discourse, the documents of the Anglo-Irish conflict also confirm that a colonial discourse contains a language of mystification as well as a language of resistance.

A constitutionalist perspective on early Ireland is one that modern historians have only recently begun to develop.[81] Nevertheless, this perspective, and the discourse on which it depends, is readily accessible in the vast amount of Irish material available, including *The Chronicle of Ireland* in Holinshed's *Chronicles of England, Scotland, and Ireland* (1587),[82] a multivocal work which tells the story of the Anglo-Irish struggle in detail over many years, and often with considerable sympathy for the Irish. This source also corroborates how deeply rooted in English culture was the story of the Irish struggle and also how constitutional issues had come to be a staple of this subject. Another set of documents that contains this discourse are letters, pamphlets, and speeches from the early years of the reign of James that record the plans for and problems with planting Ulster. This latter group of documents (many of which are contained in the *Calendar of State Papers, Ireland*)[83] demonstrates how much attention was being given to the Irish project during the period contemporary with the writing of *The Tempest* and, again, how standard a part of this discourse were constitutional issues.

That plantation is the focal point of *The Chronicle of Ireland* is apparent at the outset, for the chronicle is dedicated to Sir Henry Sidney, Sir Philip Sidney's father, who developed the system in the 1560s for planting Ireland and held the position of lord deputy of Ireland at the time this chronicle was being prepared.[84] The authors largely responsible for the chronicle were Richard Stanyhurst and John Hooker alias Vowell, both of whom displayed an intimate knowledge of the idiom of colonization.

Stanyhurst, a Dubliner by birth, wrote two sections of *The Chronicle of Ireland*, one on the reign of Henry VIII and the other a digressive "Description of Ireland." No more conventional here than in his translation of Virgil,[85] Stanyhurst scattered citations of the *Aeneid* all through the "Description"; at one point, in describing the building of the walls of Ross, he quoted fifteen fourteeners from Thomas Phaer's translation of Virgil's description of the building of the walls of Carthage (p. 31). Because glorification was not Stanyhurst's style, the citation suggests a debunking of what the English planters were attempting; it also gives us another example of how aspects of Virgil's text, in this case its colonizing motifs, could be variously appropriated.

While Stanyhurst's personal point of view is difficult to discern,[86] it is clear that his stake in this story was a political one; he places himself in relationship to the narrative of Irish history by identifying his father, James Stanyhurst, Speaker of the House in the Irish Parliament (1557, 1560, and 1568), as a man known for "his exact knowlege in the common lawes," and as one who had challenged in Parliament both Sir Henry Sidney and Thomas Earl of Sussex, Sidney's predecessor (pp. 64–65). Moreover, in the "Description," Stanyhurst included many stories of the trouble the native Irish had had with the "English conquerors" (p. 33). Typical of these narratives, and of their vituperative tone, is the account of how an Irishman charged the English lord deputy with being "the meane and instrument by which his majesties subjects are dailie spoiled. Therefore I as a loyall subject saye traitor to thy teeth" (p. 49). Later this "loyall" Irishman charged that the lord deputy was "content to wink at the miserie" of the subjects as long as "your mouth were stopt with briberie" (p. 51).

John Hooker alias Vowell, who oversaw the editing and revision of the 1587 edition of Holinshed's *Chronicle*, had an even closer association with the constitutional issues and language of colonization. Known to have made a speech in the 1569 Irish House of Commons defending the royal prerogative,[87] he is identified in *The Chronicle of Ireland* as "one of the citizens for the citie of Excester at the parlement holden at Westminster" in 1571 and 1560 (p. 345). Most of the narratives he recounts deal with confrontations between the representative of the English Crown and the representatives of the Irish people, with debates over what each owes to each, features that allow us to recognize how ideologically and discursively akin were the ongoing project of colonization and the early seventeenth-century quarrels between King James and Parliament.

For *The Chronicle of Ireland*, Hooker covered the period of Irish history that included Henry Sidney's tenure as lord deputy and James Stanyhurst's tenure as speaker of the house. Typical of the power struggles during this period was the stormy session of Parliament in 1568. There was Stanyhurst's confrontation with the lord chancellor, in which, answering the opening oration on how order in society depends on obedience to law and the queen, Stanyhurst cited those aspects of law that preserve the "liberties and freedoms" of every Parliament. He enumerated the Commons' demands that members of the lower house have free and safe passage to and from Parliament, that only Parliament have the right to punish its members for wrongdoing, and, like the Commons in 1610, that Parliament "have libertie to speak their minds freelie to anie bill . . . & matter" (p. 342). On subsequent days, there were heated debates on the subject of supply, and specifically of impositions, which, as in the Parliament of 1610, turned into a discussion of the "authoritie of a prince, and what was the dutie of a subject" (p. 344). There was also fierce dispute over whether or not the various burgesses had proper representation in Parliament and how such a matter should be determined. Among the disputants was one Edmund Butler, "who in all things which tended to the queenes majesties profit or common-wealth . . . was a principall against it" (p. 343). So disorderly did these debates become that they seemed "more like to a bearebaiting of lose persons than an assemblie of wise and grave men in parlement" (p. 345).

Resistance to plantation, especially in the form of arguments about liberty or law, marks many of the stories Hooker tells. There is the stubbornly subversive response of the city of Waterford, which, upon being requested by the lord deputy to send him military assistance, "did verie insolentlie and arrogantlie returne an answer by waie of disputing their liberties with hir majesties prerogative, and so sent him no aid at all" (p. 365). The power struggles were not limited to contention between the Irish and the English, however; some of the most serious were those between the English settlers themselves and the lord deputy. The Englishmen in Munster, for example, rebelled against another matter of supply, this time cess ("the prerogative of the prince to impose upon the countrie a certain proportion for the feeding of men and horses in the military"), and defended their recalcitrance by claiming that this imposition "was against reason and law" (p. 390), the same argument used in 1610 to challenge James. This matter was settled, in the Crown's favor, only after representatives were sent to Queen Elizabeth, who, like James after her, took the standard position that subjects had to supply the monarch because supply provided them with protection (pp. 391–94).

Just how contemporary an issue Irish colonization was at the time of *The Tempest* is indicated in part by its inclusion—immediately after an update of the Virginia venture—in John Stow's *Abridgment* (1611). According to the *Abridgment*, the next phase of the plantation of Ireland was "The plantation of the north of Ireland by Citizens of London," a project that would involve three hundred persons, who, being "furnished with all things necessary, and with all conveniency were sent to Ulster."[88] James's March 1610 speech to Parliament also documented the attention Ireland was receiving; here James singled out Ireland as one of the projects that was draining the treasury, a point to which others repeatedly returned during this long year of debating.

But among the most compelling Anglo-Irish documents from this period are those which recount the actual plantation effort and the implications of it as it was being experienced. These documents include the correspondence from Sir Arthur Chichester to King James, Salisbury, and the Privy Council. As lord deputy of Ireland, Chichester was, from the beginning, involved in James's plans to plant Ulster. He wrote instructions on how to proceed and sent descriptions of the various counties and the resources available in each; he also warned against the difficulties that might arise. In other words, he gave more than one view; he wrote of the glory the project would bring to king and nation but also of the problems it could cause the people.

How plantation would enhance the king's power is the theme of Chichester's letter to James on October 14, 1608, in which he proclaimed James to be "the sole proprietor" of Ulster "as the native lords thereof were formerly" and announced that he might retain these lands "in his Crown for ever, for his honour and increase of his revenues" (p. 68). In his letter of March 10, 1609, he acknowledged the financial advantages of the project to the "private persons whom His Majesty intends thereby to encourage and gratify" (p. 157). But in this same communication he also warned that "few here will bear any part of this intended plantation," all being "either not able or not content to undergo the conditions" (p. 161). Chichester knew, too, that the discontent came not only from the Irish. A month earlier, he had complained to the Privy Council that "The treasury here is emptied long since . . . the soldiers of necessity are forced . . . to cess upon the countries adjoining . . . with incredible bitterness and grudging of both sides." Urging the council to an immediate remedy, Chichester insisted, "The King saves nothing by this protraction of time, and yet the subject is much damnified and discontented" (pp. 143–44). Surely, James had to be remembering such requests when, in his March 1610 speech to Parliament, he referred to the supply he needed to carry on his projects in Ireland (McIlwain, pp. 319-20).

Two other motifs dominating Chichester's communications had to do with fair division of lands and fair payments to the king, the issues of *meum et tuum* that also occupied the Parliament of 1610. Writing of the County of Armagh in 1608, Chichester explained the tenacity with which the natives were holding on to their land: "many of the natives in each county claim freehold in the lands they possess" (p. 63). But he also expressed concern for the rights of the planters, suggesting that they pay no rent to the king until "after the expiration of certain years of freedom" (p. 63). Two years later, on January 27, 1610, Chichester was yet more specific about how to balance what the king got against what the English subject in Ireland got: "The King's greatest advantage will be the power, wealth, and prosperity of the new undertakers. Therefore he [Chichester] likes not that the undertaker should be bound to pay so present a rent as is projected; but . . . have three years' absolute freedom, and the following three years to pay but half the rent, and after that, the whole" (p. 356). Meanwhile, the Irish natives were uneasy too. As Chichester wrote to Salisbury on September 27, 1610, the natives "repine greatly at their fortunes and the small quantity of land left to them upon the division" (p. 502).

Consequently, their thoughts were turning again to the rebel Tyrone and possibly also to his son, for "they will rather die than be removed to the small proportions assigned to them" (p. 503). In 1610, some in Parliament spoke as though they felt nearly the same way.

Because our own historical period is especially interested in discourses of colonization, and in what these discourses disguise, the presence of such a discourse in *The Tempest* is more apparent now than at any other time in history. The value of including the Irish materials in a study of the play is that they clarify the point that inherent in the colonial discourse was a critique of the implications of absolutist and imperialist subjection. Insofar as the play is cut through with a colonial discourse, it does indeed dramatize "the practice and psychology of colonization,"[89] but not only because colonization was being practiced in Ireland and Virginia; the language of colonization also imaged the impact and implications of absolutism within England itself.

The Tempest reproduces the critique of colonization that was available, but in a fictional narrative structured metaphorically, so that it represents as equivalent (makes no distinction between) an Other who is subject to an absolute king and an Other who is subject to a colonizer—in America and in Ireland.[90] Thus, Ariel's contract with Prospero, whereby Ariel will work for him in return for freedom, is as analogous to the situation of the Irish undertaker seeking a fair schedule of rent payments as to the English Parliament promising James supply in exchange for a proper settlement of their grievances. Caliban's compulsion to raise a rebellion is likewise as analogous to the native Irish inclined to call again for Tyrone as to the English Parliament refusing to grant supply when so few of their grievances had been addressed. And all of these situations are analogous to the experiences of those in Virginia whom the Indians had threatened to kill if they did not leave and who found themselves subjected to an English authority wielding martial law.

In taking time to emphasize the Irish material, I do not mean in any sense to diminish the importance of the New World context through which many of the most important new perspectives on

The Tempest and colonization have been worked out. My aim, rather, is to qualify and extend the implications of that context, and also to furnish corroborating evidence that the issues of exploitation and the structures of power relations that critics have been finding in this text can be fully accounted for through documentation from the historical period of the play. Thus, if my own argument puts emphasis on the degree to which colonization images the problem of absolutism, in so doing it also provides a critique of the *mentalité* of colonization.

Finally, however one may see the implications or effects of the colonial discourse in *The Tempest*, no argument for its presence can do without the acknowledgment that the Virgilian presence in *The Tempest* in itself would all but require some treatment of the idea of colonization. Even as the *Aeneid* celebrates the reign of the imperialist Augustus, so also is it a colonizing text—indeed the archetypical colonizing text of all time. As Richard Waswo has argued, no other work has been more important to the process by which the West has naturalized the concept of colonization; its narrative of a great destiny to be fulfilled in the founding of Rome has offered itself to all of Western culture as a paradigm for the expansion and transmission of culture and ideology from one place to another.[91]

During the Renaissance, the *Aeneid* most certainly functioned as an archive by means of which those involved in plantation could take stock of their project. If Stanyhurst could be ironic about plantation, and Strachey could be referred to as "a fytt *Achates* for such an *Aeneas*, as is our Noble & worthy Generall the lord Delawarre,"[92] someone like John Davies could use Virgil to validate his success. In a letter dated November 8, 1610, Davies, the person whose central contribution to plantation was that he developed ways to interpret the law that would increase England's ability to secure control of Ireland,[93] summarized for Salisbury the legal grounds upon which the king of England could proceed against the lands of the Irish. Having sufficiently covered the problems of and procedures for land division, he noted that the project at Colrane, where the store of timber was particularly grand, was going better than anyone had expected, a success that made him think in Virgilian terms. There were, he said, "such a number of workmen so busy in several places about their several tasks, as methought I saw Dido's colony erecting of Carthage in Virgil."[94] (Davies then quotes three lines from the *Aeneid*.) It is an expression of confidence in the imperialist motive quite like that in the report for the Council of Virginia: "Why that which to *Rome* was possible, (to us) is impossible?"

We cannot tell whether it makes any sense to ask which had more agency in the writing of *The Tempest*, the imitation of Virgil or contemporary political issues of rule and colonization. But we can say that for an imitation of the *Aeneid*, imperialism and colonization were obvious contemporary topics to play off, and for discussion of the contemporary political situation, the *Aeneid* was a most obvious precursor to rework. Ultimately, then, the political and the aesthetic fall together with a degree of compatibility and mutual dependency that calls into question any attempt to separate them, as indeed is often the case in texts of the sixteenth and seventeenth centuries. In *The Tempest*, Shakespeare both naturalized and problematized the Virgilian idiom in such a way as to bring the Virgilian text into dialogue with the problems of power as they were being experienced in his own time, and specifically as they were being expressed through the discourses of constitutionalism and colonization.[95] To make Virgil over for one's own time meant coming to terms once more with what makes civilizations possible and with what threatens that possibility.

PART 2
The Tempest as Masque and Romance

THREE SPECTACLES

THIS SECTION WILL FOCUS ON the three spectacles—the harpy banquet scene, the betrothal masque, and the glistering apparel episode—as well as the sequence of scenes, besides the betrothal masque, that feature Ferdinand. Together these scenes illustrate the high order of craftsmanship exhibited in Shakespeare's imitation of Virgil, as well as the political implications of his repetitions and incursions into the distinct but related idioms of court masque and romance.

That the language of the three scenes of spectacle is that of the court masque has been routinely acknowledged. In rewriting Virgil in that genre, Shakespeare substituted a contemporary heroic language for the heroic language of Virgilian epic, a substitution that places his work squarely in the context of contemporary articulations of ideas about royal power. For to use the language of the masque was to use the king's own language, so identified with the court and its preferred modes of self-representation had the masque come to be.[1] As is already clear, the end toward which my own discussion is moving is not to argue for a Shakespeare who wrote only to confirm and glorify James's power; all the more interesting, then, that in these sections of the play he did use the masque idiom in what can appear to be a most conventional way. Although the three spectacles legitimate the power of the ruler, that legitimation occurs in regard to nonarbitrary categories, the categories which Bourdieu describes as appearing to a society as beyond question, as "self-evident."[2] The harpy banquet scene, the betrothal masque, and the glistering apparel episodes affirm the self-evident propositions that a ruler is a figure of justice who punishes usurpers and other dangerous and evil people and provides for the future of the realm, in part by fulfilling the patriarchal functions of furnishing heirs to the throne and arranging the marriages of his children. The value of these powers to the entire nation is so clear that, as these ideas are here represented in a language that could be identified as the king's, the play would seem to be speaking in concert with the policies and priorities of James himself. The ideological self-evidence of these three sections is suitably expressed in the masque idiom and by the way in which all three are involved in imitating details from *Aeneid 6*, the book that contained explicit glorifications of Augustus. It is during his journey through the underworld that Aeneas hears the prophecy about Augustus, the emperor who will bring a return to the golden age. It is also the book in which the allegorists saw the soul as reaching its highest state of wisdom.

The authorities at issue in the play are not, however, only those of royal policy and court aesthetics. Also at issue are other authors and their idioms. If Shakespeare naturalized Virgil by recasting some sections of the play in the language of King James, he also placed these masque structures within the larger generic category of romance. This most dignified of genres, associated with epic by way of the umbrella term "heroic poetry," had more than any other become the chosen genre of poets who wished to define themselves as spokesmen for the national community,[3] a position they often claimed by appealing to the role of the poet as prophet and maker and by defining the educative role of poetry. Tasso's treatise on heroic poetry, Sidney's *Defence of Poesie*, Harington's preface to *Orlando furioso*, and Spenser's Letter to Raleigh show how discussions about romance had become a forum for poets to assert these assumptions. Shakespeare's turning to romance—as he had in *Cymbeline, Pericles,* and *The Winter's Tale*[4]—was as much an acknowledgment that he too had this stature and served this function as it was anything else. A brief survey of the characteristics of romance as they were defined in Renaissance treatises reveals the several ways in which *The Tempest*, despite its differences from Shakespeare's other late plays, conforms to romance genre expectations.

We can begin with a more specific reminder of how closely related epic and romance were considered to be. On this point no one is clearer than Tasso who, in defense of his own work, argued that the differences between romance and epic were accidental not essential, and that one category, heroic poetry, could subsume epic and romance as subcategories: "accidental differences cannot constitute different genres . . . romance imitates the same actions [as epic], imitates in the same way, and imitates by the same means; it is therefore of the same genre."[5] As is obvious from his language, Tasso's basic working assumption was that the writer of romance, practicing the art of *imitatio*, followed the Virgilian model while also transforming it.[6] His emphasis on what would be the same—"the same actions . . . in the same way . . . by the same means"—refers as well to the requirement that, like epic, romance was to have noble characters performing noble actions that would move readers to wonder. *The Tempest*, a romance which is the "same" as epic by virtue of its being made piece-by-piece out of one, also shows a commitment to the display of the noble by featuring the aristocratic Prospero, Miranda, and Ferdinand, and a commitment to the evocation of wonder (the marvelous, or "meraveglia," Tasso's word) both by its use of magic and in the very naming of Miranda.

A feature that romance writers took from Virgil, and then adapted into one of the most distinguishing characteristics of the genre, is the narrative structure in which characters wander from place to place, the feature of romance that is always identified as especially Odyssean.[7] When Spenser described Una's journey at one point in the first book of *The Faerie Queene*, it was to the archetypal journeyer Ulysses that he compared her: "Up *Una* rose, up rose the Lyon eke, / And of their former journey forward pas, / In wayes unknowne, her wandring knight to seke, / With paines farre passing that long wandring *Greeke*" (1.3.21). This feature Angus Fletcher associates with an "idea of a finally targeted quest, the return home," a concept Patricia Parker complicates by emphasizing instead how the Odyssean pattern of homecoming might also be incorporated into "romance strategies of deferral and delay," in this case "this seeming end" becomes "only a way station."[8] Virgil's variation on Homer in the first six books of the

Aeneid features first the delay and engrossing distraction of Carthage, a structure that was to be repeated by Ariosto, Tasso, and Spenser,[9] and finally the "way station" experience of the underworld, another section worked over incessantly by imitators.

In the *Aeneid*, where home no longer exists after the fall of Troy, Aeneas's nostalgia for his past has to give way to his vision of a greater future, the goal that provides the focus of the forward movement in the work. If any experience that Virgil gave Aeneas can be called a "homecoming" experience, it is the reunion with his father in the underworld and the visions he has there of the end of his journey. But, like the souls in Elysium, Aeneas cannot stay; he must go back to the world and act according to the vision he has been shown. Shakespeare structures *The Tempest* so that it is evocative of these defining narrative features. There is the deferral that Prospero's thirteen years on the island represent, the delay that the storm causes in the court party's journey home, the interruption in routine caused by the love of Ferdinand and Miranda, the sense of homecoming that Ferdinand has during the betrothal masque ("Let me live here ever"), and finally the preparation to return home at the end of the play.

A steady sequence of visionary experiences routinely punctuates this romance pattern of deferral and delay. In Spenser studies, such moments in *The Faerie Queene* have been identified as the "allegorical cores," the "temples," the "houses of recognition,"[10] but again, this feature of romance is traceable to Virgil, "the father of its visionary core."[11] Revelation—exemplified in the *Aeneid* in Aeneas's understanding that the huntress he sees is a goddess (*o dea certe*)—recurs throughout the romance tradition, and nowhere more regularly or more powerfully than in Shakespeare's late plays.[12] This tradition is continued in *The Tempest* in the three spectacles of the harpy banquet scene, the betrothal masque, and the glistering apparel episode, as well as in the "wonder" that Prospero orchestrates when he finally reveals Ferdinand and Miranda to the court party.

Shakespeare also presents the experience of the castaways on the island itself as a wandering. The Alonso group wanders around looking for Ferdinand. And twice characters compare their experience to that of being in a labyrinth, a structure important to *The Faerie Queene*[13] and also prominent in *Aeneid* 5, where Virgil sees in the complicated riding formations of Ascanius and the other children an activity that recalls both the labyrinth of Crete and the entangled past and future adventures of their fathers and their successors.[14] In *The Tempest*, Gonzalo, weary of searching for Ferdinand, complains, "Here's a maze trod, indeed, / Through forthrights and meanders" (3.3.2–3). After Alonso has been reunited with Ferdinand and after the Boatswain suddenly turns up again, Alonso, too, uses the labyrinth image, this time more metaphorically: "This is as strange a maze as e'er men trod" (6.1.242). As Gonzalo makes clear at the end of the play, the labyrinthine journey has been good for all of them; what has been found is "all of us ourselves / When no man was his own" (5.1.211–12). Like other romances, this one also claims that it has shown how characters can be drawn away from errant ways.

Another feature of the play that formally links it to both romance and Virgil and yet seems antithetical to the motif of wandering is its unity of action. In many discussions that generalize about Shakespeare's romances, this characteristic is the one that most sets *The Tempest* apart from his other late plays. If, however, one is thinking about the rules for poetry, especially for romance (as that genre was understood as a redaction from epic), then discussion of unity must have a major place. The idea that unity of action was one of the rules for epic originated with Aristotle, who said that epic should have only one action, however complex that action might be. Ben Jonson represented the sixteenth- and seventeenth-century understanding of Aristotle's position when he explained that Virgil had accomplished this goal for Aeneas by having "pretermitted many things. He neither tells how he was borne, how brought up; how he fought with *Achilles*; how he was snatch'd out of the battaile by *Venus*; but that one thing, how he came to Italie, he prosecutes in twelve books."[15] For the Italians, arguing over the new romances by Ariosto and Tasso, unity of action was considered so important a defining feature of epic that it became the central issue in the entire quarrel.[16] Some critics thought that the new romances fitted the Aristotelian rule; others, that these works had to be distinguished from epic because of their multiplicity of action. Still others, among them Tasso, Trissino, and Giraldi, argued that different handling and different combinations might still be said to constitute a unity, that if one action by one man was acceptable, so were many actions by one man or many actions by many men.[17]

The compression in *The Tempest* may, of course, be both a transformation and an adaptation of the example of Virgil, who condensed twenty-four books of the *Odyssey* and twenty-four books of the *Iliad* into only twelve books. Whatever the case, Shakespeare cast *The Tempest* in a form that adheres to the rule of unity of action as that rule would apply to drama, and in so doing managed a *sprezzatura* display of his own mastery of the language of poetry.

We can interpret this display of mastery in different ways, not least of which might be to see it as a rhetorical strategy Shakespeare employed to make his work conform to tradition and to rules and thus, by implication, offer itself as a model, even a national standard, for behavior. Throughout *The Tempest*, in the many ways in which the play presents austerity and discipline as the standards for thought and action, it can be seen to be performing just such a political platform, which, translated into the terms of contemporary high politics, would be a program for protecting the "ancient" tradition in national politics.[18] It was precisely that tradition—that royal power was limited—to which Parliament was asking James to return.[19]

In this context, the significance of the Neoplatonized allegorical commentary on the *Aeneid*, together with the strain of Neoplatonism that runs throughout *The Tempest*—but is especially present in the scenes of spectacle and in the Ferdinand scenes—acquires additional interest. Central to the idiom of the court masque, the hierarchical system of Neoplatonism, wherein a transcendent reason keeps base nature under control, was useful for justifying an absolute and transcendent political power.[20] But a competing aspect of Neoplatonism, especially among the Virgilian allegorists, was the emphasis on the acquisition of virtue and wisdom through trial, on the practicing of physical and mental discipline for the high reward of spiritual and intellectual ecstasy. Thus it becomes possible to argue that what gets as much emphasis as anything in the play as a whole, and certainly in the scenes at issue, is not only the affirmation of self-evident powers but also of ideas of correction and discipline—not, in other words, the legitimacy of absolutism, but the legitimacy of restraint. In these scenes, often written in what is ostensibly the king's language, the self-evident value of royal power exists in combination with an articulation of another value, and one that, in the arena of national political debate, was currently in direct competition with the value James had hoped would go unchallenged.[21]

In the following pages, these ideas and the transformations of Virgil through which Shakespeare presents them will occupy the discussion. The method of *imitatio* exemplified in these scenes is exactly that considered in the opening discussion of imitation, and it is important to recall it here, especially in the context of what has been suggested about how Shakespeare is also working changes on the king's language. When Sturm explained how Virgil imitates Homer, he stated simply that "the imitation of this like matter is hidden by placing, chaunging, adding, and by varying."[22] When Shakespeare imitates the "matter" of *Aeneid* 6, for example, he retains its essential ideas but selects patterns from earlier books and combines them with those from book 6 in order to represent those ideas in a new form. He moves into one place elements that in Virgil are widely separated. Sometimes he chooses a piece of Virgil's text that, however far it is from book 6, still carries a similar idea. But often he selects a Virgilian kernel opposite in idea to the one to be represented in *The Tempest*, so that the imitation requires a degree of variation that leads to reversal. Whatever the case, the Virgilian text, handled discontinuously, yields to conflation, recombination, and change.

These concepts can be as helpful to understanding the craft of the Renaissance poet as they are to attaining a better grasp of what the modification of political discourse to effect change requires. They also illustrate how Shakespeare's appropriation of Virgil is similar to what we have come to understand about the appropriations which later periods have made of Shakespeare. Like Shakespeare in later centuries, Virgil was for the Renaissance the central canonical figure; to rework Virgil signaled "the appropriation of a usable past in relation to some common pursuit of social purpose in the present."[23]

The Harpy Banquet Scene

Because the play conforms to unity of action while imitating a diverse narrative, the island, where all the action occurs, must function, in relation to the many places in the *Aeneid*, as more than one place. In Virgil and his romance successors, the hero moves physically from one geographical location to another and at each new place has another new experience. But in *The Tempest*, one place must function as, and replicate what happened in Troy, Carthage, and the underworld. Coming to the island is like being shipwrecked at Carthage, and also like arriving in Italy. And if the wandering that takes place on this island is experienced as a bewildering maze of endless journeying, it is also experienced as, and constructed in terms analogous to, the specific journey through the underworld and out again. This last characteristic, the one most apparent to Colin Still and also a feature the play shares with *The Faerie Queene*,[24] is particularly prominent in the scenes of spectacle. Beginning with the harpy banquet, and continuing in successive actions through the glistering apparel scene, Shakespeare makes prominent use of Virgil's underworld material.

Insofar as all of these spectacles are also concerned with the right uses of power, it is important to note that Shakespeare shapes his materials rhetorically so that the representation and discussion of power proceeds in these scenes of spectacle without there ever being any reason to criticize Prospero. Rather, all representations of excessive use of power, as well as the punishment that such abuse demands, are located in other characters. This play never accuses or criticizes the king. Insofar as James is homologous to Prospero, we could say, with Burke, that Shakespeare furnishes the play with a "propagandistic (didactic) strategy" that "provides the *charitable* attitude towards people that is required for purposes of persuasion and co-operation."[25]

The harpy banquet scene begins with Alonso still complaining about his lost son—that is, his lost hope—and Sebastian and Antonio still plotting an attack on Alonso, actions that began in act 2, scene 1. Then, almost immediately, follow the solemn and strange music, Prospero "*on the top* (*invisible*)," and the Shapes that carry in the banquet. The members of the court party express their amazement and, after some consideration, decide to eat. Suddenly, to the accompaniment of thunder and lightning, Ariel "like a Harpy" appears, the banquet vanishes, and the harpy addresses the "three men of sin." Then the harpy disappears, leaving the sinful men to deal with the guilt of having supplanted the "good Prospero" (3.3.70).

As we know, Shakespeare's punishing harpy originates in the Celaeno episode of *Aeneid* 3, where the harpies sweep down upon Aeneas and his men and prevent them from feeding on the cattle and goats that they have slain on the Strophades islands.[26] The best work on the correspondences between this segment of the *Aeneid* and *The Tempest* is that of T. W. Baldwin, who shows that the action of the scene, as well as the language in which it is cast, is owing to Virgil. Baldwin notices that the stage direction indicating that the harpy "claps his wings" is an action rendered in Virgil by "quatiunt . . . alas" (3.226), and he links Ariel's remark that the harpy is "invulnerable" and cannot be injured in one feather, "one dowle," to Virgil's "nec volnera . . . accipiunt" (3.242–43). For both Alonso and his party and Aeneas and his, drawing swords against the harpy is absolutely futile. Baldwin also sees parallels between the curse Celaeno pronounces on Aeneas and the threats Ariel makes, and he notes that, "just as Aeneas and his men repent, so Alonso's conscience begins to stir."

The appropriateness of a harpy and a banquet for *The Tempest* court party is especially evident when these choices are considered against the background of the allegorists' reading of the Celaeno episode. As Landino explains, this episode signifies "the vice of avarice."[27] An important vice for the struggling soul to conquer, avarice was also the sin to which tyranny and usurpation were attributed.[28] The allegorists can also help us to make sense of the particular conflation of *Aeneid* materials that are present in this scene, which can be shown to contain details from the Celaeno episode of *Aeneid* 3 while at the same time evoking an idea of hell, such as is present in *Aeneid* 6. Though these two places occur far apart in Virgil, both include details which, according to the allegorists, carry the same ideas. Bernardus, for example, does not furnish a direct gloss on the Celaeno episode in his commentary on *Aeneid* 3, but, rather, comments on the significance of Celaeno herself when he gets to *Aeneid* 6. After listing the creatures at the gates of hell and, noting the presence of a harpy among them, he pauses for a long discussion of the many aspects of greed and avarice that Celaeno and her two sisters represent.[29] Again in book 6, the concept of avarice is prominent for the allegorists in the Sibyl's description of hell's inhabitants: she refers to Ixion and Pirithous, who sit beside a banquet table but are kept from eating by an attending fury who "stays their hands from touch of the table" ("manibus prohibet contingere mensas," 6.606). While this punishment is proceeding, the other sinful creatures in hell, such as Salmoneus, Tityus, Theseus, and Phlegyas, are enduring still other everlasting pains relative to the sins of which they are guilty. When Landino glosses the action of the fury who stays the greedy hands from the table of food, he explains that in this particular punishment Virgil "could not have designated more truly nor more clearly avarice" (Stahel, ed., p. 252).

When Shakespeare uses materials from Virgil for his punishment scene, he creates a new configuration that is not exactly like the scene or situation in either *Aeneid* 3 or 6. The harpy episode from book 3 furnishes the most dramatic visual elements for the construction of the new episode, but the overall function of *The Tempest* episode is more like that of the situation in book 6. There in hell sits the judging Rhadamanthus, who, the Sibyl tells Aeneas, "chastises" the guilty, "exacting confession of crimes" from those who "in vain deceit" have put "off atonement for sin" (6.567–69). The situation of Shakespeare's court party is similar. The three men of sin have not yet faced their guilt; they are, says Ariel, "unfit to live" and certainly ripe for punishment.

In other ways, too, this scene evokes an idea of hell like that in *Aeneid* 6. One of these ways is in the explicit evocation of language used in the Sibyl's description. For example, Alonso's cry, "O, it is monstrous, monstrous! . . . it did bass my trepass" (3.3.95, 99), echoes a sentiment in the summarizing statements the Sibyl utters as she concludes what she has been telling Aeneas of hell: "All dared a monstrous sin" ("ausi omnes immane nefas," 6.624). But there are other, more general, reminders of a hellish environment. There is Prospero's remark that classifies some of those in the group as "worse than devils" (l. 35), and there is Ariel's reference to "this lower world" (l. 54). Later there is Ariel's pronouncement that, if the men do not repent, they will be punished eternally, made to suffer "Ling'ring perdition—worse than any death / Can be at once" (ll. 77-78). And near the end of the scene is Sebastian's remark, "But one fiend at a time, / I'll fight their legions o'er" (ll. 101-2). Also, throughout the scene we are aware of the presence of Prospero "*on the top (invisible)*"—a presence which in the context of hell suggests the judging power of a deity[30] but in the context of politics suggests the ruler's power and responsibility to be the chief judge in the land, as well as a model of moral rectitude.

Like the inhabitants of hell, Shakespeare's "three men of sin" are in a place where they must undergo punishment. Although the infernal imagery of this scene ties it to *Aeneid* 6, there are, however, other aspects of the scene that lend the *Aeneid* 3 context a special poignancy. The men's fate on this island is not eternal punishment but continual wandering; they must progress beyond where they are now. The character to whom this statement is most applicable is the king in the scene—Alonso—whose conscience is most immediately pricked by the harpy's performance. Present in Alonso's speech is a detail that recalls one of the most prominent features of the experience that Aeneas the wanderer has with Celaeno. In declaring to Aeneas that he should not be disturbing the inhabitants of the Strophades, the harpy instructs him: "Italy is the goal ye seek" ("Italiam cursu petitis," 3.253). The reprimand and the instruction send Aeneas and his men hurrying to their ships and the resumption of their sea journey, an adventure that will eventually lead Aeneas to seek communion with his father in the underworld and realize, according to the allegorists, a perfecting of his soul and the renewed pursuit of his destiny. Alonso, similarly impressed by his own wrongdoing, now contemplates what he must "seek" (3.3.101) and where he will seek it.

That search will involve a variation of the experience Aeneas had upon arriving in Italy. Whereas Aeneas sought his dead father, Alonso will seek his son, whose supposed death he now imagines to be a punishment for his own sins. Whereas Aeneas journeyed to the underworld, Alonso imagines his search will involve going into the ooze, the mud: "Therefor my son i' th' ooze is bedded; and / I'll seek him deeper than e'er plummet sounded, / And with him there lie mudded" (3.3.100–102). Imagining that a return to the sea will be his death, he has yet to discover that it is his awakened conscience, which will direct him to repent for having seized power that was not his, that is the sea-change that will make of him something rich and strange. Thus, Shakespeare not only includes the idea of punishment for abuse of power but the idea of manifold reward for the one who sees the error of his ways.

The Betrothal Masque

The event in the Elysium experience that provides the structure for the betrothal masque is Aeneas's meeting Anchises in the underworld and being shown what his future will hold. This incident, always regarded as an expression of Aeneas's political destiny, was for the allegorists the climax of Virgil's first six books, the point at which the soul finally achieved a union with the truth. To bring Aeneas to the Elysian Fields, said Landino, was to bring him to "the summum bonum . . . the knowledge of the divine" (Stahel, ed., p. 253), "to a knowledge of those things which are in the heavens" (p. 256). Here, said Bernardus, "heavenly things be open to the understanding" (*Commentary*, p. 106).

The variation of this episode in *The Tempest* involves replacing both the oracular Sibyl, who leads Aeneas to Elysium, and Anchises with Prospero, who will serve as both oracle and father to the young prince in this scene. Under Prospero's guidance and through the medium of his art, the betrothal masque will celebrate the public union of marriage and the political future to which that marriage leads; it will also give Ferdinand a direct experience with

The Tempest *as Masque and Romance* 79

the spirit world. Thus Shakespeare's variation on the Elysium experience retains both the public and private meanings of the Virgilian pre-text.

The art of the scene is not dependent only on patterns from *Aeneid* 6, however. While its dominating ideas and the overall structure do derive from that section of Virgil, most of the devices in it that convey the traditional meanings of Aeneas's experience have their genesis in *Aeneid* 4, the episode at Carthage. In other words, Shakespeare transforms Carthage—to the point of reversal—so that its details are the ones which present the Elysium experience in this new work. This reversal provides that Ferdinand and Miranda are simultaneously copies of Dido and Aeneas and the antitheses of the ancient lovers.

The central aspect of Virgil's story that Shakespeare reworks is the behavior of Dido and Aeneas on that fateful day when they satisfy their lust in the cave to which they are driven by Juno's storm. As the new lovers are permitted betrothal only on the condition that they remain chaste, the idea of discipline underpins the entire scene. Prospero warns Ferdinand that he must not break Miranda's "virgin-knot" until they are properly married. If he does, "No sweet aspersion shall the heavens let fall / To make this contract grow; but barren hate / Sour-ey'd disdain and discord shall bestrew / The union of your bed with weeds so loathly / That you shall hate it both" (4.1.18–22). In Prospero's warning there is an allusion to the possibility of a storm—"No sweet aspersions shall the heaven let fall"—but, unlike in Virgil, the storm is a conditional occurrence, the aftermath of, rather than the prelude to, not remaining chaste. In the new lovers' world, it is just as possible that the heavens may let "sweet aspersions" fall. Another possibility is that this "contract" may "grow" instead of turning to "barren hate," details which recall, while standing apart from, the consequences of Dido and Aeneas's false contract, one that Dido "calls . . . marriage and with that name veils her sin" ("coniugium vocat; hoc praetexit nomine culpam," 4.172).

The emphasis on discipline as the strategy for reversing tragedy and avoiding destruction is also evident when Ferdinand responds to Prospero's warning with the promise that nothing "shall . . .

melt / Mine honour into lust," not even the opportunity provided by "the murkiest den." Here Shakespeare uses *den* for Virgil's "speluncam" (4.165), the same word Stanyhurst uses in his translation of the cave episode, although both Douglas and Phaer use "cave." (In his *Thesaurus*, Thomas Cooper gives both "den" and "cave" as the English equivalents for "spelunca.")[31]

Speaking in earnest to the imposing father before him, Ferdinand explains exactly why he will stay chaste. Hoping "for quiet days, fair issue and long life, / With such love as 'tis now," Ferdinand says that he does not want to put such high hopes at risk, or ruin that great anticipated day of consummation. He does not want "to take away / The edge of that day's celebration." In "that day's celebration," Shakespeare provides an alternative to Virgil's pronouncement after the episode in the cave: "That day was the first day of death, that first the cause of woe" ("ille dies primus leti primusque malorum / causa fuit," 4.169–70). The change reverses the Virgilian declaration of woe and death; Ferdinand's love will be cause for celebration, and the reward for his restraint will be extended day, extended time.

Shortly after the betrothal masque has gotten under way, and after Iris has called Ceres to accompany her and Juno, Shakespeare turns again to the Carthage story, though this time he takes his material not from book 4 but book 1. The target of his art is Virgil's tale about the plot of Venus to bring about the fall of Dido and Carthage by causing the queen and Aeneas to fall in love (1.657–722). Her scheme involves casting a "wanton charm" (*Tmp.* 4.1.95, and cf. "occultem inspires," *Aen.* 1.688) upon them through the presence of Cupid, who, on her orders, disguises himself as Aeneas's son Ascanius, so that he can get close to Dido and work his power.[32] For Ferdinand and Miranda, Shakespeare writes a new version of this story. He has Iris assure Ceres that there is no need to fear that Venus and Cupid's mischievous interference will spoil this affair because they have already left for Paphos:

> I met her deity
> Cutting the clouds towards Paphos, and her son
> Dove-drawn with her. Here thought they to have done
> Some wanton charm upon this man and maid,

Whose vows are, that no bed-right shall be paid
Till Hymen's torch be lighted: but in vain;
Mars's hot minion is return'd again;
Her waspish-headed son has broke his arrows,
Swears he will shoot no more, but play with sparrows,
And be a boy right out.

Shakespeare gives the story a comic twist by portraying Cupid's spoil-sport reaction to having his mischievous plan foiled. Unable to lead Miranda and Ferdinand astray, he has gone off in a mad pout; he has broken his arrows and has sworn to "shoot no more." Here Cupid surrenders both his ability to arouse passion and his power to deceive. He has been defeated by lovers who, surpassing their predecessors in love, can be victimized by neither passion nor deception. The only spells that prompt their love are those cast by Prospero: "It goes on, I see, / As my soul prompts it" (1.2.422–23).

Near the end of the masque Shakespeare draws once more on the Carthage cave episode. After Dido and Aeneas have entered the cave, "Primal Earth and nuptial Juno give the sign; fires flashed in Heaven, the witness to their bridal, and on the mountain-top screamed the Nymphs. That day was the first day of death, that first the cause of woe" ("prima et Tellus et pronuba Iuno / dant signum; fulsere ignes et conscius Aether / conubiis, summopue ululo ululorunt vertice Nymphae. / ille dies primus leti primusque malorum / causa fuit," 4.166–70). Though Dido is not yet aware of it, this day seals her ruin. For Ferdinand and Miranda, a different prospect lies ahead, one that Shakespeare signals in the masque in many ways[33] but here by transforming Virgil's nymphs that scream (*ululorunt*) from the mountain-tops (*vertice*) into nymphs that come from "*the windring brooks*" and "*crisp channels*" to "*help to celebrate / A contract of true love*" (4.1.128–33).[34] The cacaphony that accompanied the false marriage at Carthage undergoes a metamorphosis into the harmony of a true contract.

Shakespeare's revision of the tragedy at Carthage includes a recasting of the roles of Venus and Juno, whose divisive quarreling provides the backdrop for the Carthage love affair; Juno wishes to foster the cause of Carthage, Venus the future of her son. Venus sends Cupid to cast a charm on Dido to weaken her, and Juno, hoping to keep Aeneas in Carthage and at Dido's service, sends the storm that will drive the lovers to the cave (4.160f). The final outcome is the departure of Aeneas and the consequent suicide of Dido. But the struggle between Venus and Juno is not over and will not end until *Aeneid* 12, where Juno finally agrees to allow Aeneas to defeat Turnus, provided that the stock of the new nation is produced by uniting the Latins and the Trojans. Besides making the new nation stronger, this union also makes it possible for Juno to become patroness of the newly established race.

Frequently in *The Tempest*, Prospero plays the roles fulfilled in the *Aeneid* by deities, but in the betrothal masque, Shakespeare incorporates the classical tradition directly by making Juno herself the focal point of the spectacle Prospero is creating; in other words, here Prospero presents and thus is represented by Juno. In the passage that describes Venus and Cupid heading for Paphos, Shakespeare suppresses the tradition of regarding Venus as supportive (especially in the *Aeneid*) and a figure of divine love and instead accents the tradition which associates Venus and Cupid with the passions.[35] By thus removing Venus to Paphos, Shakespeare allows Juno to obtain sole sovereignty. This strategy permits Juno to be for *The Tempest* and Prospero a presiding deity of union, the same identity she has in Jonson's *Hymenaei* (1606), a masque closely related in conception to Shakespeare's betrothal masque.[36] Both masques contain iconographical descriptions of Juno with her peacocks and of the rainbow Iris, a tradition which is associated for both poets with Virgil. This point is documented for Shakespeare by Baldwin, and for Jonson by the notes he left on *Hymenaei*,[37] which refer repeatedly to the *Aeneid* as his authority.

In *Hymenaei* Jonson uses Juno and the idea of unity to represent the union of the soul, the union of marriage, the unity of England and Scotland, as well as the notion of King James as the embodiment of the oneness toward which all in the cosmos strives.[38] Jonson represents James as actually surpassing the powers of Juno; he is the "more than usuall light," the "greater *dietie*" (p. 212). This style of representation resembles Virgil's hyperbolic representation of Augustus in *Aeneid* 6, where Anchises tells Aeneas, who is now to go forward and unite the Latins and the Trojans, that his greatest successor in rule "shall again set up the Golden Age in Latium" ("aurea condet / saecula qui rursus Latio," 6.792–93).

When Shakespeare has Juno and Ceres sing of the future that will belong to Ferdinand and Miranda, he reproduces these traditions of representation. Juno promises, "*Honour, riches, marriage-blessing, / Long continuance, and increasing,*" and Ceres promises that spring, not winter, will follow every harvest. This last promise forecasts a return to that golden time of no seasons, a condition that was present on earth before Ceres, prompted by Pluto's having stolen away Proserpina to the underworld, caused periods of infertility to mark the year's progress. Thus, Gonzalo's dream of a rule that would "excel the Golden Age" (2.1.164) is reintroduced, attached this time to characters who actually are and will be rulers, and whose bounteous rule will be a device for unifying previously divided peoples.

The ability to produce this vision is evidence in itself of Prospero's own capacity for reason and self-control. That Ferdinand's capacity for reason is similarly refined is validated in his articulation that he recognizes what he sees: "This is a most majestic vision, and / Harmonious charmingly. May I be bold / To think these spirits?" Here, Ferdinand displays the gaze,[39] the ultimate certification of himself as one whose access to great truths is not a struggle. For him, such knowledge is natural and instinctive.

The importance of reason and discipline is underlined again at the end of the scene where Prospero's sudden show of anger destabilizes the vision. During the dance of the Reapers: "*PROSPERO starts suddenly, and speaks*" (4.1.s.d.138). From this point in the text, through the revels speech, and up to the point where Ferdinand and Miranda exit by retiring into Prospero's cell (l. 163), *The Tempest* repeats a structural pattern from the end of *Aeneid* 6, a section that begins at the point where Aeneas, seeing the shade of young Marcellus approach, asks Anchises who he is, and one that ends at the end of the book, where Aeneas leaves the underworld through the gate of ivory (6.860–901). In both cases, the sections of text at issue come after passages where the fathers (Anchises and

Prospero) have told the young heroes (Aeneas and Ferdinand) of the glorious futures that lie ahead. And in both cases, these fathers discuss the implications and value of earthly endeavors.

The passage in Virgil is one of lamentation. Following Anchises' charge to Aeneas "to crown Peace with Law, to spare the humbled, and to tame in war the proud" (6.852–53), the older "Marcellus advances, glorious in his splendid spoils." With him is the young Marcellus, this second figure being the adopted son of Augustus and the chosen successor who died before he could attain the seat of power. When Aeneas asks Anchises who the young man is, Anchises, "with upwelling tears" ("lacrimis ingressus obortis," 6.867), pleads that he "ask not of the vast sorrow of thy people" ("ingentem luctum ne quaere tuorum," 6.868). Earthly gifts and glories do not last: "Him the fates shall but show to earth, nor longer suffer him to stay. Too mighty, O gods, ye deemed the Roman stock would be, were these gifts lasting" ("ostendent terris hunc tantum fata, nec ultra / esse sinent. nimium vobis Romana propago / visa potens, superi, propria haec si dona fuissent," 6.869–71). Anchises concludes with the wish that Aeneas might "burst the harsh bonds of fate" ("si qua fata aspera rumpas," 6.882). Virgil then brings this sixth book to a close. Aeneas ranges about the plains of the underworld for a while before exiting through one of the two gates of sleep.

In Prospero's display of anger and in the revels speech that accompanies it, Shakespeare wrote a variation on Virgil's piece on the limits of earthly life. Prospero, too, talks about the transitoriness of life. "All . . . shall dissolve," he tells Ferdinand, who has just been led to believe that he is on the brink of a great future. Everything will pass away, the towers, the palaces, the temples, "the great globe itelf." But while Anchises' words emphasize the sorrow and tragedy in human life, Prospero offers his words as comfort to Ferdinand, "You do look, my son, in a mov'd sort, / As if you were dismay'd: be cheerful, sir." In the rest of the speech, Prospero puts both his frailty and Ferdinand's future into perspective. Earthly glory, he suggests, is not an end in itself. Ultimately this life is fulfilled not on this earth but in death: "our little life / Is rounded with a sleep." The speech offers an alternative to Anchises' pre-Christian lament for man's woes, which is seasoned with the knowledge that the Rome of Virgil and Augustus had itself been a victim of the ravages of time.[40] The speech thus calls attention to the potential for misrecognition in representations and assessments of power. Prospero has access to the world of divine ideas, but that is not to say that he is immortal; he is not a god on earth.

When Shakespeare places the revels speech at the end of the long scene of celebration and prophecy, he is copying a structural characteristic of Virgil's sixth book. He places something in his text that copies the something that Virgil placed in his text at a corresponding point. One feature that makes Shakespeare's imitation different, however, is that he uses the Virgilian material that stands at the end of *Aeneid 6* to forge a link between two sharply defined sections in his own text and, still more interesting, to introduce a section of his text—the Caliban episode—which will imitate a somewhat earlier section of Virgil's text. Then, in act 5, he moves all the way back to the beginning of Virgil's epic for his material. Old art exists not merely to be reproduced, but to be dismantled and reassembled.

The Glistering Apparel Episode

Like the harpy banquet scene, the glistering apparel episode is another in which characters are punished for not setting appropriate limits. Here, too, is punishment for avarice, excess, and presumption—but with some differences, owing to the unusual combination of characteristics in Caliban, the featured character. Throughout the play, Caliban's role is that of the political subversive, simultaneously in the roles of a "displanted native" and of a "discontent subject" in bondage to an absolute power. These identities (which can themselves be variously described)[41] enrich what Caliban can represent and seriously complicate what must be said about him in other scenes and especially in the context of the politics of 1610. Nevertheless, what will seize our attention first is that at this moment in the play Caliban has come to stage a coup. He plans to kill the ruler and set up someone else in his place; obviously he must be punished. Moreover, insofar as he also fulfills the Neoplatonic categories of the play, Shakespeare links Caliban to moral defect, of which his base physical form is a representation. Thus we could say that subversion is handled rhetorically so that opposition to rule is disgraced.

One qualifier of that attitude is that the play is now set on a course where Prospero will take the initiative to decrease—or we could say, subvert—his own power. But that attitude is also qualified by the scene itself, insofar as the scene tells more than one story. It tells how a ruler gets rid of troublemakers; but it also depicts the undisciplined seizure of power as barbarism and deviance, a notion that is greatly assisted by Shakespeare's use of Virgil.

The *Aeneid* pattern that lies behind Caliban's subversive aspect is, interestingly enough, Virgil's story of the conspiracy against Troy. In this sense, Caliban's plot against Prospero is constructed like the other two conspiracy plots in the play; all of them depend on the central structural features of that fateful night when the Greeks defeated the Trojans by creeping out of the wooden horse and opening the gates to more Greek soldiers. But also in each case, political discontent from within the society itself, not foreign invasion, is involved.

When Prospero tells Miranda of their being expelled from Milan, the description features the key elements of the Trojan tragedy, a treacherous army, a night attack, and an opening of city gates:

> A treacherous army levied, one midnight
> Fated to th' purpose, did Antonio open
> The gates of Milan; and, i' th' dead of darkness,
> The ministers for th' purpose hurried thence
> Me and thy crying self.
> (1.2.128–32)

While the army belongs to the king of Naples, the person who initiates and masterminds the plot is Antonio, Prospero's brother. Later in the play, the conspiracy of Antonio and Sebastian against Alonso again repeats the Troy pattern. This repetition does not take place at night, but it does occur while King Alonso sleeps.

"What a sleep were this for your advancement" (2.1.263), says Antonio as he urges Sebastian to join him. Finally agreeing to the plan, Sebastian, Alonso's brother, calls attention himself to the recurring pattern; their deed, he notes, is analogous to an earlier one: "Thy case, dear friend, / Shall be my precedent; as thou got'st Milan, / I'll come by Naples" (2.1.285-87). Then, as they draw their swords, Ariel sings in Gonzalo's ear, repeating both the idea of conspiracy and that of sleeping: *"While you here do snoring lie, / Open-ey'd conspiracy / His time doth take"* (2.1.295-97).

When Caliban plots to kill Prospero, the familiar features are present once more: conspiracy and sleep, and also internal dissension. Allying himself with the inebriated Trinculo and Stephano, Caliban describes his plan: "I'll yield him thee asleep" (3.2.59), he tells Stephano, and later reminds him, "Why, as I told thee, 'tis a custom with him / I' th' afternoon to sleep: there thou mayst brain him, / Having first seized his books" (3.2.85-87). But, if being modeled on Troy emphasizes Caliban's antagonism to authority and his competing desire for power, it does not confirm his danger. He is easily contained both by the plot of the play, which makes Prospero and Ariel more powerful than Caliban, and also by generic and stylistic features of the play that downgrade him; in *The Tempest* his conspiratorial tendencies are discursively limited to a *stylistically* low, as opposed to high, form.

Elsewhere in the play, the same rhetorical strategies dominate the construction of Caliban's part. In his having lusted after Miranda, Caliban evokes the Carthage model, but again in a diminished form; he never possesses her. And in the glistering apparel episode, Caliban copies, and not without some irony, some of the most elevated patterns from Virgil's depiction of Aeneas. Here he becomes yet another version of Aeneas, but this time one who has been stripped of the piety that "pius Aeneas" possesses, the characteristic that legitimizes the actions he performs throughout Virgil's epic.

To have said this much is immediately to recall how thoroughly Caliban is the antithesis of the obedient Ferdinand. If the betrothal masque, where Ferdinand has an Elysium experience, gives that point a compelling clarity, it is also an action that can be put to good use for describing the craft of the glistering apparel episode. As we have seen, the central device in the betrothal masque involves a rewriting of the Carthage love affair at its darkest moment so that it becomes a most elevated moment of spiritual enlightenment, an Elysium experience. By contrast, in the glistering apparel episode, Aeneas's most lofty experience, his sojourn in the underworld, is debased so that it becomes what the allegorists would call a mere Carthage experience. This episode presents an Aeneas figure who is driven not by lofty pursuit of his destiny but by revenge and greed. The preceding two spectacles also feature patterns from *Aeneid* 6, as well as visionary experiences for the characters. In Caliban's case, Shakespeare handles the patterns from *Aeneid* 6 so that they lose their aura of transcendence. Whereas he provides the other characters with visions, he makes Caliban's episode into a mock-"temple" experience.

The central pattern for the glistering apparel episode is the section of the *Aeneid* where Aeneas finds the golden bough and enters the cave that leads to Pluto's domain. Having pleaded with the Sibyl to grant him passage to the underworld so that he might see once more his father, Anchises, Aeneas receives instruction from her on the necessity of first finding in the surrounding forest the golden bough, which he must bring with him to the underworld and present to Proserpina: "There lurks in a shady tree a bough, golden in leaf and pliant stem, held consecrate to nether Juno" ("latet arbore opaca / aureus et foliis et lento vimine ramus, / Iunoni infernae dictus sacer," 6.136–38). Praying that the bough will show itself to him in the thick forest, Aeneas spies his mother's twin doves in flight above him and follows them, knowing that they will guide him to it (6.191–205). They fly toward the River Avernus, then turn and drop to a grove of trees, lighting on the one where the bough rests. Aeneas plucks the bough and rejoins the Sibyl, who plunges into the open cave while Aeneas follows fearlessly. The howling dogs at the entrance do not deter this powerful pair.

The Shakespearean transposition of this scene involves a systematic leveling of and deflection from the noble and sacred actions of Aeneas, a process that begins with Ariel describing the Caliban group as standing in a body of stinking water:

> at last I left them
> I' th' filthy-mantled pool beyond your cell,
> There dancing up to th' chins, that the foul lake
> O'erstunk their feet.
> (4.1.181–84)

Instead of Caliban continuing on his course to Prospero's cave, Caliban, Stephano, and Trinculo all go astray. They wind up some distance from the cave and wallowing chin deep in a body of water analogous to the River Avernus, which flows near the entrance to the underworld in the forest where the golden bough is located (6.201). Thomas Phaer described Avernus as a "stinking lake" and as a "lothsome lake," while Gavin Douglas translated "stynkand hellys see" and, as is the pool in *The Tempest*, "a fowle layk." Landino's remark that "the noisome odor of Avernus" signified "the earth's contagion" (p. 220) also suits well the action that occurs at Shakespeare's foul lake.[42] Instead of being on a sojourn that has a purifying effect, Caliban and his comrades come out of the lake smelling "all horse-piss" (4.1.199).

The next section of the episode involves Prospero sending Ariel for "The trumpery in my house," the "glistering apparel," which he instructs Ariel to "hang . . . on this line." In this action is the device by which the remainder of the episode becomes a reversal of Aeneas's finding of the golden bough. The entire parody is organized around a tree[43] in which the conspirators will find something.

Virgil does not mention what kind of tree harbors the golden bough. But just after Aeneas has found the bough and before he and the Sibyl reach the ferryman Charon, they pass through a forest in the midst of which stands an elm, where "false Dreams hold here and there" ("quam sedem Somnia volgo / vana tenere ferunt," 6.283–84). Landino read this elm as representing a person steeped in "foul deeds" which "show us nothing of substance and which, although they seem great, are in fact nothing" (Stahel, ed.,

p. 227), "And in truth they are comparable to false dreams" (p. 228). Bernardus Silvestris commented similarly: "The elm . . . is leafy, as if laden with false leaves, that is, vain thoughts, under each of which deceptive ideas are conceived" (*Commentary*, p. 67).

Shakespeare transports this elm into *The Tempest* but colloquializes it by calling it a line, or linden, tree. The connection between line and elm was ready at hand in sixteenth-century herbals, where the line or linden was often referred to as an elm. In *The Herball or Generall Historie of Plantes* (1577), John Gerarde wrote that the "Line or Linden Tree seemeth to be a kinde of Elme, and the people of Essex . . . do call it broad leafed Elme." In the next century John Parkinson's discussion of the line tree in *Theatrum Botanicum: The Theater of Plants* (1640) acknowledged that there are both male and female trees and recorded that "many have judged it to be rather a kind of Elme," citing for evidence the sixteenth-century herbal of Johann Bauhin, who was credited with having added to the title of the masculine line the word "Ulmifolio," or elmleaf.[44] As Kermode glosses, the existence of a female line accounts for Stephano's addressing the tree as "Mistress line" (4.1.235).

In the line tree in *The Tempest*, Caliban, Stephano, and Trinculo find not a golden bough but the trumpery that Prospero has told Ariel to fetch "in my house" (4.1.186). These goods are apparently the "rich garments" (1.2.164) that Gonzalo packed on Prospero's ship when he fled Milan.[45] The parallel in Virgil to these goods is the precious raiment that Aeneas took with him when he left Troy and that he has Achates bring from his ship to present to Dido as gifts. Those gifts include a scepter, a necklace, a jeweled diadem, as well as both a mantle trimmed with gold and a veil fringed with acanthus that had once belonged to Helen (1.643–56). When transformed in Shakespeare's play to "stale to catch thieves," such items furnish a suitable reduction of the golden bough that gained Aeneas entrance to the underworld and that represented for Landino "wisdom" (p. 212), for Bernardus Silvestris "philosophy" (p. 57), and for Ficino "the light of the intelligence poured in from above."[46] In *The Tempest* that elevated moment has been

The Tempest *as Masque and Romance* 91

downgraded to an episode that demonstrates appetite. Unlike Ferdinand, whose journey on the island includes an Elysium experience, no such experience awaits the Caliban group. Their journey is just an unending sequence of Carthage episodes.

The banter about the line tree that goes on while the apparel is being picked off it emphasizes the parody simply by keeping the word *line* ringing in our ears: "Mistress line. . . . Now is the jerkin under the line . . . we steal by line and level." All of these references have been glossed by Kermode. The one that can bear most scrutiny in the context of Shakespeare's imitation is Trinculo's comment, "Monster, come, put some lime upon your fingers, and away with the rest" (4.1.245). Kermode points out that putting sticky bird lime on their hands will help them hold on to the goods, bird lime also being a commonplace in proverbs on thieving. But we also know that one plant that was compared to bird lime was mistletoe, the plant to which Virgil compared the golden bough when he described the moment that Aeneas laid eyes on it: "As in winter's cold, amid the woods, the mistletoe, sown of an alien tree, is wont to bloom with strange leafage, and with yellow fruit embrace the shapely stems: such was the vision of the leafy gold on the shadowy ilex" ("quale solet silvis brumali frigore viscum / fronde virere nova, quod non sua seminat arbos, / et croceo fetu teretis circumdare truncos: / talis erat species auri frondentis opaca / ilice," 6.205–9). Phaer's marginal gloss on these lines clarifies the connection we are pursuing: "mysteltew callid of some mistelden growing on trees in winter with a yelow slimy berry clamy like byrd lyme, it commeth by donging of birds on the trees" (I4^v).[47] Consistent with the structure of the entire glistering apparel episode, the closest these three characters can get to the sacred bough is to find bird dung on a line tree.

Through it all, Caliban resists longer than the others—he does after all have more reason for wanting Prospero dead—but soon he too submits and, like a beast of burden, lets them load him with all their loot: "go to, carry this. And this. Ay, and this." No sooner have they loaded him up than they are interrupted by the "noise of hunters"[48] and then surrounded and driven off the stage by "divers Spirits in shape of dogs and hounds." The barking dogs again tie this action to *Aeneid* 6, evoking the dogs that bark at Aeneas as he enters the underworld but, in that case, do not deter him from his set course (6.257–63).

The victory here is Prospero's, and so that of established authority. At the same time, that victory has been won by way of a fiction that displays power-grabbing as the behavior of the Other, or we might say, as a characteristic that makes one an Other. In the harpy banquet scene, the rhetoric of exclusion for such trespassers is the language of hell's punishment; here a comic scene relies on the language and style of mockery. Recalling again that Caliban combines both the Troy conspiracy patterns and the debased Aeneas figure helps to make the point in a different way. The person who debases the proper standard for rule is the cultural equivalent of one who attacks the centers and foundations of human society.

THE EDUCATION OF FERDINAND AND THE DIALECTIC OF BONDAGE AND FREEDOM

In contrast to Caliban, who is constructed as one whose behavior disrupts normative standards, Ferdinand is constructed so that he presents a notion of the normative. Prospero chooses him as the prospective husband for his wonderful daughter. And Ferdinand responds so perfectly to the discipline Prospero requires that he comes to know the spirit world. The idealization in Ferdinand's image depends in part on the idiom of the masque, but also on the heroic romance tradition as it had developed through Sidney and Spenser, hand-in-hand with the education of princes and courtesy book traditions. Both Sidney and Spenser used love stories to organize the progress of the heroes' educational journeys and to represent and mystify the world of politics, rule, and authority. In *The Faerie Queene*, for example, the tested holiness that Red Crosse Knight must exhibit if he is to have Una, and the dependency of Arthegall on Britomart, as figured in the ideological vision at Isis Church, are both part of the same strategy of using love of a woman to represent education, political virtue, and political promise.[1] In *The Tempest*, where Ferdinand and Miranda fall in love under Prospero's tutelage, both past and contemporary (Elizabethan and Jacobean) rhetorical options for articulating ideological positions are thus present in rich combination and variation.

What distinguishes Shakespeare's rhetoric in the Ferdinand scenes, however, are the various ways in which he manages the contemporary language of royal mystification so that it remains distinctly Jamesian and yet does not replicate an absolutist rhetoric, a characteristic as well of the scenes of spectacle. In those scenes, he appropriates for his own uses the Neoplatonic codes through which absolutism had been naturalized; he acknowledges certain right uses of power while at the same time adding an emphasis on discipline. In the scenes showing the growing love between Ferdinand and Miranda, he retains the strong sense of a patriarchal system, a system central to James's articulation of absolutism,[2] but combines it with yet another emphasis available within the Neoplatonic system, the idea of service. In the central scene, while Prospero looks on, Ferdinand and Miranda in turn declare that each will be the other's servant.

Through this rhetorical move, whereby service and reciprocity (rather than dominance and subordination) become the featured aspects of love,[3] Shakespeare also makes central to the play a dialectic on the relationship between bondage and freedom. That dialectic was, of course, central to contemporary national politics: the dialectic on the relationship of authority (or sovereignty) to liberty. However, it is not only the incorporation of this dialectic into the play that is important, but also Shakespeare's handling of the dialectic so that in these scenes what is being euphemized and normalized is not a hegemonic power but a reciprocal system wherein power is shared. Instead of mystifying absolutism, he mystifies the other choice—the constitutional relationship between subject and ruler that depends on reciprocity, on *meum et tuum*. The Ferdinand scenes represent reciprocity by way of a love relationship in which both parties gain freedom by being bound to each other and in which the mutual obligation makes for perfect harmony. Like the emphasis on discipline and limit all through the play, the emphasis on reciprocity in these love scenes stands as another example of how epideictic can argue for and seek to increase adherence to a certain position by featuring a value which may, in a different constellation of values, be in danger of not prevailing, but which, when considered on its own, would not be contested.[4] By constructing reciprocity as love and service, as conflict-free, and as normative, this standard is foregrounded as the means by which to reach a perfect state of being, a return to the golden age.

The representation of reciprocity within a narrative that recounts the progress of love and education is, throughout the Ferdinand scenes, also dependent on Shakespeare's transformations of Virgil. Shakespeare sets the sequence of Ferdinand's scenes so that his progress conforms chronologically to the progress of Aeneas from books one through six. At the beginning of the play, Ferdinand shipwrecks on the island, just as Aeneas shipwrecks at Carthage in *Aeneid* 1. He immediately meets a woman with whom he falls in love (1.2), he works for her as Aeneas works for Dido at Carthage (3.1), and he eventually has an Elysium experience by way of the show of spirits that Prospero's art provides (4.1). But through this presentation of Ferdinand as an idealized version of Aeneas, the entire presentation can be understood to be passing judgment, however implicitly, on king and court.

Ferdinand and Miranda

Shakespeare begins the process of charting Ferdinand's way through the play by recasting for his first moments on stage some of the experiences Aeneas had when he first arrived at Carthage. Here, as elsewhere when Ferdinand is involved, Shakespeare's rewriting suppresses the stronger Virgilian language which presents Aeneas as a blemished and anxious hero. In Ferdinand's first speech, the emphasis is on a dissipating anguish rather than on that sustained state of hopelessness experienced by Aeneas. Aeneas appears calm as he speaks words of encouragement to his men, but Virgil's narrator comments: "So spake his tongue; while sick with weighty care he feigns hope on his face, and deep in his heart stifles the anguish" ("Talia voce refert, curisque ingentibus aeger / spem voltu simulat, premit altum corde dolorem," 1.208–9).[5] In contrast, Ferdinand feels a calm settle over him as soon as the supernatural music starts:

> Sitting on a bank,
> Weeping again the King my father's wrack,
> This music crept by me upon the waters,
> Allaying both their fury and my passion
> With its sweet air.
> (1.2.392–96)

We know that the Neoplatonists regarded sight and hearing as "reason's ministers,"[6] as a means to move the soul to higher knowledge. The music that emanates through Ariel is Ferdinand's introduction to the contact with divine things available to him on this island:[7] "sure it waits upon / Some god o' th' island."

In the next two speeches, the Virgilian model is from the place where Aeneas, newly arrived at Carthage, addresses Venus, disguised as a huntress. In his initial greeting to her, in which he remarks that she appears to be a goddess (*o dea certe*), he prays that she "lighten this our burden" by telling him and Achates where they have landed: "O goddess surely! . . . Inform us, pray, beneath what sky, on what coasts of the world, we are cast; knowing naught of country or of people, we wander hither driven by wind and huge billows" ("o dea certe! . . . sis felix nostrumque leves, quaecumque, laborem, / et quo sub caelo tandem, quibus orbis in oris / iactemur, doceas; ignari hominumque locorumque / erramus, vento huc vastis et fluctibus acti, 1.328–33). Ferdinand, too, first addresses Miranda as a goddess—"Most sure the goddess / On whom these airs attend"—and then prays for her assistance: "Vouchsafe my prayer / May know if you remain upon this island; / And that you will some good instruction give / How I may bear me here" (1.2.424–28).

In linking Miranda to Venus (in one of the most audible of all echoes of the *Aeneid*),[8] Shakespeare enhances Miranda's double function of being the one who arouses Ferdinand's passion and also leads him to knowledge of divine things. Landino understood Virgil's use of Venus—in this very meeting with Aeneas—similarly. Recalling Plato's discussion in the *Symposium* of the soul as possessing two Venuses, Landino explains that the first is "caught up in apprehending the beauty of God" and the second is that associated with procreation.[9] For Ferdinand to love Miranda is to discover for himself the best woman to marry and, at the same time, to pursue the truths that the allegorists saw represented in the educational progress of Aeneas.

Such achievement depends, however, on Ferdinand's compliance with Prospero's plan for testing and disciplining him,[10] a plan that features from the very beginning the loss of freedom: "I'll manacle thy neck and feet together." There will be no banquet for Ferdinand like the one Dido provided for Aeneas. Instead, Prospero puts him on an austere diet: "Sea-water shalt thou drink; thy food shall be / The fresh-brook mussels, wither'd roots, and husks / Wherein the acorn cradled." Ferdinand finds such restrictions liberating, defined as they are within the context of Miranda's love: "Might I but through my prison once a day / Behold this maid: all corners else o' th' earth / Let liberty make use of; space enough / Have I in such a prison." Throughout the rest of the play, Ferdinand accepts every opportunity for more discipline, more self-containment. Never is he an unbridled youth, but, from the outset, a tidied-up Aeneas with passions in check.

We know the extent to which the praise of Prince Henry, self-created as a figure of conquest and chastity,[11] had an idealizing quality similar to the extensive idealizing of Ferdinand. Ferdinand's portrait departs from the preferred image of Henry in its emphases on a reciprocal love and on restriction, differences that are especially marked in the context of contemporary complaints about Henry's excesses. During the debates on supply, when James was using the issue of the prince as one way to woo Parliament and to secure a larger supply,[12] anxiety was expressed about the large amount that Henry (his investiture, his palace, his household) was going to cost the nation, expense that would effectively deprive subjects of liberty. A record of the debates on October 27, 1610, acknowledges that the cost of supporting Henry had already grown so great that this cause alone would have necessitated the calling of a parliament.[13] Other records of his "elaborate regulations for diet and service indicate the luxury by which Henry was surrounded, while his impressive patent roll shows the extensive range of income and patronage rights which he could deploy."[14]

In 1610, when Salisbury was making his last efforts to reach an agreement with king and parliament on the matter of supply, he instructed James that a necessary part of the "remedy" to James's financial problems was more discipline or, as Salisbury put it, "abatement," by which he meant "the stay of bounty and the stay of your expense." Only James himself, he emphasized, could control these two aspects: "it is your hand that holdeth that sluice, which being opened at large, or shut up, will make the stream of all your charges and expenses whatsoever either to keep within the bank or to run over."[15]

In *The Tempest* Prospero is the stern father who teaches Ferdinand the value of the prize he seeks by first putting him through trials of abatement. In the real world, Salisbury had told James that, in financial matters, too, he should follow an ideal model: "it is for your Majesty to do as the Roman emperor did . . . when public treasure was much exhausted" (p. 294). Actually, the play has the capacity to say the same thing.

Log-Carrying

The scene of *The Tempest* (3.1) where Ferdinand carries logs for Prospero and in service to Miranda is the fifth of the play's nine scenes and thus also the centerpiece of the play. The chosen language for the surface texture of the scene is again that of Neoplatonism, but especially as it had developed in the Neoplatonic sonnet and heroic love treatise.[16] This language is conspicuous in Ferdinand's repeatedly calling Miranda "mistress," the word Neoplatonists used to refer to that for which the soul longs. The references he makes to his heart flying to Miranda's service (3.1.65)[17] and his realization in this scene that Miranda's name means "wonder" (or "meraveglia," the heroic principle of the marvelous)[18] are part of the same strategy of composition:

> Admir'd Miranda!
> Indeed the top admiration! worth
> What's dearest to the world.

One distinguishing aspect of Shakespeare's replication of these idioms is the degree to which he has humanized, materialized, and literalized these intellectual and spiritual concepts, a process through which he also changes the terms so that they are compatible with the constitutionalist argument of the play. Central to this shift is that this love scene exhibits no struggle to keep passion under control; in other words, the scene does not present a struggle to dominate the base. The component of struggle and discipline, so important to the Neoplatonic system, is nonetheless present, but is displaced to the experience and reward of performing difficult physical work in the world, and for a worthy end:

> some kinds of baseness
> Are nobly undergone; and most poor matters
> Point to rich ends. This my mean task
> Would be as heavy to me as odious, but
> The mistress which I serve quickens what's dead,
> And makes my labours pleasures.
>
> (3.1.1–7)

Moreover, that work is explicitly and repeatedly redefined in the scene as service, and so also as that which defines the relationship of Ferdinand to Miranda. Ferdinand, a prince and future ruler who here performs the same work Caliban does elsewhere in the play, declares that his "heart [did] fly to your service" where it remains a "slave"; "for your sake / Am I this patient log-man." He is eager to commit himself to laboring in the world and for someone else. Nevertheless, Miranda insists that she be his helper: "If you'll sit down, / I'll bear your logs the while . . . give me that; / I'll carry it to the pile." When Ferdinand denies her request, explaining that it would make him look "lazy," she counters that the work is mutually becoming. "It would become me / As well as it does you." Near the end of the scene, when she declares, "I'll be your servant," he reciprocates with, "And I thus humble ever." Understanding his declaration of humility as a definition of the terms of their relationship, she asks for confirmation: "My husband then?" And in his affirmative reply, "Ay, with a heart as willing / As bondage e'er of freedom,"[19] he alludes to the normative terms which this play privileges. Even as freedom is the most desired condition of existence, so the contractual relationship of marriage is what Ferdinand desires above anything else.

As we consider the implications of Shakespeare's having placed this display of reciprocity at the very center of the play, it is important not to lose sight of the patriarchal structures that surround it.[20] Prospero, who has arranged the love and assigned the tasks, is even present during this scene. The love proceeds visually and linguistically within the context of patriarchal guidance, and thus also within the context of the language of absolutism, to which patriarchy and its analogous metaphors of dominance and subordination were central. To King James, the king's relationship to the kingdom was analogous to being the head of the body, the god on earth, the father of the family, and even the husband to the wife: "I am the Husband, and all the whole Isle is my lawfull Wife."[21]

But clearly, the particular relationship that Shakespeare constructed for Ferdinand and Miranda is not one that is accounted for in this Jamesian language of dominance, nor in the language of dominance and subjection present in many contemporary treatises on marriage.[22] Nor does the language of this scene belong to the Petrarchan language of love, popular during the reign of Elizabeth and central to the differently gendered political language of that earlier reign. In that language, which foregrounded the ability of the woman to retain mastery, the lover sued a woman who would not respond, would not yield.[23] Instead, Shakespeare inserts here the language of marriage as a contract (the language for marriage in the courts of law) and the language of companionate marriage (as that language had filtered down from the humanists, Catholics, and finally to the protestants).[24]

Whatever relevance that language may have had when *The Tempest* was selected for the betrothal celebration of Princess Elizabeth, outside a specific marriage context that language contains the idioms for defining the contractual theory of government, which, as J. P. Sommerville has emphasized, espoused "that the king and his subjects were bound by *reciprocal* conditions." In the early seventeenth century, when "the vocabulary of contract was almost as common as that of immemorial law," it was this consensualist theory that "struck at the central doctrine of absolutism— the contention that kings derive their power from God alone." Sommerville continues, "in the Parliament of 1610 the lawyer John Hoskins declared that while regal power itself was from God, the 'actuating thereof is from the people.' In other words, God first gave regal power to the people, who then decided on the form in which it should be exercised."[25]

For *The Tempest*, Shakespeare chooses a language of love and marriage that, in its emphasis on mutual dependency (not, we should note, equality), most closely parallels the language of constitutionalism and contract.[26] This incursion, performed as it is within a context rich in patriarchal signifiers, does not display itself as a replacement of or as a challenge to patriarchy; nor does it seem in contradiction to James's own metaphor of king as husband. Here, as often, Shakespeare's method is to speak in language compatible with that of the king—even as he is representing a position that is different from the king's. Thus, insofar as Prospero himself arranges the terms of the love, reciprocity is made to seem a natural extension of patriarchy. Nevertheless, however tactful the rhetoric, for Shakespeare to insert a representation of contract within the context of a representation of patriarchy is to alter the discursive formation so that now mutuality, reciprocity, and contract also have the imprimatur of the normative.

This maneuver is supported intertextually by the way in which this scene works off and reverses one more scene from the affair at Carthage. As Ferdinand carries logs, he is also involved in a refiguration of Virgil's story of how Aeneas, after being in the cave with Dido, turns his energies to the building at Carthage.

For Aeneas to build at Carthage is to reveal how deeply involved he is with Dido. But his building for her and for the valued Carthaginian community is, at the same time, a disregard of his duty to establish a civilization in Italy for his son. His hard work is service for the wrong cause.[27] After being scolded by Mercury for his activities, Aeneas finally orders his men to ready the ships, while Dido, having heard rumors of Aeneas's plans to depart, accosts him and rages at him for having misled her with shows of affection, predicting that he leaves her a dying woman (4.307-8, 323). Insisting that he never intended to marry her and that he must obey the gods' commands, he adds the crucial line defining his personal conflict: "Italiam non sponte sequor" (4.361); going to Italy is not something he has chosen for himself.

In changing this scene for *The Tempest*, Shakespeare retained the idea of service but altered the context so that the service is for a right cause, for a woman whose destiny is compatible with the hero's. Thus the charges of negligence and betrayal disappear and with them the accompanying tension. Instead of the reprimanding Mercury who comes to tell Aeneas to stop what he is doing, Prospero himself has ordered Ferdinand to do this work and looks on approvingly during the scene. At the end of the scene, Miranda weeps "at what I am glad of" (3.1.74), not, as Dido, for what she has lost. And Miranda's references to dying (ll. 79, 84) do not refer to an impending tragedy but to how much she loves Ferdinand and how faithful she will be. As Sturm noted, "Imitation is not in things that be all one, but in things that be like, and that which is like, must be, not the same, but another thing" (H1^v).

Still, while Ferdinand is not subject to any censure, either from Prospero or Miranda, he nevertheless speaks here a variation on that most famous of all the lines that Aeneas has in this Carthage episode, in which Aeneas admits to Dido that he resists his destiny: "Italiam non sponte sequor" ("Not of free will do I follow Italy"). Ferdinand makes a similar admission—"I am, in my condition, / A prince, Miranda; I do think, a King; / I would not so" (3.1.59-61)— an admission that injects into this scene the conflict between love and duty that also stands at the center of the Dido-Aeneas crisis. Enraptured with Miranda, Ferdinand, too, wishes he could avoid the duty that he believes now calls him back to Italy. What he does not know is that Miranda will go to Italy with him.

These several reversals contribute in various ways to the dialectic on authority and freedom. One aspect of that contribution is that this time the reversal also involves disrupting a topos—the building of Carthage—that had become a central idiom in Renaissance discourse of colonization. To describe the building of the walls of Ross, Stanyhurst had quoted Phaer's translation of the building at Carthage, a text Davies had also quoted when he compared the building that was going forward in Ireland.[28] Appropriated for the symbolization of a civilizing impulse, Virgil's text seemed to justify expansion and domination; as Waswo has written, it furnished "the founding myth that supplies [European] cultural identity."[29]

In Shakespeare's rewriting of the building at Carthage, however, he replicates the idea of work in the world, but in terms that do not emphasize the notions of expansion and domination associated with colonization. The "thousands of logs" that Prospero has Ferdinand carry are there to test his worth; he must show he can work hard. Within the context of the rest of the play, logs are for making fires, as Prospero suggests when he says that Caliban "does make our fire, / Fetch in our wood" (1.2.313–14). This emphasis on work has an interesting corollary in the plight of the Virginia colony, which was known in 1610–11 to be in a severely threatened state because the colonists had not kept discipline and had refused to do the work that would have met basic needs.[30] What was needed most in Virginia, and apparently what is needed on the island of *The Tempest*, were ways to meet the material conditions of existence.

Thus, while the scene does not emphasize domination,[31] and while the characters on the island are not there to colonize it, we are not entirely accurate in saying that it does not, or cannot, represent colonization. But once again, as elsewhere in the play, the action is shaped so that the aspect of colonization to which it might refer is one which can be represented in the same way that issues of limited power can be represented—through images of discipline and restriction. Unlike Prince Henry, a patron of the Virginia plantation project[32] and one who favored a conqueror image for himself, Ferdinand is not a conqueror of lands; nor does he sue for Miranda. Rather than one who dominates and colonizes others, Ferdinand is presented as one whose first task is to subdue or limit himself; and, in another variation on the Petrarchan and Neoplatonic tradition, it is *he* who will remain chaste, not only the woman. His own self is the project.

The Tempest as Masque and Romance   103

Thus while colonization is present in the contemporary culture and also in the precursor text, a further possibility remains that the representation of Ferdinand's subjection is yet one more way to make a discursive inroad into the language of absolutism.

Chess

At the end of *The Tempest*, Shakespeare rewrites the central episode of the Dido and Aeneas story, that of the cave. For this event, he actually places Ferdinand and Miranda in a cave, but it is the cave of Prospero, and so a place of security and regulation. The language he writes for the lovers also sets them against the motifs of betrayal, accusation, and separation that constitute the outcome for Dido and Aeneas. In this new action, falseness and wrangling make up the language of wit and game, not of passion and loss:

MIR.: Sweet lord, you play me false.
FER.:   No, my dearest love,
    I would not for the world.
MIR.: Yes, for a score of kingdoms you should wrangle.
    And I would call it fair play.
                    (5.1.172–75)

Chess, the game they are playing, is a game of discipline and negotiation that demonstrates in miniature the activities of rule.[33] This point was emphasized in Caxton's *Game and Playe of the Chesse* (1474), the main concern of which was the qualities needed for rule. According to Caxton, chess was an activity for philosophers and a game that philosophers taught to kings to help them learn the virtues they needed for good rule.[34] The same point was made in the greeting to the reader that stood at the beginning of *Ludus Scacchiae: Chesse-play* (1597), where it was explained that chess was a "kingly pastime" that "breedeth in the players, a certaine study, wit, pollicie, forecast and memorie, not onely in the play thereof, but also in actions of publike governement, both in peace and warre" (A2).[35] The educational aspect of the game also accounts for the allusion Thomas More made to it in *Utopia*, where he wrote that the game the Utopians played was "not unlike chess";

in it was "exhibited very cleverly . . . both the strife of the vices with one another and their . . . opposition to the virtues."[36]

Finally, when Prospero pulls aside the curtain to reveal Ferdinand and Miranda at chess as "a wonder" (5.1.170), there is as well a conflation of the cave episode in *Aeneid* 4 and the vision of the future Anchises draws for Aeneas in *Aeneid* 6. But Prospero, unlike Anchises, has had and will have a direct role in bringing into being this promise for the future. The education of Ferdinand in love and service to the reciprocating Miranda are the central codes in that new order. The moment is fittingly emblematic for a nation where negotiations about issues of contract had broken down between king and parliament. The Great Contract of 1610 had already failed; what would become of constitutionalism remained to be seen.

PART 3
Prospero and the Best State of the Commonwealth

PROSPERO'S NAME IN ITSELF suggests the form Shakespeare chose to construct his main character in *The Tempest*. In Cooper's *Thesaurus*, "prospero, prosperas" is glossed as "to geve prosperitie: to make prosperous: to geve success to."[1] Consistent with Prospero's godlike and patriarchal identities, and with the play's strategies for praise, is this explicit naming of the ruler as the one on whom civil life depends for its goodness. But while the representation of Prospero proceeds by a demonstration of exemplary choices and actions, implicit in this demonstration is always an element of persuasion.

This linking of praise and persuasion is present in George Puttenham's instructions concerning the appropriate style for praise; there must be, he says, "decencie" and "comelinesse" both "in prayse or dispraise" and in "praise & perswasion."[2] When Brian Vickers discusses the persuasive function of epideictic, he recalls Aristotle's explanation of the connection between praise and action: "To praise a man is in one respect akin to urging a course of action. The suggestions made in the latter case become encomiums when differently expressed. . . . Consequently, whenever you want to praise any one, think what you would urge people to do" (1367^b35ff).[3] In *The Tempest*, the support of and persuasion to constitutionalism is richly and diplomatically packaged in a godlike and fatherlike ruler who nevertheless chooses to give up his transcendent power.

The following discussion focuses on three aspects of Shakespeare's construction: the transformed Virgilian patterns that present Prospero's transcendence, the representation of the political controversy through Prospero's relations with Ariel and Caliban, and the implications of Prospero's granting of mercy and suspension of power.

THE VIRGILIAN PATTERNS IN PROSPERO

The Virgilian patterns that Shakespeare refigured for Prospero's role place *The Tempest* directly in the line of earlier imitators of the *Aeneid*. Following the practice of Tasso, who, like Homer, was understood to have used two different characters to present the images of the public and private man,[4] Shakespeare created the private man, Ferdinand, primarily from patterns in the Dido and Aeneas love story. But he constructed Prospero in such a way that he embodies the idea of rule associated with Aeneas in and after book 6 (that is, Aeneas as one who will be an ideal governor), and also so that he carries, *but transforms*, the ideas of wrath, revenge, and destruction associated with the Troy story in *Aeneid* 2 and 3. Thus, in the part of Prospero, as in other instances in *The Tempest*, Shakespeare conflates widely separated sections of Virgil's text.

This method dominates the composition of Prospero's first scene (1.2) where he, like Aeneas in *Aeneid* 2 and 3, speaks a long narration of the past that establishes him as the figure who holds the memory of the culture and is haunted by its tragedies. But as he speaks to a daughter who recalls only that "Four or five women once . . . tended me" (1.2.44), the tone of his narrative has none of the hesitancy and grief that marks Aeneas's story, conserving only a sense that there is no time for delay: "Tis time I should inform thee farther" (1.2.22–23), he says; "The hour's now come" (1.2.36).

Various features of this conversation show how Shakespeare combined earlier Virgilian patterns with later ones. Prospero speaks here not as Aeneas did to Dido—as visitor to stranger—but as father to child, a fact that also recalls Anchises' words to Aeneas in the underworld, "I will teach you your fate" ("te tua fata docebo," 6.759). At another point in the scene there is a variation on the familiar paradox that Troy had to fall in order for Rome to come into being. Questioning the significance of having been thrust from Milan, Miranda asks: "What foul play had we, that we came from thence? / Or blessed was't we did?" (1.2.60–61). Prospero's reply—"Both, both"—is an appreciation of the paradox that Aeneas did not grasp about his own situation until he had heard the prophecies of Anchises in *Aeneid* 6 and could begin to imagine his destiny.

In the final passage of Prospero's conversation with Miranda, he again expresses an attitude reminiscent of Aeneas in *Aeneid* 6:

By accident most strange, bountiful Fortune,
(Now my dear lady) hath mine enemies
Brought to this shore; and by my prescience
I find my zenith doth depend upon
A most auspicious star, whose influence
If now I court not, but omit, my fortunes
Will ever after droop.

(1.2.178–84)

Here Prospero claims for himself two of the most important characteristics with which Virgil associated Aeneas. In the phrases that contain the words "Fortune," "zenith," "auspicious star," and "fortunes," he declares himself to be a man whose destiny is at hand, as was Aeneas's upon arriving in Italy. He too possesses the "fatum" that set Aeneas apart from all others. Second, in his reference to his "prescience," Prospero declares that he also possesses knowledge of the future, a characteristic Virgil does not assign to Aeneas until *Aeneid* 6, where, after listening to the prophecy of the Sibyl, he replies, "I have foreseen [*praecepi*] and thought all in my soul"[5] ("omnia praecepi atque animo mecum ante peregi," 6.105). In a conflation of characteristics of the heroic Aeneas which in Virgil stand several books apart, Prospero appears in his first scene as a man of memory, vision, and wisdom.

The dignity that such conflation confers upon Prospero's character is further stabilized by Shakespeare's making him a magician. Because of James I's cultivated reputation as a philosophic ruler, a Hermes Trismegistus,[6] the first association of the magus figure for the Jacobean court audience would no doubt have been with the tradition of the philosopher-king. Earlier, in *Gesta Grayorum*, the entertainment prepared by Gray's Inn for the Christmas revels of 1594, this tradition had been articulated in terms that others have also seen as relevant to *The Tempest*. In that entertainment, one of the counselors describes the king as a magician who engages in "the exercise of the best and purest part of the mind." "Antiquity . . . informeth us," he says, "that the [governments of] kingdomes have always had an affinity with the secrets and mysteries of learning." The Persian magi and the gymnosophists of Asia exemplified the tradition that the happiest kingdoms are those whose rulers were "most addicted to philosophy."[7] To pursue that same end, the prince should collect a perfect library, devise a magnificent garden as "a model of universal nature," possess a "hugh cabinet" full of examples of both man's and Nature's finest creations, and acquire "a still-house, so furnished with mills, instruments, furnaces, and vessels, as may be a palace fit for a philosopher's stone," so that he may become a Hermes Trismegistus and "be left the only miracle and Wonder of the world" (p. 335).

Shakespeare made his magician both Virgilian and Jamesian by arranging that Prospero's magic be articulated through patterns that Virgil used for his gods, a method that also plays off the similitude that kings are like gods. Like Aeolus, Prospero has "Put the wild waters in this roar" (1.2.2); like Neptune, he has "safely ordered" (1.2.29), so that the victims of the storm do not suffer great harm; and like Jupiter, who comforted the fearful Venus ("Spare thy fear," *parce metu*, 1.257), he tells Miranda, "Be collected . . . tell your piteous heart / There's no harm done" (1.2.12–14). Later in the scene Prospero replicates more godlike patterns when he oversees the young love of Ferdinand and Miranda, as Venus and Juno oversaw that of Dido and Aeneas and, when he issues commands to Ariel, as Jupiter did to Mercury.

Shifting the godlike powers in this play to a mortal also accommodates the problem of trying to achieve in Christian times a successful imitation of Virgil's epic machinery.[8] Shakespeare models Ariel, the aerial spirit every renowned magus would have in his company,[9] on the pattern of Mercury. When Mercury, in the *Aeneid*, carries Jupiter's message to Aeneas to leave Carthage, he puts wings on his feet so that he can fly, he drives the winds, skims the clouds, and speeds down to the waves (4.238–58). So, in Ariel's first speech of the play, the daemon offers "to fly, / To swim, to dive into the fire, to ride / On the curl'd clouds" (1.2.190–92) in order to do Prospero's bidding. Also, like Virgil's Mercury, who "gives or takes away sleep" ("dat somnos adimitque," 4.244), Ariel later uses sleep to quiet Alonso and Gonzalo and then awakens them to save them from their enemies (2.1.292–300).[10]

In these actions Ariel represents, at least in part, what Mercury was to the allegorizers. For Ficino, he was "the one who carried and revealed the hermetic mysteries,"[11] and for Bernardus he represented " 'the activity of the mind,' because he revealed contrived matters. And thus he was also called Hermes, that is *interpres*, 'explanation.' "[12] As an aerial spirit doing the bidding of a magus, Ariel manifests the degree to which Prospero is the master of his own soul. A version of an Aeneas figure who has completed much of his journey but who is now about to reenter (rather than enter) the active, governing aspect of his life, Prospero also displays through Ariel the magisterial control he can exercise over everything around him.

Such control, especially in the early scenes, may present a character seemingly static in conception. Yet it is a conception that exactly fits the language that Bacon, Salisbury, and other contemporaries used when they "translated" James's similitude about kings being gods. In his power and in his effect on the kingdom, the king was the *principale agens*, the *primum mobile*, the *primus motor*, the *primum movens*.[13] Or, as James put it, kings could "make and unmake their subjects . . . have power of raising, and casting downe: of life, and of death."[14] It would seem that, in these aspects at least, Shakespeare's representation of Prospero is of "the sacred and authoritarian word . . . with its indisputability, unconditionality, and unequivocality," a sacredness characterized by "its inertness, its withdrawal from dialogue."[15]

OCCASIONAL PATTERNS IN ARIEL AND CALIBAN

What disrupts the static quality of his presentation is the presence of the two nonhuman characters, Ariel and Caliban, whom Prospero commands. This triangle of characters acts out a complex set of power relations that share a conceptual similarity with those between king and Parliament in 1610. Like James and Parliament arguing over supply, Ariel and Caliban talk to Prospero about what they must do for him and what they will get in return. Shakespeare's method here depends primarily on the skillful assignment and management of voice. Even as Prospero speaks with the flat, impenetrable voice of the gods, so Ariel and Caliban speak with the various voices of subjects.

Ariel's is the voice of humility and obedience, as advocated by Puttenham: "in negotiating with Princes we ought to seeke their favour by humilitie & not by sternnesse" (p. 293), and "in speaking to a Prince the voyce ought to be lowe" (p. 294). Clearly, this was the standard form of address to use with the monarch. Caliban, on the other hand, speaks in a rude voice of challenge, complaint, and accusation, an alternative style that Puttenham advises against: "Princes may be lead but not driven, nor they are to be vanquisht by allegation, but must be suffred to have the victorie and be relented unto: nor they are not to be chalenged for right or justice, for that is a maner of accusation. . . . Likewise in matter of advise it is neither decent to flatter him for that is servile, neither to be to rough of plaine with him, for that is daungerous" (pp. 293, 295).

On the surface, such assignments of voice to Ariel and Caliban may seem simple. But even as Puttenham knew that the voice selected comprised a technique (hence his reference to the courtier as the "faire semblant," p. 299), so there is a great deal of equivocation, amounting to paradox,[16] in the effect and implication of these two voices being present, and present in characters of such opposite (Ariel/high; Caliban/low) natures. Thus, even though humility can suggest an obedient and respectful attitude, it can also disguise a self-interested motive. But a rude voice can be a disguise too,[17] and especially in a work of fiction written for a culture where the standards for decency and comeliness predisposed the assumption that someone with a rude voice was not only imprudent but discreditable. Thus, in *The Tempest*, where this rude voice fits Caliban's subhuman status, it becomes both representative of baseness (that is, what is not normative and so not to be valued), and a disguise for the voice of challenge and accusation—or, to shift back to the terms of epideictic, the voice of vituperation and blame.[18] In other words, in this situation, ironically and paradoxically, the voice of blame (and the character who speaks with it) is discountable for its indecency and uncomeliness yet *is* creditable and compelling insofar as the vices it enumerates are recognizable as those of a ruler who has insufficient regard for the freedom of subjects.

Whatever the case at any one moment in the play, Caliban and Ariel can best be understood when, in the context of their dealings with Prospero, they are read relationally,[19] not allegorically. We would not, for example, want to fix our reading so that we always saw Ariel as the properly obedient subject and Caliban as the disobedient one deserving of punishment. Nor does the project involve matching a speech of Ariel or Caliban with a particular speech or speaker in Parliament. The object instead is to see how the issues that Parliament and James were debating, the idioms in which they cast this debate, and the forms of address they used when they responded to each other have been given concrete representation in a parodic fictional setting. In the process, we witness both the means by which controversy can be fictionalized, and also another example of the "expansion of the literary language that results from drawing on various extraliterary strata of the national language."[20]

Before proceeding to the ways in which Ariel and Caliban represent conflict and struggle, we should first acknowledge how exactly they iterate the common ground shared by all those who participated in the argument over royal power—namely, the assumption, central to the very concept of English monarchy, that in certain areas no one could interfere with the king's exercise of power. In the heated sessions that took place at the end of June, Henry Martin, discussing the issue of whether the king had any "absolute power," argued that, if he did, "it is in matters of justice, or in matters of treason or felony" (Gardiner, p. 89). Thomas Hedley made the same point, only he emphasized that some prerogatives did not need to be disputed because they were not as easily abused as were impositions. His list of such indisputable prerogatives, similar to and yet more complete than Martin's, included "making war and peace, enhancing or debasing coin, pardoning of felons and offenders, making of judges, etc." (Foster, 2:183).[21] When Shakespeare shows Ariel stopping the treasonous attack of Antonio and Sebastian on Alonso, has the harpy-Ariel denounce the three men of sin in the banquet scene, and routs the treasonous Caliban in the glistering apparel scene, he is acknowledging these necessary and acceptable prerogatives of the king.

Beyond this acknowledgment of the rightful powers of the king, the basic issue that Ariel and Caliban represent in relation to Prospero is that of reciprocity, that is, *meum et tuum*, the principle that the Commons urged on the king from the very beginning of the session. When he asked for supply, they responded by asking what the king would, in turn, give to them. In his March speech James made this same point, though emphasizing his own needs, when he explained that "Duetie I may justly claime of you as my Subjects; and one of the branches of duetie which Subjects owe to their Soveraigne is Supply" (McIlwain, p. 317). In *The Tempest*, both Ariel and Caliban are shown as deeply beholden to Prospero, and likewise he to them. In exchange for having set him free from a pine tree, Prospero now requires Ariel to fulfill all of his commands. The obedient Ariel is also aware that the relationship is a reciprocal one: "Is there more toil? Since thou dost give me pains, / Let me remember thee what thou hast promis'd, / Which is not yet perform'd me. . . . My liberty" (1.2.242–45). Likewise, Prospero says that upon coming to the island he treated Caliban very well ("us'd thee with human care . . . lodg'd thee / In mine own cell," 1.2.347–49), though now he needs Caliban more than the belligerent Caliban thinks he needs Prospero. "We cannot miss him," Prospero tells Miranda; "he does make our fire; / Fetch in our wood, and serve in offices / That profit us" (1.2.312–14). In other words, although he is now offering resistance to Prospero's demands ("There's wood enough within," "I must eat my dinner," 1.2.316, 332), Caliban's basic function is to supply Prospero.

All during the debates on impositions, the central issue for the Commons was the need to protect the property of the subject. This is the point around which Nicholas Fuller, invoking, like others, Magna Carta, organized his entire speech of June 23, where he explained that his "arguments for the freedom of the subject" would show "that by the laws of England the subjects have such property in their lands and goods as that without consent the king can take no part of" (Foster, 2:152). This argument was in effect one that opposed the concept of absolute monarchy by setting against it a concept of absolute property (and hence an argument for the absolute rights of subjects).[22] One way of articulating the argument about property was to distinguish the status of a subject from that of a slave, the former having a status before the law that protects him and gives him rights, the latter not. When some members of the Lower House protested the king's system of impositions, they argued that impositions had the effect of making the people slaves. James Whitelocke, in his speech arguing the "essence" of the kingdom and his fear of subjects becoming "tenants at [the king's] will," cited a precedent from the reign of Richard III when "the Commons of this his Realme . . . have been put to great servitude" (*A Learned and Necessary Argument*, C3). "We are," Whitelocke said, emphasizing the consensualist position, "masters of our own and can have nothing taken from us without our consents." At one point, Thomas Edmondes wrote William Trumbull that the object of Parliament had now to be "to redeem a greater burden and thralldom" (Foster, 1:47). One of the strongest statements of this sort was that of Hedley, who argued that "the liberty of the subject" exists principally "in matter of profit and property" (Foster, 2:191). Therefore, "take away the liberty of the subject" in these matters "and you make a promiscuous confusion of a freeman and a bound slave, which slavery is as repugnant to the nature of an Englishman as allegiance and due subjection is to his own proper and peculiar" (Foster, 2:192).

This promiscuous confusion is replicated in the patterning of Caliban's role on that of a displanted native. Actually named in the list of actors as "a savage and deformed slave," he is an exaggerated representation of that debased and deformed state that some parliamentarians claimed they would be reduced to were subjects to lose their rights. And because Shakespeare had at hand the other contemporary context of plantation, especially that of Ireland where slavery was also an issue, he could superimpose the image of the enslaved and colonized native upon that of the subject who is no longer, as Whitelocke would say, his own "master."

All these images, and their accompanying languages, are simultaneously written into Caliban's protest that Prospero has taken what is not his:

> This island's mine, by Sycorax my mother,
> Which thou tak'st from me . . .
> For I am all the subjects that you have,
> Which first was mine own King.
> (1.2.332–33, 342–44)

According to Bakhtin, such superimposition virtually defines the nature of parody: "in parody two languages are crossed with each other, as well as two styles, two linguistic points of view, and in the final analysis two speaking subjects. It is true that only one of these languages (the one that is parodied) is present in its own right; the other is present . . . as an actualizing background for creating and perceiving."[23] In the vituperative Caliban, who characterizes Prospero's power as strong enough to reduce even the god Setebos to the status of "vassal" (1.2.376), the language "present in its own right" is that of the opposition parliamentarians, to whose position Shakespeare gives dramatic actuality when he provides Caliban with an identity that they insisted an English subject was not to have. However, this does not mean that scholars are mistaken in finding here a colonialist discourse; on the contrary, Bakhtin's explanation of parody helps to confirm its presence.

Parody, a method of composition that Greene speaks of as one of the dominant modes of imitative writing,[24] is also a method that hides intent. As Bakhtin stresses, "Theoretically it is possible to sense and recognize in any parody that 'normal' language, that 'normal' style, in light of which the given parody was created. But in practice it is far from easy and not always possible."[25] And in *The*

Tempest, the act of recognition required by parody is continually complicated by Shakespeare's switching, as it were, the sides on which the norm and its parody might be expected to be found.

One aspect of the normal language of the parliamentary debates, for instance, was the citation of precedents by which could be measured the regularity or irregularity of King James's actions. On the issue of impositions, a frequently cited precedent was that no impositions had been levied in England for one hundred and eighty years, from the time of Edward III until the time of Queen Mary.[26] Especially important in this context was the fact that Elizabeth herself had levied impositions, as Salisbury was eager to remind Parliament when he spoke to them on July 10, 1610, referring to "the impost upon the currants (set in the Queen's time, and then carried in a monopolie)" (Gardiner, p. 157). The Commons also referred to this precedent in the Petition of Temporal Grievances, issued just days before Salisbury spoke, where they admitted that impositions "were in some use in the late Queen's time, and not then much impugned, because the usage of them being more moderate, gave not so great occasion of offense." Moreover, Parliament urged that the king not "continue any grievance upon your people, because you found them begun in your predecessor's time" (Foster, 2:257).

In *The Tempest*, Shakespeare displaces these arguments about the preceding monarch onto Prospero's female predecessor, Sycorax, whose behavior Prospero describes to Caliban:

> too delicate
> To act her earthy and abhorr'd commands,
> Refusing her grand hests, she did confine thee,
> By help of her more potent ministers.
> (1.2.272–75)

This description of how an earlier authority, in this case a female, also tried to control Caliban would seem to make Sycorax into a parody of Queen Elizabeth, as Ariel and Caliban are of Parliament. Even though elsewhere Caliban appeals to her precedent for his own legitimacy, here it is her precedent for taking power and containing her opposition that receives emphasis.

It should be admitted that the political story we are considering has a confusing aspect, in that it is Caliban, not Prospero, who evokes Sycorax to claim his own legitimacy. While it might be possible to make sense of this confusion by positing that what is being referred to is the legitimacy of Parliament's status under Elizabeth, the outcome of our efforts is just as likely to shake our confidence in our ability to identify equivalencies. At any point, we may feel, our ability to distinguish between legal and illegal ruler, master and slave, could falter, so fluid and abstract is the play's referential method. And if we grasp, for security, the notion that Sycorax is the black magical alternative to Prospero as magus, that confidence will also disappear when we reach, much later, the speech where Prospero gives up his magic, a speech modeled on an Ovidian passage spoken by the witch Medea.

This is not the only place where Shakespeare manipulates categories and displaces language.[27] In a passage that follows shortly after this one, where Caliban speaks of Prospero's having usurped the island which was his "by Sycorax my mother," he also tells of how Prospero, upon first coming to the island, had been kind to him: "When thou cam'st first, / Thou strok'st me, and made much of me . . . and then I lov'd thee, / And show'd thee all the qualities of the isle, / The fresh springs, brine-pits, barren place and fertile; / Curs'd be I that did so" (1.2.334–41). Here again, one starting point for grasping the referent is the perspective of the Commons in the Petition of Temporal Grievances, where they recalled for the king how *they* had treated *him* when he first came to their land. They reminded James that the people then expressed their "cheerful affections . . . by their joyful receiving of your Majesty at your happy entrance into this kingdom . . . as also by their extraordinary contributions granted since unto you, such as never have been yielded to any former prince upon the like terms and occasions" (Foster, 2:258). Once again, master and slave seem to have exchanged languages. In this play it is the foreigner, Prospero, who initiated the kindness to the native, Caliban.

Shakespeare's technique might, therefore, be compared to the "world upside down" iconography popular in the sixteenth, seventeenth, and eighteenth centuries. These metaphoric graphics picture a series of inversions—a man carrying a beast of burden, a servant beating his master, and so on. The ideological ambivalence of such a picture permits either the interpretation that the picture supports the existing ideology by mocking its inversion or that it mocks the existing ideology as in itself a perversion.[28] On the one hand, Prospero's thoroughgoing domination of both Ariel and Caliban can be taken as representing the significance of the royal prerogative, which nothing, not even the Great Contract, should be allowed to diminsh. Moreover, the representation of parliamentary positions in two nonhuman figures can be taken as having a satiric thrust; these diminutive others can suggest an uncomplimentary caricaturing of Parliament. But the opposite reading is also possible. Even as a cartoonist may draw a caricature of the ideological position he favors as well as of that he disfavors, so can the caricaturing of Ariel and Caliban be understood as reflecting the right role of Parliament. In this reading, Ariel and Caliban are again structures that function collaboratively, with Ariel representing Parliament's high role as counselor to the king and Caliban the essential role that opposition to authority plays in the commonwealth. In this regard, we may note with some interest the statement made by Sir Julius Caesar, drawn up on December 20, 1610, urging that Parliament be prorogued rather than dissolved; "notice of another parliament," Caesar said, would indicate "a dislike of these parliament men 'who are held amongst the common people the best patriots that ever were,' most valued for their greatest contempts to the King" (Foster, 2:348).

We need this grasp of Shakespeare's shiftiness in his manipulation of rhetorical structures—a grasp, that is, of the potential ideological ambivalence of his caricatures of the ruler-subject relationship—in order to consider two other central political issues in the 1610 parliamentary proceedings, the related terms of *complaint* and *restraint*. In the March speech, James took the position that Parliament could not dispute the royal prerogative; it was "sedition in Subjects, to dispute what a King may do in the height of his power . . . I will not be content that my power be disputed upon" (McIlwain, p. 310). He also spoke at some length about grievances and the necessity that the Commons bring the people's grievances to him. But he then turned again to the topic of their disputing his prerogative, instructing the Commons, "doe not meddle with the maine points of Government; that is my craft," and "I would not have you meedle [*sic*] with such ancient Rights of mine, as I have received from my Predecessors," and "beware to exhibit for *Grievance* anything that is established by a settled Law" (p. 315). Parliament's response to this position was firm. They had always had the right to dispute, as Wentworth explained: "Is not the king's prerogative disputable? Do not our books in 20 cases argue what the king may do and what not do by his prerogative. . . . Nay if we shall once say that we may not dispute the prerogative, let us be sold for slaves" (Foster, 2:82–83). The Commons's more formal response to the king was to issue the Petition of Right, dated May 23, and, in July, the Petition of Temporal Grievances.

In *The Tempest*, Shakespeare replicates the debate over the right to dispute and the right to issue grievances by inventing actions and speech that concretize the two terms of restraint and complaint that were so central to this aspect of the debate and recur in both petitions, as well as in the speeches of James and the debates in Parliament.

The code word *restraint* entered the Petition of Right when Parliament addressed the fact that they "have received, first by message and since by speech from your Majesty, *a commandment of restraint* from debating in Parliament your Majesty's right of imposing" and then informed the king that the "prerogatives of that king concerning directly the subject's right . . . have been ever freely debated . . . both in this and all former Parliaments, *without restraint*" (Tanner, p. 246, italics added). "Restraint" and the variant "restrain" also occurred repeatedly in the debates when the Commons argued whether or not the king could levy impositions, the idea being that to levy an imposition, or to impose, was itself a form of restraint.[29] This point was made in a slightly different way by Fuller when he argued that because impositions were illegal, to levy them was to restrain the law, or, as he put it, "the power of the law in this land is not to be restrained by the power of the king" (Foster, 2:153).

In *The Tempest*, Prospero exercises his power by restraining or confining those on the island. He threatens to return Ariel to confinement in a tree, this time an oak instead of the weaker pine tree that Sycorax had used; and he has "confin'd" Caliban "into this rock" (1.2.363). Later he casts a spell on the Alonso party that leaves them, as Ariel says, "Confin'd . . . all prisoners. . . . They cannot budge" (5.1.7–11).

In addition to using forms of confinement, Prospero also restrains by silencing or threatening to silence Ariel and Caliban, a pattern that duplicates James's attempt to silence his opposition by forbidding the Commons to dispute. Prospero warns Ariel that imprisonment in an oak will be the result "if thou more murmur'st" (1.2.294), and he threatens Caliban with "Side-stitches that shall pen thy breath up" (1.2.328). The implications of these threats, especially as they reflect what was happening in Parliament, extend even beyond the issue of disputing to include the fear that, should the Great Contract be passed and the king's revenue thereby guaranteed, then the king would not have to summon Parliament at all, in which case it would be completely silenced. In his speech of May 21, James certainly had done nothing to allay such fears, as he declared, "be not misled that the more wayward you shall be I shall be the more unwilling to call you to parliament, for such behavior will make me call you the seldomer to council" (Foster, 2:105). In *The Tempest*, Prospero threatens to silence Ariel, but he also keeps summoning him to do his bidding, even as James had originally summoned the Parliament of 1610 to settle the matter of his supply. In 1611, people were wondering when the king would call his counselors together again.

We get a somewhat clearer idea of how complicated and tense the entire situation in 1610 had become when we find references in the records of Parliament to occasions on which fear so overcame everyone that no one dared speak: knowledge that "speeches in the House of Commons critical of royal policy were instantly reported to the crown . . . 'brought so base a fear amongst them, no man dareth speak freely' " (Foster, 2:46n.), and "It seemeth by this great silence men do not think it safe to speak" (Foster, 2:88). In such an atmosphere, it is even more understandable that fuller should focus his entire speech of June 23 upon "arguments for the freedom of the subject" (Foster, 2:152), and that Shakespeare, in imitating this discourse, should punctuate the play with lines in which Ariel and Caliban cry out for their liberty and freedom.

As even these cries suggest, the counterbalance to restraint and silencing, in Parliament as in *The Tempest*, was the insistence on the right to issue grievances, or to complain. How closely associated are the ideas of restraining and complaining in this context is obvious from the way they fall together in James's speech of May 21: "I told you my meaning was [not] to forbid you to complain if their were inconvenience or heaviness, inequality, disproportion or disorder in matter of trade; from this I mean not to restrain you" (Foster, 2:102; her brackets). In the Petition of Temporal Grievances, the Commons explained that the people, "perceiv[ing] their common and ancient right and liberty to be much declined and infringed in these late years, do with all duty and humility present these just complaints thereof to your view" (Foster, 2:257), and asked that "we may receive to these our complaints your most gracious answer" (Foster, 2:258). The Commons matched this insistence on verbalizing their griefs with language that expressed the effect of those griefs. In the Petition of Right, they complained that the king's actions caused them to "languish in much sorrow and discomfort" (Tanner, p. 247). Fuller called this abuse of power a "hurt" (Foster, 2:152) and a "burden" (2:26, 75). James, too, on May 21, used the word *hurt* to refer to "any just grievance" (Foster, 2:102).

Shakespeare conflates and reifies this complaint and hurt by developing for Caliban a coarse and cursing language of complaint about all the physical ills that Prospero inflicts upon him:

> All the infections that the sun sucks up
> From bogs, fens, flats, on Prosper fall, and make him
> By inch-meal a disease! his spirits hear me,
> And yet I needs must curse . . .
> For every trifle are they set upon me;
> Sometime like apes, that mow and chatter at me,
> And after bite me; then like hedghogs, which
> Lie tumbling in my barefoot way, and mount
> Their pricks at my foot fall; sometime am I
> All wound with adders, who with cloven tongues
> Do hiss me into madness.
>
> (2.2.1–14; cf. 1.2.327–32)

In giving such angry and vociferous representation to Parliament's own complaining, Shakespeare dramatizes *both* the idea that a king could do great hurt to a subject, and Parliament's reputation at court for growing entirely too insolent and contemptuous in their attitude toward the king. On May 21, James remarked that they were "peevish and undutiful subjects that will petition to the king for that wherein they know his mind already, it is both superfluous and a piece of contempt" (Foster, 2:105). And Thomas Egerton, Lord Ellesmere, writing "Special Observations Touching all the Sessions of the Last Parliament," referred to the "very audacious and contemptuous speeches" given "against the King's regal prerogative" in the Lower House, to the Commons's desire only "to quarrel," and to the "irregular and insolent course of their proceeding."[30]

If Shakespeare represents through Caliban one view of the Commons, he sometimes represents through Ariel an ideally obsequious Commons such as the king himself would have preferred. Such a subservient (Puttenham would say "comely") persona was actually available in the language that the Commons used in representing themselves officially to the king. That persona was the one adopted for the Petition of Right, where the Commons addressed James as "Most gracious Sovereign" and referred to themselves as "your humble subjects" who "do with all humble duty make this remonstrance to your Majesty," "your Majesty's most humble, faithful, and loyal subjects [who] shall ever (according to our bounden duty) pray for your Majesty's long and happy reign over us" (Tanner, pp. 245-47). Ariel is also able to speak in this voice: "All hail, great master . . . I come / To answer thy best pleasure" (1.2.189-90); "What would my potent master? here I am" (4.1.34); "Thy thoughts I cleave to. What's thy pleasure?" (4.1.164).

Despite the similarity in style here, the opponents of the king were not, like Ariel, asking what they could do for him but, as we have said before, what he could do for them. The effect on James of their insistent complaining was that he became by May 19 (two days before he would speak again to Parliament and four days before the date of the Petition of Right) "extremely disquieted with our long forbearing" (Foster, 1:96). Said Wentworth politely, "We all had cause to be sorry that the King should be disquieted with any proceedings of ours" (Foster, 1:97).

Caliban has the same disquieting effect on Prospero. In the midst of celebrating the betrothal of Miranda and Ferdinand, Prospero suddenly flies into a "passion that works him strongly." The masque disintegrates, the spirits leave. Prospero, as sure of Caliban's treasonous intents as James was of the seditiousness of some members of the Commons, prepares to punish him and his cohorts. First they are led through a stinking swamp; then they are shown to be so petty that they can be distracted from their seditious intents by clothes hanging on a line. If one feels that Shakespeare gives Caliban rough treatment here for being a debased mutation of the Aeneas pattern, one may also feel (to the extent that one sees Caliban figuring them) that the poet is presenting the predicament of those in his own culture who challenge absolute authority. For whoever one sees as these characters run off the stage chased by a ruler's hunting dogs, the final point is the same: the person who is forced to run is the person who confirms the hunch that one person on the island has more power than anyone else.

Of the several achievements of the Ariel and Caliban material, then, the primary one remains the opportunity to voice blame while at the same time appearing not to blame. These constructions allow no sacrifice of attention to contemporary issues and yet they avoid accusation. The resultant validation of all sides provides the attitude within which the play can suggest a resolution to conflicts.

THE GIVING OF MERCY AND THE SUSPENSION OF POWER

The successful routing of Caliban is followed immediately in the next scene by two actions in which Prospero sets his own passions aside. First he grants mercy and then he surrenders his magic. The problems that these actions have caused critics can be resolved to some extent by appealing to generic requirements of comedy and romance, two genres that must produce happy endings. But it is possible to reauthenticate the ending and reduce its transparency by contextualizing this section, too, taking note once again of the political field of parliamentary discourse. Also, again at issue here are the authorities of ancient texts, first the tradition of mercy-giving as it had been transmitted by the *Aeneid* and next the tradition of magic as it had been handled by Ovid in his story of Medea.

Of the several places in Virgil's poem where showing mercy is an important issue, the two episodes that seem most relevant for Shakespeare's text are the ending of the epic—Aeneas's refusal to extend pity to Turnus—and the chronological beginning of the poem, where Priam makes the mistake of extending pity to Sinon, thereby bringing on the destruction of Troy. To the extent that we describe the ending of *The Tempest* in terms of Virgil's ending, it can represent one more reversal of Virgil; for Prospero extends mercy and thus breaks the pattern of revenge that Aeneas could only perpetuate by acting out the role of the furious Achilles who denied mercy to Hector. If, on the other hand, it is the Priam story that we see behind Shakespeare's mercy-giving scene—and there are several details here evocative of Virgil's telling of that story—we may find another kind of variation on Virgil, another bold rearrangement of parts. Shakespeare's ending might here be described as a rewriting of Virgil's beginning.

In the context of the Virgilian Troy patterns that we have noticed elsewhere in the play, several details of Shakespeare's mercy-giving scene are interesting. First of all, the court group to whom Prospero extends mercy is made up of characters who have earlier mounted conspiracies that replicate an aspect of the Greek conspiracy against Troy; Alonso was implicated in Prospero's being hustled out of Milan at night, and Antonio and Sebastian tried to undo Alonso while he slept.[31] Moreover, just as Sinon was bound as a prisoner when he was brought to Priam, so does Ariel in this scene describe these characters as "all prisoners, sir. . . . They cannot budge till your release" (ll. 9–11). Then, too, both Priam and Prospero justify their decisions, and with the same argument. Priam defends himself by saying that the Trojans should accept Sinon as one of them: "He is ours" ("noster eris," 2.149); Prospero explains to Ariel: "shall not myself, / One of their kind . . . be kindlier mov'd than thou art." A significant variation on Virgil's story is that the supplicative role that the wily Sinon played is here taken over by Ariel, Prospero's trusted companion and guide.[32]

The experience of reading Shakespeare's ending in the context of Virgil's beginning is not necessarily a clarifying one, however. In this context, too, there may indeed be a reversal of the *Aeneid*; Priam's pity issued in disaster, Prospero's issues in renewal. But the very presence in Shakespeare's text of the Sinon episode, in which Virgil told of a well-meaning gesture that turned out to be a mistake of catastrophic proportions, destabilizes that text no matter how we might want to see it differently. This element of instability is all the more interesting when considered in relation to Shakespeare's historical present, the deteriorated relationship of king and Parliament that we have been pondering, and, more specifically, the options James had in dealing with the situation.

Indeed, at this very time in history, there were the fear and the possibility that James might take revenge on those who had opposed him in Parliament. As early as his March speech, James himself addressed this possibility, being careful to present himself as one who would not use an arbitrary power outside the law in order to punish anyone. Nevertheless, he made it clear that within the law he could still get even with those who did not support him: "For although I will be no lesse just, as a King, to such persons, then any other . . . yet ye must thinke I have no reason to thanke them, or gratifie them with any suits or matters of grace, when their errand shall come my way" (McIlwain, p. 318). Several months later, on October 25, Salisbury spoke suggestively—and, despite his disclaimers, even threateningly—of how the king's withholding of "favor" and "grace" would not be inconsistent with "justice": "No necessity is such as may make a king do unjustly; but there may be cause to make a king not to extend his favor; he oweth his justice, not his favor" (Foster, 2:300), and, "I speak not by way of menace . . . I do not speak anything by way of threat; the King will not do injustice to his subject; he will not do all he may do" (Foster, 2:301). There is no question that people who had opposed James perceived that they were in a dangerous position. For example, on

November 16, a few weeks after Salisbury's speech, Samuel Lewknor began a speech with some remarks about the danger in which he might be placing himself by taking a stand against the king: "Dangerous I account it to contradict or expose himself against his prince's will or demand. . . . The fury of the king, saith the wise man, is the messenger of death and I know that one word evil taken, though not evil spoken, may blot out the remembrance of many years' deserts" (Foster, 2:400). Later in the speech, he acknowledged that he, too, wished that this king could have all the money he wanted, "that as he is a prince *Troiano melior* so he might be *Augusto felicior*" (p. 401)—but his good wishes for the king were not sufficient to allow him to change his position on the issue of supply.

Implicit in these threats and fears of threat is the assumption that reciprocity was to characterize the relationship between king and Parliament. As long as the king felt that Parliament was not being sufficiently cooperative with him, he believed it injudicious to consent to all their demands and felt it necessary to remind them that they were placing their own power in jeopardy by challenging his. Meanwhile, Parliament wanted the king to moderate his demands, but they were at the same time aware that their recalcitrance had its costs. In this climate of contention, more than one speaker likened the situation to the Trojan War, where men fought for years over Helen, "a goodly treasure," said Roger Owen, "but not worth the destruction of Troy" (Foster, 2:398; cf. 401).

In the passage in which Prospero declares that he will grant them mercy, the point is made that the mercy is, to some degree, contingent on his enemies' being repentant (the reciprocity theme again): "they being penitent, / The sole drift of my purpose doth extend / Not a frown further."[33] The wise governor does not, as a rule, give mercy to those, like Virgil's Sinon, who are confirmed in their intention to undermine him (although in this case, it should be noted, Prospero also forgives the unrepentant Antonio). Still, because the ruler is the only one who possesses a great power, that power can be felt as a most fearsome thing. All subjects—those who always cooperate and those who do not—long for assurance that the full strength of that power will never be made to work to their detriment. Hence the counseling Ariel directs Prospero to recognize what it is to be subject to such a power as his: "Your charm so strongly works 'em, / That if you now beheld them, your affections / Would become tender." And a little later, the faithful Gonzalo cries out, "some heavenly power guide us / Out of this fearful country" (5.1.105-6).

Although Salisbury was entirely able, as we have seen, to speak threats to the Commons, he recommended that James speak to them in a different voice, and especially at a time when the king was seeking to make more demands on his people. Salisbury himself was quite eloquent and precise in explaining what was at stake, and why the king's rhetoric should be the tempered voice of "clemency and moderation":

> whensoever there is cause to draw any extraordinary supplies from vulgar people, then it is the highest wisdom to observe such courses as generate greatest love, and cherish greatest hopes. . . . Neither do we draw these arguments from grounds Machiavell, as meaning to make use of virtue, as of an art. . . . But we use them as Christian counsellors, for a Christian and religious king, persuading ourselves that those princes are most happy and those counsellors most worthy where clemency and moderation is the object of princes' actions, as well as law and justice.[34]

Prospero's dispensing mercy may be a satisfying ending for a romance, but it is also an ending that accommodates itself to the tensions in the king-subject relationship. The play does not, of course, show what the consequences of that mercy actually will be. Yet it permits one to conclude that although giving pity once led to the destruction of Troy, it is far from clear that not being merciful (Aeneas and Turnus notwithstanding) is the way to vitalize an island community or, for that matter, a weary national community. Thus, it is the restraining of power, not the exercise of it, that this scene represents.

Immediately after the mercy episode comes the speech in which Prospero relinquishes his magic: "Ye elves of hills, brooks, standing lakes, and groves." His plan to reassume his dukedom requires that he leave this exclusive and removed world of the mind and immerse himself again in the give-and-take of civic life.

Seen from this point of view, the relinquishing of the magic is the logical next step in a plot where characters are to return home at the end. At this important political moment in Jacobean England, the notion that a ruler has the option of not using all of the power available to him was commanding a lot of attention. This context makes it all the more interesting that the speech in which Prospero dismisses his magical powers is modeled on a speech Ovid wrote for Medea.

As has probably always been known, Shakespeare's model for Prospero's speech is the speech Medea gives when she uses her magic to restore Jason's aged father to youth.[35] Having prepared a potion, she drains out Aeson's blood and refills his veins with a magic elixir that turns his white hair black, his wrinkled and withered body to a lusty and fair condition. T. W. Baldwin's analysis of Shakespeare's transformation of this passage emphasizes that he omitted any detail that would suggest the darker realms and purposes with which Medea was associated.[36] So altered, the passage suits the white magic that Prospero has wielded, while the original context of the Medea passage (a story of restoration and renewal) still matches nicely the theme of restoration and renewal that dominates Prospero's efforts to reform his island visitors.

As clear as this sense of the action may be, for Prospero to give up a quality that has assured his success on the island is to acknowledge the tension between utopian vision and the reality of everyday experience. Another complication derives from the precursor text itself. While Shakespeare has reshaped it to fit Prospero's white magic, he retains enough of the old passage to make its influence easily identifiable, and this means that his passage, despite the use to which it is now put, alludes rather forthrightly to a magic that has been known for its sinister capacities. Thus, even if Prospero speaks here to all good intents, the image that accompanies and haunts the one he now projects is the image of a magic, a power, that can destroy—the type of magic with which Medea was primarily associated and that has been brought to mind earlier in this play in the lines recalling the ruling days of the "damn'd witch Sycorax."

The capacity that a transcendent power has for destruction was also an issue, probably the central issue, for the Parliament of 1610. If the king were allowed to levy impositions without consulting Parliament, then his power could grow to the point of their destruction. The king might be *primum movens, principale agens*, a god on earth, but these aspects of his identity did not permit him to do anything he wanted to do; they did not give him unlimited power—hence Parliament's declaration in the Petition of Grievances that there was nothing more important to them than "to be guided and governed by the certain rule of the law" by which they avoided "any uncertain or arbitrary form of government" (Foster, 2:258). When Martin argued that the king's imposing showed "an arbitrary, irregular, unlymited, and transcendent power" (Gardiner, p. 88), and Hoskyns observed that "an unlimited power is contrary to reason" (Gardiner, p. 76), they were asserting the same thing.[37]

This argument, which, from a constitutional perspective, is of more interest than any other in a consideration of Prospero's actions, was also made by Hedley. Hedley framed his argument within an issue of law, and specifically of common law, which he defined as "more than bare reason." Common law, which governs both the king and Parliament, is, said Hedley, "tried reason, or the quintessence of reason" (Foster, 2:175). He then proceeded to show that these new impositions were against the common law and so also against reason, the implication being that, for a king to impose them would be for him to exercise his power in a manner contrary to reason (Foster, 2:171–90).

It would, of course, be possible to read the moments during which Prospero surrenders his magic as signifying that a king may be depended upon to know when he should curb his power. As James, who had argued that levying impositions was legal, had told Parliament, in the final analysis it was necessary for them to trust the king not to abuse his power: "If a king be resolute to be a tyrant, all you can do will not hinder him. . . . Kings must be trusted . . . I would not have you judge in general of my prerogative" (Foster, 2:103–4).

But it is also possible to see in Prospero's echo of Medea's speech a replication of Parliament's argument. For the right and good

Prospero and the Best State of the Commonwealth   129

king, the quintessence of reason is to bow to the common law. To curb power, to limit it, and to subject the royal prerogative to dispute in Parliament is, the Commons believed, the way to make oneself the best of rulers. In this reading, Prospero's surrendering of magic is less a giving up than it is a going forward to a condition that surpasses the "rough magic" on which he has been relying.

In structuring his play so that Prospero follows mostly the model of Aeneas but other models too, Shakespeare presents a complex reconstitution of the current dialogue on the nature and implications of political power. If the shadow of Medea carries by implication some rather stern warnings, the still more dominant Aeneas prototype, the ideal pattern to which the play always returns, presents the means by which a great political figure can move unfalteringly toward the fulfillment of his destiny. Cast as one whose greatness is in part owing to his ability to steel himself against excessive self-indulgence and self-interest, Aeneas faces at Carthage and again at Elysium the necessity of abandoning places of pleasure and sanctuary. Prospero's final actions, where he gives mercy and suspends his power, involve a like sacrifice. Readers and audiences have always sensed in these actions a quality of loss, what David William calls a "deprivation" and "contraction" of the self, born of necessity and yet somehow also desired.[38] Like Aeneas, who leaves both Carthage and Elysium to pursue his destiny, Prospero, too, bends his will at the end and therein serves a higher cause. In *The Tempest*, Shakespeare offers the option of retrenchment as the most noble and heroic of choices.

DISCASEMENT AND REUNION

Once through the two important decisions that stand at the beginning of act 5, all that Shakespeare has left to do is to arrange to let his play run joyously on to the end with actions that show the consequences of right choice. In the lines immediately following Prospero's suspension of power, Shakespeare moves his story forward by again immersing his text in that of Virgil. For the sequence during which Prospero exchanges his magician's robes for the everyday cloak of a duke and then reveals his presence to the Alonso group, Shakespeare refashions a moment in Virgil where Aeneas has a similar experience. That episode occurs after Aeneas's encounter with Venus at Carthage. Upon leaving her son, Venus makes Aeneas and his companion Achates invisible in order to ensure their safety: "Venus shrouded them, as they went, with a dusky air, and enveloped them, goddess as she was, in a thick mantle of cloud" ("Venus obscuro gradientis aëre saepsit / et multo nebulae circum dea fudit amictu," 1.411–12). As Aeneas and Achates proceed on their way through Dido's land; they view her city from a hilltop and finally come to the temple of Juno, where they observe first Dido approaching and then a group of their forlorn Trojan comrades. They listen to Ilioneus telling Dido of their shipwreck, the hostile reception they have had from the Carthaginians, and their great but now missing king, Aeneas, and they hear Dido promise the Trojans safety. Only then is Aeneas revealed to them. Suddenly, Virgil writes, the cloud that has enshrouded him separates and dissipates and Aeneas speaks, "I, whom ye seek, am here before you, Aeneas of Troy" ("coram, quem quaeritis, adsum, Troius Aeneas," 1.595–96). Aeneas praises Dido for pitying Troy's woes and welcoming the Trojans to her city and then he "grasps his dear Ilioneus with the right hand, and with the left Serestus; then others, brave Gyas and brave Cloanthus" ("amicum / Ilionea petit dextra laevaque Serestum, / post alios, fortemque Gyan fortemque Cloanthum," 1.610–12).

The last scene of *The Tempest* reproduces all of the central elements of this reunion of the Trojans with their king. First the Alonso group enters, as confused and fearful of their surroundings as were the Trojans at Carthage. Ilioneus's plea to Dido becomes Gonzalo's prayer that they will be rescued from the confusion they find on this island: "All torment, trouble, wonder and amazement / Inhabits here: Some heavenly power guide us / Out of this fearful country" (5.1.104–6). And just as the cloud that has robed or mantled (*amictu*, 1.412) Aeneas disperses so that Aeneas can be seen, so does Prospero now "discase" (5.1.85) himself.[39] In words that echo what Aeneas says to Dido, Prospero steps forward and speaks to the group: "Behold, sir King, / The wronged Duke of

Prospero and the Best State of the Commonwealth   131

Milan, Prospero" (5.1.106–7). Just as Aeneas grasps the hands of his men, so Prospero embraces Gonzalo, thereby assuring him that what he is seeing has a corporeal reality: "For more assurance that a living Prince / Does now speak to thee, I embrace thy body." Finally, like Dido welcoming the Trojans, Prospero welcomes his visitors: "And to thee and thy company I bid / A hearty welcome" (5.1.110–11). As in the *Aeneid*, the reunion in *The Tempest* speaks of a situation that has been restored to a right order, one in which the Alonso group cooperates but which ultimately relies, as does so much else in the play, on the ruler's having taken the initiative.

As Shakespeare draws his play to the close, he emphasizes the reliance of his story on old forms, and also its novelty, by writing into the dialogue that runs to the end of the play several reminders that a new story has been told—or, as the dialogue has it, that Prospero now has a new story to tell. The pattern for all of these lines is that ancient moment when, at Dido's banquet, Aeneas at last responds to her urgings and finally recounts the tale of the destruction of Troy.

Dido's insistent plea, "tell us, my guest, from the first beginning the treachery of the Greeks, thy comrades' misfortunes, and thine own wanderings" ("immo age et a prima dic, hospes, origine nobis / insidias inquit Danaum casusque tuorum / erroresque tuos," 1.753–55), reappears in the last scene of *The Tempest* in the lines of Alonso, who keeps insisting that Prospero tell them his story: "this must crave . . . a most strange story" (ll. 116–17), "Give us particulars of thy preservation; / How thou has met us here" (ll. 135–36), and finally, "I long / To hear the story of your life, which must / Take the ear strangely" (ll. 311–13). Also, three times in the scene Prospero mentions the tale he now has to tell. Unlike Aeneas's tale, which could be told at the end of that first banquet with Dido, Prospero says of his story, "'tis a chronicle of day by day, / Not a relation for a breakfast, nor / Befitting this first meeting" (ll. 163–65). Later he promises Alonso, "I'll resolve you . . . of every / These happen'd accidents" (ll. 248–50). And finally, he invites his visitors to enter his cell and promises to make the time pass quickly by telling them "the story of my life" (l. 304).

Prospero's story will not, of course, be a replication of the tragic narrative Aeneas told to Dido; rather, it will be a story of the renovation of a mind and the union of self and society that is made possible thereby. But, as we have seen, Shakespeare's text contains stories other than this one. It included as well, for the audience who was living through it, a chronicle of national politics, the ending of which had not yet been seen and which still depended on the choices that king and subjects would make in the months and years to come. The tentativeness that one always senses in the ending of *The Tempest* reflects the uneasiness of the contemporary political scene. The questions that are inevitably asked about the ending— will Prospero succeed when he goes back to Milan? will the ruler succeed once the play is over?—are the right ones.

EPILOGUE

I

I have been arguing that *The Tempest* is not a transcendent, indifferent text and that Shakespeare was not an apologist for monarchy. There are many reasons that assumptions other than these have often governed readings of this play and other Shakespeare plays. The explanation that receives the most emphasis in this study centers around the matter of style. In the sixteenth and seventeenth centuries, the approved manner of address for both high literature and high politics was a style characterized by an indirection that only a practiced skill in rhetoric could produce. In this culture, skill in rhetoric could purchase not only safety, but respect, authority, and power. Thus such skill was as useful to writers engaged in oppositional politics as to those who were apologists for the established authority. As is true of all situated discourse, the position any of these writers assumed within a particular political controversy cannot be fully appreciated by later readers unless a text has been sufficiently historicized. Hence, it has been easy for readers who would emphasize the "transcendent" Shakespeare to misrecognize the passion for resistance that Shakespeare exhibited in many plays and throughout his career, but that perhaps appears nowhere more cunningly than in *The Tempest*.

II

Because *The Tempest* was Shakespeare's last play before he left London, it has always occupied a special place in the canon, one made all the more secure by the feeling, shared by many, that the play has an autobiographical dimension. Shakespeare's choice to imitate Virgil in it also has relevance to this issue.

For the Renaissance poet, it was always true that imitation of Virgil was a way to claim one's place in the company of the great poets. There is nothing to belie the assumption that Shakespeare would have understood his own imitative act, as he left London, as an opportunity to identify the place he saw himself as having acquired, through stagecraft, in the ranks of England's poets. One could even take this line of thought one step further, in the direction of a Bloomian hypothesis, and see *The Tempest* as Shakespeare asserting himself over the poet whom he had confronted and rewritten almost obsessively throughout his career; even in *The Comedy of Errors* he modeled on Virgil.

Given the public meanings of *The Tempest*, along with the challenge of trying to assess the Virgilian impact on it, it is especially interesting to turn to the epilogue, and to what may be described as one of the most private moments in the entire work—the moment when Prospero steps forward and sues the audience for its applause and also, it seems, for prayers for forgiveness:

> Now my charms are all o'er thrown
> And what strength I have's mine own
> Which is most faint. . . .
>   Now I want
> Spirits to enforce, Art to enchant;
> And my ending is despair,
> Unless I be reliev'd by prayer,
> Which pierces so, that it assaults
> Mercy itself, and frees all faults.
> As you from crimes would pardon'd be,
> Let your indulgence set me free.

Ten of Shakespeare's plays end with epilogues. There are similarities among them. They typically express, in one way or another, the hope that the play has pleased the audience, and they ask for applause. In *A Midsummer Night's Dream* we hear: "If we shadows have offended, / Think but this and all is mended. . . . Give me your hands, if we be friends, / And Robin will restore amends." In *As You Like It*, Rosalind urges the audience to "like as much of this play as please you." In *All's Well*, the king assures the audience that the play is "well ended" and instructs them, "That you express content / Your gentle hands lend us and take our hearts." Sometimes Shakespeare expresses more diffidence than others, as for example in the epilogue to *Henry V*: "Thus far, with rough and all-unable pen, / Our bending author hath pursu'd the story."

As a group, the epilogues seem similar, and yet each is tailored to fit the particular play that it ends. The epilogue to *Henry V* speaks about the death of this Henry and the coming to rule of the child, Henry VI. In *2 Henry IV*, the epilogue has the actor speak of having acted earlier in a play that displeased the audience. In *Troilus and Cressida*, Pandarus talks about the diseases in himself and in the audience. In *Pericles*, Gower summarizes and moralizes about the story. In the epilogue to *The Tempest*, Shakespeare includes the standard request for applause, but he also writes more particularly.

One of the striking features of the epilogue is its capacity to suggest that different voices are speaking at the same time, a characteristic also of numerous other passages in this play. Some of the voices here, as earlier, are political. Prospero speaks as the duke on his way back to Naples, who, having given up his magic, is thinking about his new frailty ("what strength I have's mine own") and considering his need for mercy, an important reconceptualization of the *meum et tuum* formula that is at the center of the king-subject relationship. But because the epilogue moves away from the action of the play, Prospero also speaks as an actor, one who has played the part of a ruler but who now, about to finish that part, suddenly stands as a subject—and, at a court performance, as a subject before his own king. Then, too, Prospero is the dramatist himself, who has used his art to enchant but must now ask for approval, and then for forgiveness. In *The Tempest* Shakespeare has exercised fully his prerogative as public poet, and the ending would seem to ask that no one judge his use of this authority harshly.

These various resonances in the epilogue work simultaneously and so share in the multivocality of the play as a whole. Nevertheless, it is possible, especially in combination with the potential for an autobiographical reading, to wonder whether the personal voice that Shakespeare has allowed to emerge in *The Tempest* may, in part, also be contrived—that is, part of the imitation of Virgil. Or, as Frank Kermode remarks in considering the possibility of seeing in the play a personal allegory, such a reading "is almost inevitable; why should it not attach itself to Shakespeare as it did to Homer, Virgil, and Ovid?"[1]

What Kermode is referring to are those lines of the ancient poets which have been understood as comments on their art. Of these, Ovid's remarks at the end of the *Metamorphoses* are among those which represent the voice of the poet directly. They are also among the most self-congratulatory: "Let comme that fatall howre / Which (saving of this brittle flesh) hath over mee no powre. . . . For looke how farre so ever / The Romane Empyre by the ryght of conquest shall extend, / So farre shall all folke reade this work. And tyme without all end / (If Poets as by prophesie about the truth may ame) / My lyfe shall everlastingly bee lengthened still by fame." In contrast, Virgil adopts a self-deprecatory tone. Like the speaker of Shakespeare's epilogue in *Henry V*, the narrator in the *Georgics* declares his modest aims: "Not mine the wish to embrace all the theme within my verse, not though I had a hundred tongues, a hundred mouths, and a voice of iron" ("non ego cuncta meis amplecti versibus opto, / non mihi si linguae centum sint oraque centum, / ferrea vox," 2.42–44).

Although in this case Virgil speaks through a general narrator, in other instances he chooses a more specific character. One example occurs in *Eclogue* 9, where the poet-shepherd Lycidas remarks on his unworthiness as a poet: "Me, too, the Pierian maids have made a poet; I, too, have songs; me also the shepherds call a bard, but I trust them not. For as yet, methinks, I sing nothing worthy of a Varius or a Cinna, but cackle as a goose among melodious swans" ("et me fecere poetam / Pierides, sunt et mihi carmina, me quoque dicunt / vatem pastores; sed non ego credulus illis. / nam neque adhuc Vario videor nec dicere Cinna / digna, sed argutos inter strepere anser olores," 9.32–36). The self-deprecating tone that characterizes this statement is regularly associated with Virgil. Robert Durling shows that it was a stance imitated by other poets, including Tasso, and David Coldwell suggests that Gavin Douglas was also imitating Virgil when he wrote, in his first and ninth prologues to his translation of the *Aeneid*, of his failure to match the artistry of the master, Virgil.[2] There he begs forgiveness of God, and of Virgil too:

> Lat all my faltis with this offens pass by.
> Thou prynce of poetis, I the mercy cry,
> I meyn thou Kyng of Kyngis, Lord Etern
> Thou be my muse, my gydar and alnd stern,
> Remittyng my trespass and every myss . . .
> Forgif me, Virgill, gif I thee offend.
> Pardon thy scolar, suffer hym to ryme
> Sen thou was bot ane mortal man sum tyme.
> (Prol. 1.451–55, 472–74)

Whatever other readings or resonances we may find in the epilogue to *The Tempest*, it is to this long and rather disparate tradition wherein the poet humbles himself before his audience that it ultimately belongs. Writing after and alongside the diffident Virgil, Shakespeare furnished an epilogue that declares his fallibility and inadequacy. It is the comeliest of departures and the surest of rhetorical gestures. The poet who has imitated Virgil and has, in the same work, intervened in national politics ends his play gracefully and yet with authority. The closing language, however humble, invokes the authority of Virgil, which Shakespeare has made his own.

ABBREVIATIONS

AHR	*American Historical Review*
BIHR	*Bulletin of the Institute of Historical Research*
CI	*Critical Inquiry*
ELR	*English Literary Renaissance*
HLQ	*Huntington Library Quarterly*
JBS	*Journal of British Studies*
JWCI	*Journal of the Warburg and Courtauld Institutes*
NLH	*New Literary History*
NS	*Die Neueren Sprachen*
RES	*Review of English Studies*
RQ	*Renaissance Quarterly*
RS	*Renaissance Studies*
SEL	*Studies in English Literature*
ShakS	*Shakespeare Studies*
ShS	*Shakespeare Survey*
SQ	*Shakespeare Quarterly*
TLS	*Times Literary Supplement*

NOTES

PREFACE

1. "The Haddington Masque," in *Ben Jonson*, ed. C. H. Herford, Percy Simpson, and Evelyn Simpson, 11 vols. (Oxford: Oxford University Press, 1925–52), 7 (1941): 256, l. 214.
2. See Howard Erskine-Hill, *The Augustan Idea in English Literature* (London: Edward Arnold, 1983), pp. 106–7. For more on this association with Augustus in poems, plays, masques, and coins, see Erskine-Hill, pp. 123–29; Graham Parry, *The Golden Age restor'd: The Culture of the Stuart Court, 1603–42* (New York: St. Martin's Press, 1981), pp. 1–39; and Jonathan Goldberg, *James I and the Politics of Literature: Jonson, Shakespeare, Donne, and their Contemporaries* (Baltimore: Johns Hopkins University Press, 1983), pp. 28–54.
3. William Strachey, "A True Reportory of the Wrack," in *Samuel Purchas, Hakluytus Posthumus or Purchas His Pilgrimes* (Glasgow: James MacLehose and Sons, 1906), 19:54, 56, 57.
4. John Davies, "The Plantation of Ulster," in Henry Morley, ed., *Ireland under Elizabeth and James the First* (London: Routledge and Sons, 1890), p. 390.
5. *The Journals of the House of Commons*, 1:430. Hereafter cited in the text as *CJ*.
6. Kenneth Burke, *Attitudes Toward History*, 3d ed. (Berkeley: University of California Press, 1984), p. 209.
7. Ibid., p. 224.
8. See Marilyn Butler, "Against Tradition: The Case for a Particularized Historical Method," in *Historical Studies and Literary Criticism*, ed. Jerome J. McGann (Madison: University of Wisconsin Press, 1985), p. 43.
9. Frank Lentricchia, *Criticism and Social Change* (Chicago: University of Chicago Press, 1983), p. 128.

INTRODUCTION

1. J. M. Nosworthy, "The Narrative Sources for *The Tempest*,"

RES 24 (1948): 281–94; Jan Kott,"The *Aeneid* and *The Tempest*, *Arion*, n.s. 3 (1978): 425–51; idem, "*The Tempest*, or Repetition," in *Shakespeare Today*, ed. Ralph Berry, *Mosaic* 10 (1977): 9–36; and Colin Still, *Shakespeare's Mystery Play: A Study of "The Tempest"* (London: Cecil Palmer, 1921), later revised and reprinted as *The Timeless Theme* (London: Ivor Nicolson and Watson, 1936); all of my references to Still are to *The Timeless Theme*.

2. Gary S. Schmidgall, *Shakespeare and the Courtly Aesthetic* (Berkeley: University of California Press, 1981); John Pitcher, "A Theatre of the Future: "The *Aeneid* and *The Tempest*," *Essays in Criticism* 34 (1984): 193–215; Barbara Bono, *Literary Transvaluation: From Vergilian Epic to Shakespearean Tragedy* (Berkeley: University of California Press, 1984), pp. 220–24; Robert Miola, "Vergil in Shakespeare: From Allusion to Imitation," in *Vergil at 2000*, ed. John D. Bernard (New York: AMS Press, 1986), pp. 254–56; Robert Wiltenburg, "The *Aeneid* in *The Tempest*," *ShS* 39 (1986): 159–68; Peter Hulme, *Colonial Encounters: Europe and the Native Caribbean, 1492–1797* (London: Methuen, 1986), pp. 109–15; and Stephen Orgel, ed., *The Tempest* (Oxford: Clarendon Press, 1987), pp. 39–43. Wiltenburg's essay is especially fine; it came out after I had completed my own work on the relationship between the *Aeneid* and *The Tempest*.

3. The theoretical essay on *imitatio* that has most influenced my own work is Marion Trousdale, "Recurrence and Renaissance: Rhetorical Imitation in Ascham and Sturm," *ELR* 6 (1976): 156–79. The recent Shakespeare scholar who has most repeatedly urged that, in many cases (including *The Tempest*), the procedures of *imitatio* are more relevant to discussions of Shakespearean citation than other terms is Robert Miola: see his *Shakespeare's Rome* (Cambridge: Cambridge University Press, 1983); "Vergil in Shakespeare: From Allusion to Imitation," pp. 241–58; and "Shakespeare and His Sources: Observations on the Critical History of *Julius Caesar*," *ShS* 40 (1988): 69–76. See also T. W. Baldwin, *William Shakspere's small Latine & lesse Greeke*, 2 vols. (Urbana: University of Illinois Press, 1944), for both the theory of imitation and detailed illustrations of imitation (of Virgil and Ovid) in *The Tempest*.

See also Thomas M. Greene, *The Light in Troy: Imitation and Discovery in Renaissance Poetry* (New Haven: Yale University Press, 1982); G. W. Pigman III, "Versions of Imitation in the Renaissance," *RQ* 33 (1980): 1–32; Daniel Javitch, "The Imitation of Imitations in

Orlando furioso," *RQ* 38 (1985): 215–39; Gordon Braden, *The Classics and English Renaissance Poetry* (New Haven: Yale University Press, 1978); Terence Cave, *The Cornucopian Text: Problems of Writing in the French Renaissance* (Oxford: Clarendon Press, 1979); D. J. Gordon, "The Renaissance Poet as Classicist: Chapman's *Hero and Leander,*" in *The Renaissance Imagination,* ed. Stephen Orgel (Berkeley: University of California Press, 1980), pp. 102–33; Marguerite Waller, *Petrarch's Poetics and Literary History* (Amherst: University of Massachusetts Press, 1980); Richard S. Peterson, *Imitation and Praise in the Poems of Ben Jonson* (New Haven: Yale University Press, 1981); Clark Hulse, *Metamorphic Verse: The Elizabethan Minor Epic* (Princeton, N.J.: Princeton University Press, 1981); Howard Erskine-Hill, *The Augustan Idea in English Literature* (London: Edward Arnold, 1983); David Quint, *Origin and Originality in Renaissance Literature* (New Haven: Yale University Press, 1983); Davis P. Harding, *The Club of Hercules: Studies in the Classical Background of "Paradise Lost,"* Illinois Studies in Language and Literature (Urbana: University of Illinois Press, 1962); and Francis Blessington, *"Paradise Lost" and the Classical Epic* (London: Routlege and Kegan Paul, 1979).

4. *Letters from Petrarch,* trans. Morris Bishop (Bloomington: University of Indiana Press, 1966), p. 199; and quoted in Greene, *The Light in Troy,* p. 95.

5. Sir John Harington, trans., *Ludovico Ariosto's "Orlando furioso,"* ed. Robert McNulty (Oxford: Clarendon Press, 1972), p. 572. In the marginalia for *Orlando furioso,* Harington occasionally notes the author whom Ariosto is imitating, as, for example, "Virgil hath the like. But this is described with more particulars," book 23, canto 90, p. 260. I am indebted to Marion Trousdale for these references.

6. Michael Riffaterre, *Text Production,* trans. Terese Lyons (New York: Columbia University Press, 1983), p. 6. This position leads also to Riffaterre's interest in "the rhetorical doctrine of imitation," which provides that "one writes according to models, so that one's reader will simultaneously experience the pleasure of discovery and the pleasure of rediscovery" (p. 133). Compare Greene, *The Light in Troy,* p. 31: "The relationship to the subtext is deliberately and lucidly written into the poem as a visible and acknowledged construct."

7. Riffaterre, *Text Production,* pp. 111, 112.

8. See, for example, Harold Bloom, *A Map of Misreading* (New York: Oxford University Press, 1975).

9. Greene, *The Light in Troy*, pp. 43, 178.
10. Ibid., p. 47.
11. M. M. Bakhtin, *Speech Genres and Other Late Essays*, trans. Vern W. McGee, ed. Caryl Emerson and Michael Holquist (Austin: University of Texas, 1986), p. 99: "addressivity, the quality of turning to someone, is a constitutive feature of the utterance; without it the utterance does not and cannot exist."
12. Ibid., p. 92.
13. See ibid., p. 98: "This question of the concept of the speech addressee (how the speaker or writer senses and imagines him) is of immense significance in literary history. Each epoch, each literary trend and literary-artistic style, each literary genre within an epoch or trend, is typified by its own special concepts of the addressee of the literary work, a special sense and understanding of its reader, listener, public, or people." See also Marilyn Butler, "Against Tradition: The Case for a Particularized Historical Method," in *Historical Studies and Literary Criticism*, ed. Jerome J. McGann (Madison: University of Wisconsin Press, 1985), pp. 25-47.
14. Bakhtin, *Speech Genres and Other Late Essays*, p. 93: "The topic of the speaker's speech, regardless of what this topic may be, does not become the object of speech for the first time in any given utterance; a given speaker is not the first to speak about it. The object, as it were, has already been articulated, disputed, elucidated, and evaluated in various ways. Various viewpoints, world views, and trends cross, converge, and diverge in it."
15. On the notion of text as event, see J. G. A. Pocock, "Texts as Events: Reflections on the History of Political Thought," in *Politics of Discourse: The Literature and History of Seventeenth-Century England*, ed. Kevin Sharpe and Steven H. Zwicker (Berkeley: University of California Press, 1987), pp. 21-34; and Edward Said, *The World, the Text, and the Critic* (Cambridge, Mass.: Harvard University Press, 1983), p. 4 and passim.
16. See O. B. Hardison, *The Enduring Monument: A Study of the Idea of Praise in Renaissance Literary Theory and Practice* (Chapel Hill: University of North Carolina Press, 1962); Brian Vickers, "Epideictic and Epic in the Renaissance," *NLH* 14 (1983): 497-537; Brian Vickers, *In Defence of Rhetoric* (Oxford: Clarendon Press, 1987), pp. 52-63; James D. Garrison, *Dryden and the Tradition of Panegyric* (Berkeley: University of California Press, 1975).
17. See the work of Stephen Orgel: *The Jonsonian Masque* (Cam-

bridge, Mass.: Harvard University Press, 1965); Ben Jonson, *The Complete Masques*, ed. Orgel (New Haven: Yale University Press, 1969); *The Illusion of Power* (Berkeley: University of California Press, 1975); and Orgel and Roy Strong, *Inigo Jones: The Theater of the Stuart Court*, 2 vols. (Berkeley: University of California Press, 1973).

18. On criticism of court and king in masques, see Orgel, *The Jonsonian Masque*, and the work of Leah Sinanoglou Marcus: " 'Present Occasions' and the Shaping of Ben Jonson's Masques," *ELH* 45 (1978): 201–25; "The Occasion of Ben Jonson's *Pleasure Reconciled to Virtue*," *SEL* 19 (1979): 271–93; "Masquing Occasions and Masque Structure," *Research Opportunities in Renaissance Drama* 24 (1981): 7–16; *The Politics of Mirth: Jonson, Herrick, Milton, Marvell, and the Defense of Old Holiday Pastimes* (Chicago: University of Chicago Press, 1986); on Jonson's *Love Restored* as a response to the politics of 1610–11, see Marcus, *The Politics of Mirth*, pp. 30–38. See also Orgel and Strong, *Inigo Jones*, 1:63–65; Louis Adrian Montrose, "Celebration and Insinuation: Sir Philip Sidney and the Motives of Elizabethan Courtship," *Renaissance Drama* 8 (1977): 3–35; and Kevin Sharpe, *Criticism and Compliment: The Politics of Literature in the England of Charles I* (Cambridge: Cambridge University Press, 1987), pp. 1–53, 296. For the masque, topicality, and *The Tempest*, see Glynne Wickham, "Masque and Anti-masque in *The Tempest*," *Essays and Studies* 28 (1975): 1–14; and for an emphasis on subversion, Ernest B. Gilman, " 'All eyes': Prospero's Inverted Masque," *RQ* 33 (1980): 214–30.

19. See J. W. Williamson, *The Myth of the Conqueror: Prince Henry Stuart, A Study of Seventeenth-Century Personation* (New York: AMS Press, 1978), pp. 75–107; and Stephen Orgel, "Making Greatness Familiar," in *The Power of Forms in the English Renaissance* (Norman, Okla.: Pilgrim Books, 1980), p. 44. Jonson had, of course, used the chivalric terms for representing Henry in *Speeches at Prince Henry's Barriers*, but for *Oberon*, Williamson comments (p. 95), "the vocabulary and imagery of militarism was quite thoroughly eliminated." See also Marcus, "Masquing Occasions and Masque Structure," who finds some of the same political significances in the rhetorical devices in *Oberon* that I find in the rhetorical devices in *The Tempest*.

20. See Lloyd F. Bitzer, "The Rhetorical Situation," *Philosophy and Rhetoric* 1 (1968): 1–14.

21. For discussion, see Parry, *The Golden Age restor'd*, pp. 18–20,

see also pp. 16–17; Goldberg, *James I and the Politics of Literature*, pp. 43–50; and Erskine-Hill, *The Augustan Idea in English Literature*, pp. 122–33.

22. For discussion, see Parry, *The Golden Age restor'd*, p. 26.

23. "A Collection of Severall Speeches and Treatises of the Late Lord Treasurer Cecil and of Several Observations of the Lords of the Council Given to King James Concerning his Estate and Revenue in the Years 1608, 1609, and 1610," ed. Pauline Croft, in *Camden Miscellany, Vol. XXIX*, Camden Fourth Series (London: Royal Historical Society, 1987), 34:294.

24. For example, see Vickers, *In Defence of Rhetoric*, pp. 55–58.

25. Chaim Perelman and L. Olbrechts-Tyteca, *The New Rhetoric: A Treatise on Argumentation* (Notre Dame, Ind.: University of Notre Dame Press, 1969), p. 51..

26. See Daniel Javitch, *Poetry and Courtliness in Renaissance England* (Princeton, N.J.: Princeton University Press, 1978).

27. George Puttenham, *The Arte of English Poesie*, ed. Gladys Doidge Willcock and Alice Walker (Cambridge: Cambridge University Press, 1936), p. 293. For discussion, see Javitch, *Poetry and Courtliness in Renaissance England*, pp. 76–106, and passim; and Frank Whigham, *Ambition and Privilege: The Social Tropes of Elizabethan Courtesy Literature* (Berkeley: University of California Press, 1984).

28. Puttenham, *The Arte of English Poesie*, p. 262.

Part 1: Imitation and Occasion

IMITATION AND *THE TEMPEST*

1. *Ben Jonson*, ed. C. H. Herford, Percy Simpson, and Evelyn Simpson (Oxford: Oxford University Press, 1947), 8:639. For a discussion of the standard metaphors for imitation, see Pigman, "Versions of Imitation in the Renaissance," and Greene, *The Light in Troy*, pp. 98–99, 147, and passim.

2. *Letters from Petrarch*, trans. Bishop, pp. 198–99, and quoted in Greene, *The Light in Troy*, pp. 95–96.

3. Trousdale, "Recurrence and Renaissance," p. 165. For another discussion of Sturm, one that cites his later work, *De imitatione oratoria* (1574), see Pigman, "Versions of Imitation," p. 11. All references to Sturm in the text are to *A Ritch Storehouse or Treasure for Nobilitye and Gentlemen* (London, 1570).

4. See the discussion of concealing and revealing in Trousdale, "Recurrence and Renaissance."

5. *Letters from Petrarch*, trans. Bishop, pp. 182-83, and quoted in Greene, *The Light in Troy*, pp. 99.

6. *Ben Jonson*, ed. Herford, Simpson, and Simpson, 7:281.

7. Greene, *The Light in Troy*, p. 99.

8. See Baldwin, *William Shakspere's small Latine & lesse Greeke*, 2:495-96; and R. K. Root, *Classical Mythology in Shakespeare*, Yale Studies in English (1903; rpt. New York: Gordian Press, 1965), p. 4.

9. Incidentally, despite the explanation by Orgel, ed., *Tempest*, pp. 40-41, it may not be necessary to go to a non-Virgilian tradition to understand the references to Widow Dido. Dido was a widow when Aeneas came to Carthage; upon leaving Carthage, after the cave incident which Virgil says they called a marriage, Aeneas in effect became a widower because Dido committed suicide. Still, see Lee Patterson, "Virgil and the Historical Consciousness of the Twelfth Century: The *Roman d'Eneas* and *Erec et Enide*," in *Negotiating the Past: The Historical Understanding of Medieval Literature* (Madison: University of Wisconsin Press, 1987), pp. 157-95, for an important consideration of Virgil and the Dido tradition, expressed in terms that are admittedly compelling for anyone interested in Shakespeare and Virgil.

10. Kermode, ed., *Tempest*, pp. 46-47, discarding the older assumption that the references to Dido and Aeneas are trivial, comments, "*The Tempest* is far from being a loosely built play; and nowhere in Shakespeare, not even in his less intensive work, is there anything resembling the apparent irrelevance of lines 73-97. It is a possible inference that our frame of reference is badly adjusted, or incomplete, and that an understanding of this passage will modify our image of the whole play."

11. These phrases are from Greene, *The Light in Troy*, pp. 37, 19.

12. Compare ibid., p. 50: "If the topos has been everywhere, then it derives specifically from nowhere."

13. Riffaterre, *Text Production*, p. 92.

14. Thomas Cooper, *Thesaurus* (London, 1565), p. 63, defines *incumbo* as "to leane upon: to fall on a thyng: to sink downe on a thyng: to be inclined to: to geve diligence or studie to: to indevour earnestly." Surrey incorporates *incumbunt* in his translation by writing "With rered brest lift up above the sea," p. 63. See also Charles Knapp, *The Aeneid of Vergil* (Chicago: Scott, Foresman and Co., 1928), who also

translates *incumbunt* as "are breasting" and, by way of explanation, refers the reader to the appropriate sections on grammar elsewhere in this textbook (p. 75) to explain the translation. I am indebted to Linda Wallace for this reference.

15. Thomas Phaer, *The XIII Bookes of Aeneidos. The first twelve beeinge the worke of the divine Poet Virgil Maro, and the thirteenth the Supplement of Maphaeus Vegius* (London, 1584), sig. V^v; Richard Stanyhurst, *The First Foure Bookes of Virgil His Aeneis Translated intoo English heroical verse* (Leiden, 1582), sig. A2; and Edmund Spenser, *Works*, ed. Edwin Greenlaw, Charles Grosvenor Osgood, and Frederick Morgan Padelford (Baltimore: Johns Hopkins University Press, 1932), 1:168.

16. Philip Sidney, "Defence of Poesie," in *Elizabethan Critical Essays*, ed. G. Gregory Smith (Oxford: Clarendon Press, 1904), 1:179. See the discussion of Aeneas as an "idea" in James Nohrnberg, *The Analogy of "The Faerie Queene"* (Princeton, N.J.: Princeton University Press, 1976), pp. 29–30.

17. William Webbe, "Discourse of English Poetrie," *Elizabethan Critical Essays*, 1:237. In the same volume, compare Thomas Lodge, "Defense of Poetry, Music, and Stage Plays," p. 65: "under the person of Aeneas in Virgil the practice of a diligent captaine is described."

18. Torquato Tasso, *Discourses on the Heroic Poem*, trans. and notes by Mariella Cavalchine and Irene Samuel (Oxford: Clarendon Press, 1973), p. 49.

19. See D. C. Allen, *Mysteriously Meant: The Rediscovery of Pagan Symbolism and Allegorical Interpretation in the Renaissance* (Baltimore: Johns Hopkins University Press, 1970), pp. 135–62; Michael Murrin, *The Allegorical Epic: Essays in Its Rise and Decline* (Chicago: University of Chicago Press, 1980), especially pp. 27–50; T. H. Stahel, ed. and trans., "Cristoforo Landino's Allegorization of the *Aeneid*: Books III and IV of *Camaldolese Disputations*" (PhD. diss., Johns Hopkins University, 1968), introduction, pp. 1–39; Anna Cox Brinton, ed., *Maphaeus Vegius and His Thirteenth Book of the Aeneid: A Chapter on Virgil in the Renaissance* (Stanford: Stanford University Press, 1930), pp. 24–40; Leslie George Whitbread, ed. and trans., *Fulgentius the Mythographer* (Columbus: Ohio State University Press, 1971), pp. 105–53; Bernardus Silvestris, *Commentary on the First Six Books of Virgil's "Aeneid,"* intro. and trans. Earl G. Schreiber and Thomas E. Maresca (Lincoln: University of Nebraska Press, 1979), pp. xi–xxxiii; William Harris Stahl, trans. and intro., Macrobius,

Commentary on the Dream of Scipio (New York: Columbia University Press, 1952), pp. 3–65; J. W. Jones, Jr., "Allegorical Interpretation in Servius," *Classical Journal* (1961): 217–26. All references to the works by Landino, Fulgentius, Bernardus, and Macrobius in the text are to the editions cited here.

20. See Allen, *Mysteriously Meant*, p. 149; and Schreiber and Maresca, introduction to *Commentary on the First Six Books of Virgil's "Aeneid,"* p. xi.

21. For a discussion of the relationship between a medieval poem and the commentary tradition as one that gives a poem two outlines, see Judson Boyce Allen, *The Ethical Poetic of the Later Middle Ages* (Toronto: University of Toronto Press, 1982), pp. 117–50. On the commentary on the *Aeneid* by Bernardus Silvestris, see pp. 89–91, 133–35.

22. Merritt Hughes, *Virgil and Spenser* (Berkeley: University of California Press, 1929), p. 402; Allen, *Mysteriously Meant*, p. 142. For further discussion of Landino's currency in the Renaissance, see Craig Kallendorf, "Cristoforo Landino's *Aeneid* and the Humanist Critical Tradition," *RQ* 36 (1983): 519–46.

23. See, for example, Vergilius Maro, *Opera* (Nuremberg, 1492); and Vergilius Maro, *Opera* (Venice, 1532). The *Camaldolese Disputations*, cited throughout my own study, should not be mistaken for the commentary in such editions of Virgil. The *Disputations* are a separate work, published separately. For a list of some editions of Virgil and the commentaries each includes, see Sears Jayne and Frances R. Johnson, *The Lumley Library: The Catalogue of 1609* (Cambridge: Cambridge University Press, 1956).

24. All references to and citations of the *Camaldolese Disputations* are from the translation by Stahel, "Landino's Allegorization of the *Aeneid*"; citations appear in the text. For summaries of Landino, see Allen, *Mysteriously Meant*, pp. 146–54; Murrin, *The Allegorical Epic*, pp. 197–202; and Kallendorf, "Cristoforo Landino's *Aeneid* and the Humanist Critical Tradition."

25. See Florence Ridley, ed., *The "Aeneid" of Henry Howard Earl of Surrey* (Berkeley: University of California Press, 1963), pp. 43–46.

26. Gavin Douglas, *Virgil's "Aeneid,"* ed. David F. C. Coldwell, Scottish Text Society, 4 vols. (Edinburgh: Wm. Blackwood, 1957–64), 2:29, n. 100. For other notes to Landino, see 1:154; 2:31, n. 49; and 2:35, n. 28; references to notes to Servius are reproduced in 1:144ff.

27. Readers who have always allegorized *The Tempest* will rec-

ognize much in this reading that is similar to their approach to the play. See A. D. Nuttall, *Two Concepts of Allegory: A Study of Shakespeare's "The Tempest" and the Logic of Allegorical Expression* (New York: Barnes and Noble, 1967); Derek Traversi, *Shakespeare: The Last Phase* (London: Hollis and Carter, 1954), pp. 193-272; G. W. Knight, *The Crown of Life* (1947; rpt. London: Methuen, 1948), pp. 203-55; Murray W. Bundy, "The Allegory in *The Tempest*," *RS* 32 (1964): 189-206; D. C. Allen, *Image and Meaning: Metaphoric Traditions in Renaissance Poetry*, rev. ed. (Baltimore: Johns Hopkins University Press, 1968), pp. 77-101; Howard Felperin, *Shakespearean Romance* (Princeton, N.J.: Princeton University Press, 1972), pp. 249-50.

28. Greene, *The Light in Troy*, p. 47.

29. Kott, "The *Aeneid* and *The Tempest*," p. 444.

OCCASION AND *THE TEMPEST*

1. Greene, *The Light in Troy*, pp. 66-67.

2. Erskine-Hill, *The Augustan Idea in English Literature*, p. xv, comments, "If formal panegyric is at one extreme of the tradition of the Augustan idea, and Tacitean analysis at the other, the literary imitation holds the centre. Imitation is, at the literary level, that retrieval and incorporation of what is to be admired from the past which panegyric recommends. . . . But genuine imitation, great imitation . . . can draw from both the idealizing and the analytic extremes of the Augustan idea. . . . To recreate so that one can both agree and disagree, at times identify and at other times stand separate—that is the highest measure of imitation."

3. See Harington, trans., *Ludovico Ariosto's "Orlando furioso*," ed. McNulty, 35.25.1-2; and "The Answer of Mr. Hobbes to Sir William Davenant's *Preface* before *Gondibert*," in *A Discourse upon Gondibert. An Heroick Poem by Sir William Davenant With an Answer to it by Mr. Hobbes* (Paris, 1650), sig. F7. See Howard Weinbrot, *Augustus Caesar in "Augustan" England: The Decline of a Classical Norm* (Princeton, N.J.: Princeton University Press, 1978), pp. 120-49, for eighteenth-century treatment of Virgil as a court poet.

4. Boccaccio, "Genealogy of the Gods," in Charles G. Osgood, *Boccaccio on Poetry*, (1930; rpt. New York: The Liberal Arts Press, 1956), p. 69.

5. W. F. Jackson Knight, *Roman Vergil* (1944; rpt. New York:

Barnes and Noble, 1971), pp. 125–30, discusses the predecessors Virgil may have relied on for this section. See also Kenneth Quinn, *Virgil's "Aeneid"* (Ann Arbor: University of Michigan Press, 1969), pp. 55 and 152, for the idea that the Cleopatra–Julius Caesar affair be listed with the Antony–Cleopatra affair among the "possible transfers of significance." For Quinn, "an element of uncertainty always remains, to intrigue the reader and arouse his responsiveness to the text; it permits a degree of guarded frankness otherwise unachievable, and it guarantees the integrity of the poet by enabling him to stop short of final one-sided judgments" (p. 55).

6. See John Dryden, "Dedication of the *Aeneis*," *Essays of John Dryden*, ed. W. P. Ker (Oxford: Clarendon Press, 1926), 2:174 and 179; and Quinn, *Virgil's "Aeneid,"* pp. 54–55.

7. Dryden, "Dedication of the *Aeneis*," p. 196.

8. See ibid., pp. 186–88, for a defense of Aeneas's action against the complaints "by the ladies," and pp. 195–96, for a defense against Ovid's condemnations.

9. Michael C. J. Putnam, *The Poetry of the "Aeneid"* (Cambridge, Mass.: Harvard University Press, 1966), p. 192.

10. *Giraldi Cinthio on Romances*, trans. Henry L. Snuggs (Lexington: University of Kentucky Press, 1968), p. 168.

11. Putnam, *The Poetry of the "Aeneid,"* p. 192.

12. See Dryden, "A Discourse Concerning the Original and Progress of Satire," *Essays*, 2:88, for discussion of how Augustus had usurped the peoples' "freedom," and of "the violent methods which he had used, in the compassing that vast design . . . the slaughter of so many Romans" and other "horrible action[s]."

13. *Londons Love, To the Royal Prince Henrie, Meeting Him on the River of Thames, at his returne from Richmonde . . . on Thursday the last of May, 1610* (London, 1610). For more on the pageants and masques written for Henry, see Parry, *The Golden Age restor'd*, pp. 70–77; and C. E. McGee and John C. Meagher, "Preliminary Checklist of Tudor and Stuart Entertainments: 1603–1613," in *Research Opportunities in Renaissance Drama* 27 (1984): 95–99.

14. See Parry, *The Golden Age restor'd*, pp. 64–94; and Roy Strong, *Henry, Prince of Wales and England's Lost Renaissance* ([London]: Thames and Hudson, 1986).

15. Parry, *The Golden Age restor'd*, p. 68.

16. Daniell Price, *The Creation of the Prince. A Sermon Preached in the Colledge of Westminster, on Trinity Sunday, the day before the*

Creation of the most Illustrious Prince of Wales (London, 1610), sig. D2.

17. Samuel Rawson Gardiner, ed., *Parliamentary Debates in 1610*, Camden Society, 81 (Westminster: John Bowyer Nichols and Sons, 1862), p. 48; hereafter cited in the text as Gardiner. For another description of these proceedings in Parliament, see *The Order and Solemnitie of the Creation of the High and mightie Prince Henrie, Eldest Sonne to our sacred Sovereign, Prince of Wales* (London, 1610). For the investiture to occur in Parliament was also to emphasize Henry's position as heir apparent not to Wales alone but to the realm of England; this point is from J. G. A. Pocock.

18. See Elizabeth Read Foster, ed., *Proceedings in Parliament, 1610*, 2 vols. (New Haven: Yale University Press, 1966), 2:127.

19. See the important discussion in Pauline Croft, ed., "A Collection of Several Speeches," pp. 257–59.

20. Croft, ed., "A Collection of Several Speeches," p. 259.

21. Burke, *Attitudes Toward History*, p. 166.

22. See Wickham, "Masque and Anti-masque in *The Tempest*," pp. 10–12; David Bergeron, *Shakespeare's Romances and the Royal Family* (Lawrence: University Press of Kansas, 1985), pp. 186–87; and Orgel, ed., *Tempest*, p. 30. See Williamson, *The Myth of the Conqueror*, pp. 133–40, for a review of the details of these negotiations.

23. *Calendar of State Papers, Venetian, 1610–1613*, ed. Horatio F. Brown (London: Mackie and Co., 1905), p. 126.

24. Ralph Winwood, *Memorials of Affairs of State in the Reigns of Q. Elizabeth and K. James I* (London, 1725), 3:308–9.

25. See *Calendar of State Papers, Venetian, 1610–1613*, pp. 216–17, 226–27. For more on these negotiations from March through November 1611, see pp. 126–27, 130–31, 180–82, 201, 211–12.

26. Walter Raleigh, "A Discourse Touching a Match Propounded by the Savoyan between the Lady Elizabeth and the Prince of Piedmont" and "A Discourse Touching a Marriage between Prince Henry of England and a Daughter of Savoy," *Works* (Oxford: Oxford University Press, 1829), 8:223–52. Sir John Holles claimed that money was the motive in the negotiations to marry Henry to a Savoyan princess, " 'supposed the best receivable mean for the clearing the King's debts. . . . But why should the heir of England be sold?' "; quoted in Linda Levy Peck, " 'For a King not to be bountiful were a fault': Perspectives on Court Patronage in Early Stuart England," *JBS* 25 (1986): 51.

27. At 2.1.241-49, Antonio once more describes the tenuousness of a situation wherein the princess "dwells / Ten leagues beyond man's life."

28. Raleigh reminded James that one of the most skillful of Catholic and Spanish politicians when it came to dealing in "matrimonial trafficke" (p. 232) had been Emperor Charles V, who had inherited the crowns of the Spanish kingdom in 1516, and who had conquered Tunis for the Spanish and attempted to spread his power to Algiers (pp. 232-33). Within this context, both "Africa" and "Tunis" may be seen to carry specifically Catholic associations. See Annabel Patterson, *Censorship and Interpretation: The Conditions of Writing and Reading in Early Modern England* (Madison: University of Wisconsin Press, 1984), p. 17, for the reminder that Philip Massinger's *Believe as You List*, "clearly critical of Caroline appeasement of Spain, was licensed for production after the most trivial gesture of 'submission,' the deletion of all references to Spain and its replacement with Carthage." Also, in the *Aeneid* Carthage is the city that represents a constant threat to the Virgilian ideal.

29. See Bergeron, *Shakespeare's Romances and the Royal Family*, pp. 186-87; and Parry, *The Golden Age restor'd*, pp. 95-107. Parry (p. 95) comments, "Princess Elizabeth did not attract a great deal of literary or artistic attention until the great moment of her marriage."

30. Abner Cohen, *The Politics of Elite Culture: Explorations in the Dramaturgy of Power in Modern African Society* (Berkeley: University of California Press, 1981), p. 158.

31. On the art of political storytelling, see especially Patterson, *Censorship and Interpretation*; and Albert Braunmuller, "*King John* and Historiography," *ELH* 55 (1988): 309-22.

32. See Bakhtin, *Speech Genres and Other Late Essays*, pp. 68-70, 99.

33. M. M. Bakhtin, *The Dialogic Imagination*, ed. Michael Holquist, trans. Caryl Emerson and Michael Holquist (Austin: University of Texas, 1981), pp. 274, 279, 280.

34. See, especially, Goldberg, *James I and the Politics of Literature*; and the work of Orgel: *The Jonsonian Masque*; "The Poetics of Spectacle," *NLH* 2 (1970-71): 367-89; *The Illusion of Power*; "The Royal Theatre and the Role of King," in *Patronage in the Renaissance*, ed. Guy Fitch Lytle and Orgel (Princeton, N.J.: Princeton University Press, 1981), pp. 261-73; Orgel and Strong, *Inigo Jones*, introduction; and Orgel, ed., *Tempest*, pp. 37-39.

35. See especially G. L. Harriss, "Medieval Doctrines in the De-

bates on Supply, 1610-1629," in *Faction and Parliament: Essays on Early Stuart History*, ed. Kevin Sharpe (Oxford: Clarendon Press, 1978), pp. 73-103.

36. See, for example, Neil Cuddy, "The Revival of the Entourage: The Bedchamber of James I, 1603-1625," in David Starkey et al., *The English Court: From the Wars of the Roses to the Civil War* (London: Longman, 1987), p. 202; and Bruce Galloway, *The Union of England and Scotland 1603-1608* (Edinburgh: John Donald Publishers, 1986).

37. The following account of the Parliament of 1610 is in essential agreement with the view of this Parliament taken by James Spedding, ed., *The Letters and the Life of Francis Bacon* (London: Longmans, Green, Reader, and Dyer, 1868), 4:148-238; Wallace Notestein, *The House of Commons 1604-1610* (New Haven: Yale University Press, 1971); Harriss, "Medieval Doctrines in the Debates on Supply"; Alan G. R. Smith, "Crown, Parliament and Finance: The Great Contract of 1610," in *The English Commonwealth 1547-1640; Essays in Politics and Society*, ed. Peter Clark, Alan G. R. Smith, and Nicholas Tyacke (New York: Barnes and Noble Books, 1979), pp. 111-27; Linda Levy Peck, *Northampton: Patronage and Policy at the Court of James I* (London: George Allen and Unwin, 1982), pp. 198-205; J. P. Kenyon, *Stuart Constitution 1603-1688: Documents and Commentary* (Cambridge: Cambridge University Press, 1966), pp. 53-57; and J. R. Tanner, *Constitutional Documents of the Reign of James I 1603-1625 with an Historical Commentary* (Cambridge: Cambridge University Press, 1930), pp. 243-45.

See also J. P. Sommerville, *Politics and Ideology in England, 1603-1640* (London: Longman, 1986); Corinne Comstock Weston, *English Constitutional Theory and the House of Lords, 1556-1832* (New York: Columbia University Press, 1965); Corinne Comstock Weston and Janelle Renfrow Greenberg, *Subjects and Sovereigns: The Grand Controversy over Legal Sovereignty in Stuart England* (Cambridge: Cambridge University Press, 1981); and Croft, ed., "A Collection of Severall Speeches."

38. See Spedding, ed., *Life and Letters*, 4:148-53; Harriss, "Medieval Doctrines in the Debates on Supply," pp. 80-81; and Kenyon, *Stuart Constitution 1603-1688*, p. 54. See also Louis A. Knafla, "Kingship and the Problem of Sovereignty," in *Law and Politics in Jacobean England: The Tracts of Lord Chancellor Ellesmere* (Cambridge: Cambridge University Press, 1977), pp. 65-76.

39. On Bates's Case, see Tanner, *Constitutional Documents of the Reign of James I*, pp. 244, 338.

40. See Donna B. Hamilton, "*The Winter's Tale* and the Language of Union, 1604–1610," *ShakS* (forthcoming).

41. *The Political Works of James I*, ed. C. H. McIlwain (Cambridge, Mass.: Harvard University Press, 1918), p. 307; hereafter cited in the text as McIlwain.

42. See Sharpe, ed., *Faction and Parliament*, pp. 1–42; and Conrad Russell, *Parliaments and English Politics 1621–1629* (Oxford: Clarendon Press, 1979), pp. 1–26, on the matter of how revisionist historians of parliamentary history have shifted from an emphasis on the Crown-Parliament relationship as being one of conflict toward seeing it as based primarily on a desire for cooperation. Arguing that the Commons man was, when he returned home, primarily a representative of the Crown, Russell concludes that "the court-country, or government-opposition split assumed by Parliamentary historians was not only institutionally impossible. Under James and Buckingham, it was also ideologically impossible" (p. 9). This perspective is not necessarily in conflict with my own, although I have insisted on retaining the term "opposition" to refer to those who were disagreeing with James. There were still debates on political issues in Parliament, and in 1610 there were those who opposed the proposals of the king. For a discussion of the issue of "opposition" in Parliament as that issue has now been clarified but also distorted by the revisionists, see Galloway, *The Union of England and Scotland 1603–1608*, pp. 161–69. Cuddy, "The Revival of the Entourage," p. 202, writes succinctly, "First, whatever the 'revisionists' may argue, there *was* opposition . . . and it was focused explicitly on the two key issues of government policy: Union . . . and fiscal reform." See also Sommerville, *Politics and Ideology in England, 1603–1640*; Weston and Greenberg, *Subjects and Sovereigns*; Marc L. Schwarz, "James I and the Historians; Toward a Reconsideration," *JBS* 13 (1974): 114–34; Conrad Russell, "Parliamentary History in Perspective, 1604–1629," *History* 61 (1976): 1–27; and Paul Christianson, "The Causes of the English Revolution: a Reappraisal," *JBS* 15 (1976): 40–75.

43. See Ernest W. Talbert, *The Problem of Order* (Chapel Hill: University of North Carolina Press, 1902); and Donna B. Hamilton, "The State of Law in *Richard II*," *SQ* 34 (1983): 5–17.

44. I am indebted to Peter Blayney for this detail.

45. Croft, ed., "A Collection of Several Speeches," pp. 252–53.

For more on the availability of information, see Derek Hirst, *The Representative of the People? Voters and Voting in England under the Early Stuarts* (Cambridge: Cambridge University Press, 1975), pp. 166–70, 178–79; Clive Holmes, "The County Community in Stuart Historiography," *JBS* 19 (1980): 54–73; F. J. Levy, "How Information Spread among the Gentry, 1550–1640," *JBS* 21 (1982): 11–34; Richard Cust, "News and Politics in Early Seventeenth-Century England," *Past and Present*, no. 112 (1986): 60–90; and R. Malcolm Smuts, *Court Culture and the Origins of a Royalist Tradition in Early Stuart England* (Philadelphia: University of Pennsylvania Press, 1987).

46. *The Letters of John Chamberlain*, ed. Norman Egbert McClure (Philadelphia: American Philosophical Society, 1939), 1:301.

47. James Whitelocke, *A learned and necessary argument To prove that each subject hath a Propriety in his Goods* (London, 1641); and William Hakewill, *The Libertie of the Subject: Against the Pretended Power of Impositions* (London, 1641). On the place of Whitelocke's speech in the debates of 1610, see Notestein, *The House of Commons 1604–1610*, pp. 378–81. For the texts of other speeches given during June and July 1610, see Foster, 2:152–248.

48. Croft, ed., "A Collection of Several Speeches," p. 252, writes "the importance of the events of 1610–12 in stimulating public awareness must not be overlooked, for these were crucial years in focussing national attention on high politics."

49. Frederick R. Jameson, "The Symbolic Inference: or, Kenneth Burke and Ideological Analysis," in *Representing Kenneth Burke*, ed. Hayden White and Margaret Brose, English Institute Papers, n.s. 6 (Baltimore: Johns Hopkins University Press, 1982), p. 74.

50. See Pocock, "Texts as Events: Reflections on the History of Political Thought," pp. 21–33; J. G. A. Pocock, *Virtue, Commerce and History: Essays on Political Thought and History, Chiefly in the Eighteenth Century* (Cambridge: Cambridge University Press, 1985); and John E. Toews, "Intellectual History after the Linguistic Turn: The Autonomy of Meaning and the Irreducibility of Experience," *AHR* 92 (1987): 879–907.

51. Andrew Gurr, *Playgoing in Shakespeare's London* (Cambridge: Cambridge University Press, 1987), p. 114.

52. See Sommerville, *Politics and Ideology in England, 1603–1640*, pp. 9–56.

Notes to Pages 50-53   157

53. For the text of the Petition of 1610, see *Commons Journals*, p. 431, or Tanner, *Constitutional Documents of the Reign of James I*, p. 245-47, or any one of the original printed copies. For one record of how the Commons handled the petition, see Foster, *Proceedings in Parliament 1610*, 2: 112-13. For the tradition of the petition from the time of Elizabeth to 1628, see Elizabeth Read Foster, "Petitions and the Petition of Right," *JBS* 14 (1974): 21-45.

54. Tanner, *Constitutional Documents of the Reign of James I*, p. 246; hereafter cited in the text as Tanner.

55. See Foster, ed., *Proceedings in Parliament 1610*, 2: 253-54; for the text of the Petition of Temporal Grievances, see pp. 257-71.

56. Ibid., p. 258; hereafter cited in the text as Foster.

57. Bacon, *Life and Letters*, ed. Spedding, 4:192; hereafter cited in the text as Spedding.

58. On the importance of Julius Caesar's arguments, see Harriss, "Medieval Doctrines in the Debates on Supply," p. 84.

59. Obviously this statement acknowledging the relationship between king and law is markedly different from the statements James makes in *The Trew Law of Free Monarchies* (1598). Anxious to show Parliament that he understood that relationship and was willing to listen to counsel in regard to it, he issued *A Declaration of His majesties Royall pleasure, what sort He thinketh fit to enlarge, Or reserve Himselfe in matter of Bountie* (London, 1610), in which he insisted that he did not want anything "by which Our People in generall may be impoverished or oppressed" and yet also nothing that would "turn to the diminution of our Revenew and setled Receipts" (A4^v). Moreover, "to prevent the passing or graunting of any thing which should be contrary to our Lawes, We have made Our choice of persons severally qualified, both in the understanding of our Lawe, and other knowledges" (B3^v).

60. The context of this remark is interesting; James is assuring Parliament that he respects the common law, and that anyone who reports that James is known privately not to respect it is wrong.

61. Harriss, "Medieval Doctrines in the Debates on Supply," pp. 83-85, explains that traditionally the position of Parliament had been that the king could ask for supply for "the necessity of the realm" but not for his own personal needs.

62. Smith, "Crown, Parliament and Finance: The Great Contract of 1610," p. 127. Failure of the Great Contract, Smith continues,

"demonstrated the inability of Crown and Commons to reach agreement on a fundamental overhaul of an outmoded and unpopular financial system. The consequences were very apparent in the rest of early Stuart history right up to the outbreak of the Civil War." See also Eric Lindquist, "The Failure of the Great Contract," *JMH* 57 (1985): 617–51.

63. Harriss, "Medieval Doctrines in the Debates on Supply," p. 99. Harriss, pp. 99–100, n. 1, also cites the quotation from Bacon that immediately follows in my own text.

64. Cf. the remark of Hoskyns in Parliament on Nov. 23, 1610, as recorded in Gardiner, ed., *Parliamentary Debates in 1610*, p. 144: "Henry the 7th and Tiberius bothe rich, but not taking all from the people. Tacitus."

65. See especially Thomas Cartelli, "Prospero in Africa: *The Tempest* as Colonialist Text and Pretext," in *Shakespeare Reproduced: The Text in History and Ideology*, ed. Jean E. Howard and Marion F. O'Connor (London: Methuen, 1988), pp. 99–115; and Rob Nixon, "Caribbean and African Appropriations of *The Tempest, CI* 13 (1987): 557–78.

66. See especially Stephen J. Greenblatt, "Learning to Curse: Aspects of Linguistic Colonialism in the Sixteenth Century," *First Images of America: The Impact of the New World on the Old*, ed. Fredi Chiappelli (Berkeley: University of California Press, 1976), pp. 561–80; Francis Barker and Peter Hulme, "Nymphs and Reapers Heavily Vanish: The Discursive Con-texts of *The Tempest*," in *Alternative Shakespeares*, ed. John Drakakis (London: Methuen, 1985), pp. 191–205; Walter Cohen, *Drama of a Nation: Public Theater in Renaissance England and Spain* (Ithaca, N.Y.: Cornell University Press, 1985), pp. 398–406; Richard Marienstras, *New Perspectives on the Shakespearean World*, trans. Janet Lloyd (Cambridge: Cambridge University Press, 1985), pp. 160–84; Peter Hulme, *Colonial Encounters*, pp. 89–134; Stephen Orgel, "Shakespeare and the Cannibals," in *Cannibals, Witches, and Divorce: Estranging the Renaissance*, ed. Marjorie Garber (Baltimore: Johns Hopkins University Press, 1987), pp. 40–66; and Stephen Greenblatt, *Shakespearean Negotiations: The Circulation of Social Energy in Renaissance England* (Berkeley: University of California Press, 1988), pp. 147–58.

See also Philip Brockbank, "*The Tempest*: Conventions of Art and Empire," in *Later Shakespeare*, Stratford-upon-Avon Studies 8 (London: Edward Arnold, 1966), pp. 183–201; D. G. James, *The Dream* of *Prospero* (Oxford: Clarendon Press, 1967), pp. 72–123; Kermode, ed., *Tempest*, pp. xxv-xxx; Felperin, *Shakespearean Romance*, pp. 260–57; Charles Frey, "*The Tempest* and the New World," SQ 30 (1979): 29–41; and Orgel, ed., *Tempest*, pp. 31–36.

The bibliography on *The Tempest* and colonization is now large and important; for listings, see Hulme, *Colonial Encounters*, pp. 292–93; Alden T. Vaughan, "Shakespeare's Indian: The Americanization of Caliban," SQ 39 (1988): 137–53; and Meredith Skura, "The Case of Colonialism in *The Tempest*," SQ 40 (1989): 42–69.

67. *A True Declaration of the Estate of the Colonie in Virginia, With a confutation of such scandalous reports as have tended to the disgrace of so worthy an enterprise*, in *Tracts and other Papers, Relating Principally to the Origin, Settlement, and Progress of the Colonies in North America*, 4 vols. (New York: Peter Smith, 1947), 3:5, 6. For the argument about lawfulness, see also William Crashaw's sermon to the Virginia Company, February 21, 1610, in Alexander Brown, *The Genesis of the United States*, 2 vols. (New York: Russell & Russell, 1964), 1:363; and John Parker, "Religion and the Virginia colony, 1609–1610," in *The Westward Enterprise: English Activities in Ireland, the Atlantic, and America 1480–1650*, ed. K. R. Andrews, N. P. Canny, and P. E. H. Hair (Liverpool: Liverpool University Press, 1978), pp. 245–70.

68. Robert Gray, *A Good Speed to Virginia* (London, 1609), ed. Wesley F. Craven (New York: Scholars Facsimiles and Reprints, 1937), sig. C3^v.

69. See Wesley Frank Craven, *Dissolution of the Virginia Company: The Failure of a Colonial Experiment* (Gloucester, Mass.: Peter Smith, 1964); and Edmund S. Morgan, *American Slavery, American Freedom: The Ordeal of Colonial Virginia* (New York: W. W. Norton and Company, 1975), pp. 79–80. W. Moelwyn Merchant, "Donne's Sermon to the Virginia Company: 13 November 1622," in *John Donne: Essays in Celebration*, ed. A. J. Smith (London: Methuen, 1972), pp. 433–52, remarks, "These years [1609–1624], when John Donne and Sir Thomas Roe became most intimately concerned in the affairs of the Company, had a complexity of troubles which very accurately reflected in the New World some of the most characteristic problems of the Stuarts in England and Europe" (p. 436). For the place of Sir Edwin Sandys and the earl of Southampton as defenders of the colonists' political rights, see Merchant, p. 436–37; M. J. Brown, *Itinerant Ambassador: The Life of Sir Thomas Roe* (Lexing-

ton: University of Kentucky, 1970), p. 109; and Wesley Frank Craven, *Dissolution of the Virginia Company*. Alexander Brown, *The First Republic in America* (Boston: Houghton Mifflin and Company, 1898), p. 85, comments (and without giving the documentation), "The party in England calling themselves 'advocates of English right,' 'opponents of Spain,' 'the best effected to the English religion and liberty,' 'patriots,' etc., was not satisfied with the 'barring our trade to the West Indies,' or with 'the advancement of absolute power then aimed at in England by King and court.' 'Whereupon many worthy *Patriots*, Lords, Knights, gentlemen, Merchants, and others held consultation . . . and laid hold on this expectation of Virginia as a providence cast before them,' and in the petition for the new charter they determined to ask for several privileges which would aid them in carrying out 'their ends.'

"Sir Thomas Smythe was selected as the treasurer of the new company in England because he had sympathized with the Earl of Essex 'when his Lordship went to appeal to the citizens of London.' Lord De la Warr, another friend of that Earl's, was chosen to be captain-general in Virginia, and Sir Thomas Gates, who commanded the first expedition, had won his spurs under Essex. The leading managers of the movement under the company in England and in Virginia were members of 'the patriot party.' "

On the role of Sir Edwin Sandys in the Parliament of 1610, see Notestein, *The House of Commons, 1604–1610*, index. I am grateful to Marion Trousdale for the Southampton references in Merchant and M. J. Brown.

70. "The Second Charter," in *The Three Charters of the Virginia Company of London, with Seven Related Documents, 1606–1621*, ed. Samuel M. Bemiss, Jamestown 350th Anniversary Historical Booklet 4 (Williamsburg, Va., 1957), p. 52. For discussion, see Warren M. Billings, "The Transfer of English law to Virginia, 1606–50," in *The Westward Enterprise*, pp. 215–44.

71. See David H. Flaherty, ed., *Lawes Divine, Morall and Martiall, etc.: Compiled by William Strachey* (Charlottesville: University Press of Virginia, 1969); Warren M. Billings, "The Transfer of English Law to Virginia 1606–50," in *The Westward Enterprise*, pp. 215–44; Canny, "The Permissive Frontier: The Problem of Social Control in English Settlements in Ireland and Virginia 1550–1650," in *The Westward Enterprise*, pp. 17–44; James Curtis Ballagh, *White Servitude in the Colony of Virginia: A Study of the System of Identured*

Labor in the American Colonies (New York: Burt Franklin, 1969), pp. 9, 22–23. For another discussion of *The Tempest* and martial law in the Virginia colony, see Greenblatt, "Martial Law in the Land of Cockaigne," in his *Shakespearean Negotiations*, pp. 147–58.

72. Billings, "The Transfer of English Law to Virginia," p. 218. See also Flaherty, ed., *Lawes Divine, Morall and Martiall, etc.*, pp. ix-xxxvii; Flaherty remarks (pp. xxxi-xxxii): "It is evident that those responsible for the *Lawes Divine, Morall and Martiall* did exceed the letter of the Virginia charter of 1609 and of the earlier charter and instructions. They went far beyond the definite limits in the instructions of 1606 on the number of offenses which were to bear the death penalty. The various charters had also guaranteed English laws to the residents of Virginia. Only a liberal reading of the charter provisions could justify some of the stipulations of the laws here reprinted. The considerable discretion granted the Virginia Company and its governors by the 1609 charter did not wholly legitimize some of these enactments."

73. *The New Life of Virginea* (London, 1612), in *Collections of the Massachusetts Historical Society*, vol. 8, 2d ser. (Boston: Sewell Phelps, 1819), p. 214.

74. *Calendar of State Papers, Colonial, 1574–1660*, ed. W. Noel Sainsbury (London: Longman, Green, Longman, and Roberts, 1860), p. 67; and see Flaherty, ed., *Lawes Divine, Morall and Martiall, etc.*, p. xxx.

75. For related discussions of the characteristics of metaphor in *The Tempest*, see Greenblatt, "Learning to Curse," pp. 574–75; Hulme, *Colonial Encounters*, pp. 108–9, 123; and Paul Brown, " 'This thing of darkness I acknowledge mine': *The Tempest* and the Discourse of Colonialism," in *Political Shakespeare: New Essays in Cultural Materialism*, ed. Jonathan Dollimore and Alan Sinfield (Ithaca, N.Y.: Cornell University Press, 1985), p. 66.

76. Paul Ricoeur, "The Metaphorical Process as Cognition, Imagination, and Feeling," *CI* 5 (1978): 144.

77. On Ireland as a context for *The Tempest*, see the important essay by Brown, " 'This thing of darkness I acknowledge mine': *The Tempest* and the Discourse of Colonialism," pp. 48–71. On Shakespeare, Ireland, and *Henry V*, see Jonathan Dollimore and Alan Sinfield, "History and Ideology: The Instance of *Henry V*," in Drakakis, ed., *Alternative Shakespeares*, pp. 224–26.

78. See, for example, the letter of Arthur Chichester, Lord Deputy

of Ireland, written from Ulster in September 1608, explaining that plans were to proceed there "as if His Majesty were to begin a new plantation in America," in *Calender of State Papers, Ireland, 1608–1610*, ed. C. W. Russell and John Prendergast (1874; rpt. Nendeln: Kraus-Thomson Organization Limited, 1974), p. 64. See also David Beers Quinn, "Ireland and America Intertwined," in *The Elizabethans and the Irish*, Folger Monograph on Tudor and Stuart Civilization (Ithaca, N.Y.: Cornell University Press, 1966), pp. 106–22; Nicholas P. Canny, "The Permissive Frontier: The Problem of Social Control in English Settlements in Ireland and Virginia 1550–1650," in *The Westward Enterprise*, pp. 17–44; Karl S. Bottigheimer, "Kingdom and Colony: Ireland in the Westward Enterprise," in *The Westward Enterprise*, pp. 45–63; Nicholas P. Canny, *The Elizabethan Conquest of Ireland: A Pattern Established 1565–76* (New York: Barnes and Noble Books, 1976), pp. 128–36.

79. For another discussion of the inadequacy of the definition of colonialist discourse provided by critics whose focus is *The Tempest* in relation to the New World, see Skura, "The Case of Colonialism in *The Tempest*," pp. 52–57.

80. See especially Hans S. Pawlisch, *Sir John Davies and the Conquest of Ireland: A Study of Legal Imperialism* (Cambridge: Cambridge University Press, 1985); Brendan Bradshaw, *The Irish Constitutional Revolution of the Sixteenth Century* (Cambridge: Cambridge University Press, 1979); and Canny, *The Elizabethan Conquest of Ireland*.

81. Brendan Bradshaw, reviewing Pawlisch, *Sir John Davies and the Conquest of Ireland*, in *TLS* (July 5, 1985), p. 742, remarks, "What is the historian of Ireland to do who sets out to explode the nasty historical myths that have bedevilled Anglo-Irish relations in the modern period, and discovers that the myths correspond with the truth?"

82. Citations in my text are to Raphael Holinshed, *Chronicles of England, Scotland, and Ireland* (1808; rpt. New York: AMS Press, 1965), vol. 6.

83. Citations in my text are to *Calendar of State Papers, Ireland, 1608–1610* (n. 78 above). See also Constantia Maxwell, *Irish History from Contemporary Sources* 1509–1610 (London: George Allen and Unwin, 1923). For a detailed bibliography of primary materials on Ireland, see Pawlisch, *Sir John Davies and the Conquest of Ireland*, pp. 213–22.

84. On Henry Sidney's role in Ireland, see Canny, *Elizabethan Conquest of Ireland*, pp. 45–65.

85. But see Richard Helgerson, "Barbarous Tongues: The Ideology of Poetic Form in Renaissance England," in *The Historical Renaissance: New Essays on Tudor and Stuart Literature and Culture*, ed. Heather Dubrow and Richard Strier (Chicago: University of Chicago Press, 1988), pp. 273–92, for the argument that an interest in quantitative meter was linked by Stanyhurst and others to interests in arguing for limits on royal power.

86. See the account of Richard Stanyhurst in *The Dictionary of National Biography*.

87. According to *DNB*, "In 1569 he spoke vehemently in the Irish House of Commons in support of the royal prerogative, and so irritated the opposition that the house broke up in confusion, and his parliamentary friends deemed it necessary to escort him to his lodgings."

88. John Stow, *The Abridgment of the English Chronicle continued . . . unto the end of the yeare 1610* (London, 1611), sig. Kk5.

89. Ngugi Wa Thiong'o, *A Grain of Wheat* (London: Heinemann, 1968); quoted in Cartelli, "Prospero in Africa," p. 106.

90. Like the tradition of othering the native Americans, the tradition of othering the Irish was well established and is well known. In *A New Description of Ireland* (London, 1610), Barnabe Riche was repeating an established tradition when he wrote that the Irish people "need to be restrained" (E). A people who had lived like barbarians without law, they were, like the "wilde and uncivill Sythians," "canibals in their cruelty," and people who "repay good Princes with grudge and contempt and disobedience" (E^v). William Camden, *Britain, or A Chorographical Description of the Most flourishing Kingdomes, England, Scotland, and Ireland*, trans. Philemon Holland (London, 1610), sig. Ffff2, described the Irish as "wilde and uncivill," given to "love idelness" and "immoderatly given to fleshly lust," people who "feed upon mans flesh in the maner as of the Sythians" ($Mmmm4^v$). For the same tradition, see Edmund Spenser, *A View of the Present State of Ireland*, in *Works*, ed. Edwin Greenlaw, Charles Grosvenor Osgood, Frederick Morgan Padelford, Ray Heffner; special ed. Rudolf Gottfried (Baltimore: Johns Hopkins University Press, 1949), 9: 39–231; and John Davies, *A Discovery of the True Causes why Ireland was never entirely subdued nor brought under obedience of the Crown of England* (London, 1612), in Henry Morley, ed., *Ireland under Elizabeth and James the First* (London: George Routledge and Sons, 1890), pp. 213–342. For discussion of this tradition, see Quinn, *The Elizabethans and the Irish*, pp. 65–66; and Brown, "'This thing of darkness I acknowledge mine': *The Tempest*

and the Discourse of Colonialism," pp. 55-58. Recent discussions of and arguments over Spenser's attitudes toward the Irish situation include Stephen Greenblatt, *Renaissance Self-Fashioning: From More to Shakespeare* (Chicago: University of Chicago Press, 1980), pp. 184-88; David Norbrook, *Poetry and Politics in the English Renaissance* (London: Routledge and Kegan Paul, 1984), pp. 139-52; and Ciaran Brady, "Spenser's Irish Crisis: Humanism and Experience in the 1590's," *Past and Present* 111 (1986), pp. 17-49.

91. Richard Waswo, "The History That Literature Makes," *NLH* 19 (1988): 541-64.

92. Letter by Richard Martin, Dec. 14, 1610, quoted in S. G. Culliford, *William Strachey, 1572-1621* (Charlottesville: University Press of Virginia, 1965), p. 124.

93. See Pawlisch, *Sir John Davies and the Conquest of Ireland*, and *A New History of Ireland*, ed. T. W. Moody, F. X. Martin, F. J. Byrne (Oxford: Clarendon Press, 1976), pp. 197-98.

94. John Davies, "The Plantation of Ulster," in Henry Morley, ed., *Ireland under Elizabeth and James the First* (London: Routledge and Sons, 1890), p. 390. See also Davies, *A Discovery of the True Causes why Ireland was never entirely subdued nor brought under obedience of the Crown of England.*

95. For discussion of the relationship between nationalism and colonialism, see Edward Said, *Nationalism, Colonialism and Literature: Yeats and Decolonization*, A Field Day Pamphlet, Number 15 (Derry: Field Day Theatre Company, 1988).

Part 2: The Tempest *as Masque and Romance*

THREE SPECTACLES

1. See especially Orgel and Strong, *Inigo Jones*, vol. 1.

2. Pierre Bourdieu, *Outline of a Theory of Practice* (Cambridge: Cambridge University Press, 1977), p. 164.

3. See, for example, Richard Helgerson, *Self-Crowned Laureates: Spenser, Jonson, Milton and the Literary System* (Berkeley: University of California Press, 1983); Patterson, *Censorship and Interpretation*, pp. 24-43; Norbrook, *Poetry and Politics in the English Renaissance*, pp. 91-96; and Louis Adrian Montrose, "The Elizabethan Subject and the Spenserian Text," in *Literary Theory/Renaissance Texts*, ed.

Patricia Parker and David Quint (Baltimore: Johns Hopkins University Press, 1986), pp. 303-40.

4. For discussion of the romance tradition in relation to Shakespeare's romances, see E. C. Pettet, *Shakespeare and the Romance Tradition* (London: Staples Press, 1949); J. H. P. Pafford, ed., *The Winter's Tale*, Arden Shakespeare (London: Methuen, 1963), pp. xxxvii-l; Carol Gesner, *Shakespeare and the Greek Romance* (Lexington: University Press of Kentucky, 1970); Hallett Smith, *Shakespeare's Romances* (San Marino, Calif.: Huntington Library, 1972); and Felperin, *Shakespearean Romance*, pp. 3-54.

5. Tasso, *Discourses on the Heroic Poem*, trans. Cavelchine and Samuel, p. 69.

6. See Bernard Weinberg, "The Quarrel over Ariosto and Tasso," *A History of Literary Criticism in the Italian Renaissance*, 2 vols. (Chicago: University of Chicago Press, 1961), 2:954-1073.

7. See Patricia Parker, *Inescapable Romance: Studies in the Poetics of a Mode* (Princeton, N.J.: Princeton University Press, 1979), p. 50.

8. Angus Fletcher, *The Prophetic Moment: An Essay on Spenser* (Chicago: University of Chicago Press, 1971), p. 28; and Parker, *Inescapable Romance*, pp. 76, 75. See also William A. Sessions, "Spenser's Georgics," *ELR* 10 (1980): 202-38.

9. For discussion of Spenser's use of the moral implications of Aeneas's delay at Carthage, see Parker, *Inescapable Romance*, pp. 62-63; for Ariosto's use of this section of Virgil's epic, see A. Bartlett Giamatti, *The Earthly Paradise and the Renaissance Epic* (Princeton, N.J.: Princeton University Press, 1966), pp. 158-60.

10. For the critical tradition, see Fletcher, *The Prophetic Moment*, p. 13.

11. A. Bartlett Giamatti, "Spenser: From Magic to Miracle," in *Four Essays on Romance*, ed. Herschel Baker (Cambridge, Mass.: Harvard University Press, 1971), p. 18.

12. Giamatti, "Spenser: From Magic to Miracle," p. 18, writes, "Ovid stands behind the Angelicas and Florimells fleeing their tormentors; Vergil behind Hermione stepping down to Perdita."

13. Fletcher, *The Prophetic Moment*, pp. 24-34.

14. *Aen.* 5.588-93: "As of old in high Crete 'tis said the Labyrinth held a path woven with blind walls, and a bewildering work of craft with a thousand ways, where the tokens of the trail were broken by the indiscoverable and irretraceable maze: even in such a course do the

Trojan children entangle their steps" ("ut quondam Creta fertur Labyrinthus in alta / parietibus textum caecis iter ancipitemque / mille viis habuisse dolum, qua signa sequendi / frangeret indeprensus et inremeabilis error: / haud alio Teucrum nati vestigia cursu / impediunt").

15. Herford and Simpson, eds., *Ben Jonson*, 8:647–48.

16. See Weinberg, *A History of Literary Criticism in the Italian Renaissance*, 2:954–1073.

17. See Giraldi Cinthio, *On Romances*, intro. and trans. Henry L. Snuggs (Lexington: University of Kentucky Press, 1968), pp. 11, 21–23, 37–38; and Tasso, *Discourses on the Heroic Poem*, pp. 64–79. On Cinthio, see Weinberg, *A History of Literary Criticism in the Italian Renaissance*, 2:969–70; and on Tasso, 2:1009–16, 1035–39, 1054–60, 1071–73. See also H. T. Swedenberg, Jr., *The Theory of the Epic in England, 1650–1800* (Berkeley: University of California Press, 1944), p. 10.

18. See Helgerson, "Barbarous Tongues: The Ideology of Poetic Form in Renaissance England," pp. 273–92, for the argument that the defense of quantitative meter was related to an argument for constitutionalism.

19. Compare Leeds Barroll, "A New History for Shakespeare and his Time," *SQ* 39 (1988): 463: "It may have been James, the new-fashioned monarchist with absolutist notions, who was in England, as he had been in Scotland, the subversive force: threatening the established power and order of a circle of oligarchs in the earldom. . . . James's theories of monarchy were not, after all, traditional ones."

20. See Orgel and Strong, *Inigo Jones*, 1:50–61, and passim.

21. See Perelman, *A New Rhetoric*, p. 51. See Bourdieu, *Outline of a Theory of Practice*, p. 168–69: "The critique which brings the undiscussed into discussion, the unformulated into formulation, has as the condition of its possibility objective crisis, which, in breaking the immediate fit between the subjective structures and the objective structures, destroys self-evidence practically. . . . It is only when the dominated have the material and symbolic means of rejecting the definition of the real that is imposed on them through logical structures . . . that the arbitrary principles of the prevailing classification can appear as such, and it therefore becomes necessary to undertake the work of conscious systematization and express rationalization which marks the passage from doxa to orthodoxy."

22. Sturm, *A Ritch Storehouse or Treasure for Nobilitye and Gentlemen*, sig. H3.

23. Robert Weimann, "Shakespeare (De)Canonized: Conflicting Uses of 'Authority' and 'Representation,' " *NLH* 20 (1988): 73.

24. On *The Tempest*, see Still, *The Timeless Theme*. On *The Faerie Queene*, see Fletcher, *The Prophetic Moment*, pp. 76-90; Isabel E. Rathborne, *The Meaning of Spenser's Fairyland* (New York: Columbia University Press, 1937), p. vii; and Thomas P. Roche, Jr., *The Kindly Flame: A Study of the Third and Fourth Books of Spenser's "Faerie Queene"* (Princeton, N.J.: Princeton University Press, 1964), pp. 38-50; and Sessions, "Spenser's Georgics." For the tradition of associating England with the Blessed Island, see Josephine Waters Bennett, "Britain among the Fortunate Isles," *SP* 53 (1956): 114-50.

25. Burke, *Attitudes Toward History*, p. 166.

26. See H. H. Furness, ed., *Tempest*, Variorum Shakespeare (New York: J. B. Lippincott, 1892), p. 181, n. 71 (citing Peck and Steevens); Root, *Classical Mythology in Shakespeare*, p. 69; Baldwin, *William Shakspere's small Latine & lesse Greeke*, 2:481-84; Kermode, ed., *Tempest*, p. 169 (n. to p. 89), and Ian Kott, "The *Aeneid* and *The Tempest*," pp. 433-37.

27. Stahel, ed. and trans., "Cristoforo Landino's Allegorization of the *Aeneid*: Books III and IV of *Camaldolese Disputations*," p. 91. Of the critics (cited in the above note) who have connected Shakespeare's harpy to Celaeno, only Kermode indicates that the harpy specifically signifies avarice.

28. For these concepts, see, for example, *Macbeth* 4.3.

29. Bernardus Silvestris, *Commentary on the First Six Books of Virgil's "Aeneid,"* trans. and ed. Schreiber and Maresca, pp. 70-72. In the Cave of Mammon episode (*F.Q.* 2.7.23), Spenser also places Celaeno in hell.

30. Critics who read the scene as evoking a context of Christian sin and judgment, as opposed to a classical context, include Robert G. Hunter, *Shakespeare and the Comedy of Forgiveness* (New York: Columbia University Press, 1965), pp. 233-36; John Doebler, *Shakespeare's Speaking Pictures* (Albuquerque: University of New Mexico Press, 1974), pp. 148-57; and Herbert R. Coursen, *Christian Ritual and the World of Shakespeare's Tragedies* (Lewisburg, Pa.: Bucknell University Press, 1976), pp. 376-80.

31. Thomas Cooper, *Thesaurus* (London, 1565). See also Furness, ed., *Tempest*, p. 191, n. 29.

32. The same trick had been played on Ceres's daughter. At the

instigation of Venus, Cupid shot an arrow to make Pluto fall in love with Proserpina.

33. See Orgel, ed. *Tempest*, pp. 43-50.

34. When Kott, "The *Aeneid* and *The Tempest*," pp. 438-39, notes the parallel between Virgil's nymphs and Shakespeare's, he does not also note the contrast, an omission that leads him to conclude that Shakespeare is also repeating in *The Tempest* the defeat and failure that characterize this moment in Virgil.

35. For the tradition of the two Venuses, one celestial and one natural, see Erwin Panofsky, *Studies in Iconology: Humanistic Themes in the Art of the Renaissance* (1939; rpt. New York: Harper & Row, 1962), pp. 142-43; and Landino, *Camaldolese Disputations*, pp. 61-64.

36. See Kermode, ed., *Tempest*, p. lxxii; Wickham, "Masque and Anti-Masque in *The Tempest*"; and Gilman, " 'All eyes': Prospero's Inverted Masque."

37. Jonson cites the *Aeneid* at many points in his notes to *Hymenaei*. Herford and Simpson, eds., *Ben Jonson*, 8:209-41 (the text cited in my study), prints these notes in the margins and around the texts of the masques. Stephen Orgel, ed., *Ben Jonson: The Complete Masques* (New Haven: Yale University Press, 1969), pp. 514-25, provides them in the more convenient form of a separate appendix.

38. See D. J. Gordon, "*Hymenaei*: Ben Jonson's Masque of Union," *JWCI* 8 (1945): 107-45; reprinted in Stephen Orgel, ed., *The Renaissance Imagination: Essays and Lectures by D. J. Gordon* (Berkeley: University of California Press, 1980), pp. 157-84. In the latter, see appendix 6, pp. 282-89, for Gordon's notes on Jonson's notes to the sources and origins of his art.

39. See Pierre Bourdieu, *Distinction: A Social Critique of the Judgement of Taste*, trans. Richard Nice (Cambridge, Mass.: Harvard University Press, 1984), p. 31.

40. In *Metamorphoses* 15, Arthur Golding, trans., *The Fifteen Books of P. Ovidius Naso Entituled Metamorphoses* (London, 1567), sig. Cc8^v, Ovid prefaces his announcement that the new city of Rome is now coming into being with the reminder that Troy, Sparta, Amphion, Thebes, and Athens have all fallen; thus, "One nation gathereth strength: / Another wereth weake: And bothe doo make exchaunge at length. / So Troy which once was great and strong as well in welth as men, / Now . . . hath nothing left . . . Save ruines." Cf. Allen, *Image and Meaning*, p. 100: "When Prospero talks about ruined towers, temples, and palaces, he may be speaking in general terms, but a tra-

velled Jacobean . . . would certainly think of the waste of Imperial Rome. No dream was ever greater than this imperial one; no dream ever passed more sadly and left grander evidence of its passing."

41. On Caliban as "doubly inscribed, a discursive monster, a compromise formation," see Hulme, *Colonial Encounters*, p. 109. See also Hayden White, "The Forms of Wildness: Archeology of an Idea," in *The Wild Man Within: An Image in Western Thought from the Renaissance to Romanticism*, ed. Edward Dudley and Maximillian E. Novak (Pittsburgh: University of Pittsburgh Press, 1972), p. 28, for sketches of "two distinct personalities" of the wild man.

42. Still, *The Timeless Theme*, p. 204, connects Shakespeare's foul lake to Cocytus (*Aen.* 6.295-97) rather than to Avernus. I emphasize Avernus because Virgil refers to it in the context of speaking of the doves that light on the tree bearing the golden bough (*Aen.* 6.190-204). But it is not necessary to insist that only one of these rivers is Shakespeare's model; Landino associates all the foul rivers in the underworld with base things; he explains, "From our concupiscense, as from a spring, flows the water which makes up the Stygian Swamp" (p. 230).

43. For summaries of the confusion caused by the word *line* in "Come, hang them on this line" (4.1.193), see Furness, ed., *Tempest*, pp. 222-25, and Kermode, ed., *Tempest*, gloss for 4.1.193.

44. John Gerarde, *The Herball or Generall Historie of Plantes* (1577; rpt. London, 1636), p. 1483; John Parkinson, *Theatrum Botanicum: The Theater of Plants* (London, 1640), pp. 1406-7.

45. Or so Kermode suggests in his gloss to 1.2.164.

46. *Marsilio Ficino: The "Philebus" Commentary*, trans. and ed. Michael J. B. Allen (Berkeley: University of California Press, 1975), pp. 448-50.

47. In his notes to *Poly-Olbion*, John Selden connects the use of mistletoe by the British Druids for their magical ceremonies to the passage in the *Aeneid* that describes the golden bough and compares it to mistletoe; see Michael Drayton, *Works*, ed. J. William Hebel, 5 vols. (Oxford: Shakespeare Head Press, 1933), 4:192-95.

48. The emphasis on the "noise of hunters" also evokes the associations of James with the hunt.

THE EDUCATION OF FERDINAND

1. See Norbrook, *Poetry and Politics in the English Renaissance*, pp. 56, 97, 109-11, 113.

2. See Sommerville, *Politics and Ideology in England 1603–1640*, pp. 27–34; Goldberg, *James I and the Politics of Literature*, pp. 85–112; and Peter Stallybrass, "Patriarchal Territories: The Body Enclosed," in *Rewriting the Renaissance: The Discourses of Sexual Difference in Early Modern Europe*, ed. Margaret W. Ferguson, Maureen Quilligan, and Nancy J. Vickers (Chicago: University of Chicago Press, 1986), pp. 123–42.

3. Norbrook, *Poetry and Politics in the English Renaissance*, p. 109, makes the distinction that, in *The Faerie Queene*, "Spenser identifies political virtue with love rather than liberty." Orgel and Strong, *Inigo Jones*, 1:57, show how the masques represent absolute power as love: "Power, say the masques, is love; rebellion, unbridled passion."

4. Perelman, *The New Rhetoric*, p. 51.

5. This topos of the Aeneas who offers comfort occurs three other times in *The Tempest*. Stephano finds comfort in liquor: "Here's my comfort" (2.2.46, 56). Alonso presents himself as one who can neither give comfort nor receive it (2.1.9, 10, 18, 166; 3.2.7–10, 11). And Gonzalo, who can offer others comfort, tells his companions that, though shipwrecked they all "have cause . . . of joy" (2.1.1–2).

6. Baldassare Castiglione, *The Book of the Courtier*, trans. Charles S. Singleton (Garden City, N.Y.: Doubleday and Company, 1959), p. 347. See also "Marsilio Ficino's Commentary on Plato's *Symposium*," intro. and trans. Sears Reynolds Jayne, *University of Missouri Studies* 19, no. 1 (1944): 13–247.

7. *Macrobius' Commentary on the Dream of Scipio*, trans. and notes by Stahl, p. 195, explains that "every disposition of the soul is controlled by song."

8. As Sessions ("Spenser's Georgics," p. 228) reminds us, "Belphoebe as the Vergilian Venus has been a commonplace in Spenser criticism since Upton. Her first appearance in the Legend of Temperance recalls the Venus of Vergil's Book One, pointing her son the way out of the forest. . . . When Belphoebe appears again in Book III to heal the wounds of Timias in the forest, Spenser again directly translates the 'O dea certe' recognition scene, using it, as he had for Elizabeth in the April eclogue, to indicate an exalted being. Belphoebe's answer also paraphrases Venus' assertion of mortality: 'Nor Goddess I, nor Angell, but the Mayde, / and daughter of a woody Nymphe.' " See also Norman Council, " 'O Dea Certe': The Allegory of 'The Fortress of Perfect Beauty,' " *HLQ* 39 (1975–76): 329–42.

9. See Panofsky, *Studies in Iconology*, pp. 142–43; *Marsilio Fic-*

ino: The "Philebus" Commentary, ed. and trans. Allen, pp. 136–38.

10. Writing about the difference in the two Venuses, Landino, *Camaldolese Disputations*, p. 64, explains that Aeneas's journey toward divine love is naturally difficult and long: "Indeed no one will completely finish this journey which abounds in sweat and labor unless, burning with a love of it, he is prepared to undergo every difficulty." *Giordano Bruno's "The Heroic Frenzies,"* trans. Paul Eugene Memmo (Chapel Hill: University of North Carolina Press, 1964), p. 184, also speaks of the labor that is called for and that is eagerly taken up: "You know very well that to men who are well disposed the love of material beauty not only does not at all delay them from the greater enterprises, but rather gives them wings to accomplish them; for love's constraint is transformed into a virtuous zeal which forces the lover to progress to the point of becoming worthy of the thing loved."

11. On Henry's preference for a style of representation that emphasized his warlike nature, see Williamson, *The Myth of the Conqueror*, pp. 23, 28–29, 64–70; for Jonson's decision to cast Henry as a figure of love in *Oberon, the Faery Prince*, see pp. 75–107. See also Orgel, "Making Greatness Familiar," p. 44.

12. Foster, ed., *Proceedings in Parliament, 1610*, 2:127, remarks, "Holding the ceremony in parliament was part of the plan to encourage contributions toward the Prince's support." Strong, *Henry, Prince of Wales*, p. 26, concurs.

13. Foster, ed., *Proceedings in Parliament, 1610*, 2:304; see also pp. 310, 354.

14. Croft, ed., "A Collection of Several Speeches," p. 259. P. R. Seddon, "Household Reforms in the Reign of James I," *BIHR* 53 (1980): 49, remarks, "The problem of an increase in costs caused by the appointment of additional officers is seen in its most acute form in Prince Henry's household." But Strong, *Henry, Prince of Wales*, p. 26, interprets the regulations on banqueting as indicating that Henry planned to run a disciplined court unlike the court of his father.

15. Croft, ed., "A Collection of Several Speeches," p. 314.

16. See *Giordano Bruno's "The Heroic Frenzies,"* trans. Memmo; John Charles Nelson, *Renaissance Theory of Love: The Context of Giordano Bruno's "Eroici furori"* (New York: Columbia University Press, 1958); Frances Yates, "The Emblematic Conceit in Giordano Bruno's *De gli eroici furori* and in the Elizabethan Sonnet Sequence," *England and the Mediterranean Tradition: Studies in Art, History, and Literature*, ed. The Warburg and Courtauld Institutes (London: Ox-

ford University Press, 1945), pp. 81–101; Rosalie Colie, *Resources of Kind* (Berkeley: University of California Press, 1973), pp. 108–11. Colie emphasizes that Bruno, "In a traditional conflation of *eros* with *heros* (love with heroism) . . . insisted on the heroic character, not of sonnets simply, but of love itself," p. 108. The tradition is exemplified for drama in the court plays of John Lyly; see Peter Saccio, *The Court Comedies of John Lyly: A Study of Allegorical Dramaturgy* (Princeton, N.J.: Princeton University Press, 1969). On Neoplatonism and the concept of reciprocity in Spenser's *Amoretti*, see J. W. Lever, *The Elizabethan Love Sonnet* (London: Methuen, 1956), p. 115; John D. Bernard, "Spenserian Pastoral and the *Amoretti*," *ELH* 47 (1980): 419–32; and Arthur Marotti, " 'Love is not love': Elizabethan Sonnet Sequences and the Social Order," *ELH* 49 (1982): 416.

17. For the metaphor of flight that Ferdinand uses, compare *Bruno's "The Heroic Frenzies*," p. 203, "it is customary to depict . . . by a pair of wings that potency of the soul that orders it to its highest good." Cf. Plotinus, who explains that the philosopher is "one who is by nature ready to respond and 'winged' " (*Ennead* 1.3.3.), and who asks, "How can one see the 'inconceivable beauty,' " and then replies, "let us fly to our dear country" (*Ennead* 1.6.8).

18. See Tasso, *Discourses on the Heroic Poem*, pp. 15–16, 37–39.

19. Kermode, ed., *Tempest*, glosses 3.1.89, with a heart "as desirous of it . . . as the bondman is to be free."

20. On patriarchy in *The Tempest*, see Stephen Orgel, "Prospero's Wife," in *Rewriting the Renaissance*, ed. Ferguson, Quilligan, and Vickers, pp. 50–64; and Marilyn L. Williamson, *The Patriarchy of Shakespeares' Comedies* (Detroit, Mich.: Wayne State University Press, 1986), pp. 111–201. See also Coppelia Kahn, "The Absent Mother in *King Lear*," in *Rewriting the Renaissance*, pp. 33–49.

21. From James's speech to Parliament, 1604, in McIlwain, ed., *The Political Works of James I*, p. 272.

22. See Kathleen M. Davies, "Continuity and Change in Literary Advice on Marriage," in *Marriage and Society: Studies in the Social History of Marriage*, ed. R. B. Outhwaite (London: European Publications, 1981), pp. 58–80.

23. See especially Marotti, " 'Love is not love' "; Ann Rosalind Jones and Peter Stallybrass, "The Politics of *Astrophil and Stella*," *SEL* 24 (1984): 53–68; and Montrose, "The Elizabethan Subject and the Spenserian Text," pp. 303–40.

24. See Martin Ingram, "Spousals Litigation in the English Ecclesiastical Courts c. 1350-c. 1640," in *Marriage and Society*, pp. 35–57; and Margo Todd, "Humanists, Puritans and the Spiritualized Household," *Church History* 49 (1980): 18–34. I am grateful to Heather Dubrow for these references.

25. Sommerville, *Politics and Ideology in England 1603–1640*, pp. 79, 66. For theories of contract as forms of resistance, see Sommerville, pp. 71 and 73.

26. One must take care not to oversimplify or overgeneralize the concepts of patriarchy and contract. For a consideration of the distortions that oversimplification of the concept of patriarchy promotes, see Margaret J. M. Ezell, *The Patriarch's Wife: Literary Evidence and the History of the Family* (Chapel Hill: University of North Carolina Press, 1987). Likewise, contract and mutual obligation, in marriage and in government, do not in themselves imply equality between the parties involved. On this point, see Davies, "Continuity and Change in Literary Advice on Marriage"; and Weston and Greenberg, *Subjects and Sovereigns*, pp. 1–34.

27. Since Carthage was for the allegorists a place where the passions held sway, the story of Aeneas's building the city walls could represent the hero's immersion in base things. Landino read the episode as an instance of how "the enticement of earthly things" leads one to "give up contemplation of the heavenly" (Stahel, p. 170).

28. Holinshed, *Chronicles of England, Scotland, and Ireland*, ed. Ellis, 6:31; and *Calendar of State Papers, Ireland, 1608–1610*, p. 501.

29. Waswo, "The History That Literature Makes," p. 545.

30. See Morgan, *American Slavery, American Freedom*, pp. 71–91; and Greenblatt, *Shakespearean Negotiations*, p. 29.

31. Compare John Pitcher, " 'In those figures which they seeme': Samuel Daniel's *Tethys' Festival*," in *The Court Masque*, ed. David Lindley (Manchester, Eng.: Manchester University Press, 1984), p. 37, who argues that Daniel is presenting "counsel against imperialism."

32. See Williamson, *The Myth of the Conqueror*, p. 51; Williamson continues, "the Virginia headland was soon sprouting with landmarks named for him: Cape Henry, Fort Henry, Henricopolis, and Henrico College." Williamson, p. 53, also notes that Henry had also been named Supreme Protector of the Northwest Passage Company.

33. A central issue also in Bryan Loughrey and Neil Taylor, "Fer-

dinand and Miranda at Chess," *ShS* 35 (1982): 113-18. Loughrey and Taylor, p. 114, also refer to the importance of the game in medieval literature.

Additionally, in "The *Aeneid* and *The Tempest*," Kott cites a reference Panofsky makes to a picture of Dido and Aeneas playing chess. Panofsky's reference (*Studies in Iconology*, pp. 19-20) refers us, in turn, to Erwin Panofsky and Fritz Saxl, "Classical Mythology in Medieval Art," *Metropolitan Museum Studies* 4, no. 2 (1933): 228-80. In this latter essay, where I expected to find it, there is no picture of Dido and Aeneas, or anyone else, playing chess. But the authors do speak of the medieval artist presenting ancient figures in medieval and frequently chivalric settings: "in all these illustrations of the Troy legend . . . the classical heroes and heroines appear as medieval knights and ladies. The typical scenes of battle, lovemaking, and mourning wholly conform to the contemporary types most common in novel illustration and religious art" (pp. 262-63). They also explain that the medieval artists, "Being familiar with the game of chess as a characteristic feature of courtly life . . . saw no incongruity in a picture of Medea playing chess" (p. 268). For more on illustrations of the Troy story, see Fritz Saxl, "The Troy Romance in French and Italian Art," in *Lectures*, 2 vols. (London: Warburg Institute, University of London, 1957), 1:125-38; vol. 1 contains Saxl's lectures, vol. 2, the illustrations. There are plates of Achilles and Patroclus playing chess in Hugo Buchthal, *Historia Troiana: Studies in the History of Medieval Secular Illustration*, Studies of the Warburg Institute 32 (London: Warburg Institute, University of London, 1971), plate 33, b and d.

34. *Caxton's Game and Playe of the Chesse*, intro. William E. A. Axon (London: Elliot Stock, 1883), pp. 10-14.

35. *Ludus Scacchiae: Chesse-Play. A Game, both pleasant, wittie, and politicke . . . Translated out of the Italian into the English tongue. Containing also therein, A prety and pleasant Poeme of a whole Game played at Chess*. Written by G. B. (London, 1597). The facsimile at the Folger Shakespeare Library was printed in London by Hardyng and Wright, n.d. Mario A. Di Cesare, ed., *The Game of Chess: Marco Girolama Vida's "Scacchia Ludus"* (Nieuwkoop: B. DeGraaf, 1975), p. 11, speaks of the "immense popularity of the poem" in England and on the Continent; it was translated into English ten times.

36. Thomas More, *Utopia*, in *Works*, ed. Edward Surtz, S.J., and J.

H. Hexter (New Haven: Yale University Press, 1965), 1:129; see also p. 408, n. 128/18.

Part 3: Prospero and the Best State of the Commonwealth

1. Thomas Cooper, *Thesaurus* (London, 1565).
2. Puttenham, *The Arte of English Poesie*, ed. Willcock and Walker, p. 276.
3. Vickers, *In Defence of Rhetoric*, pp. 55–56.
4. See "A Letter of the Authors," in Spenser, *Works*, ed. Greenlaw, Osgood, and Padelford, 1:167.
5. The translation of this line only is from C. M. Bowra, *From Virgil to Milton* (London: Macmillan, 1967), p. 63, n. 1. In discussing the meaning of *praecipere*, Bowra recalls that "Cicero uses the word when he says that the duty of a great nature is to foresee what can happen, whether good or bad [*De officiis* 1.80], and Seneca quotes Virgil's actual words to illustrate his view of a good man.—'Whatever happens he says, "I foresaw it" ' [*Ep.* 76.35]" (p. 63). In his *Thesaurus*, Cooper gives many definitions of *praecipio*, including "to foresee: to conceive in minde before," a definition he repeats again and illustrates by reference to Virgil when he cites the infinitive *praecipere*.
6. For this attribution, see Francis Bacon, *Of the Proficience and Advancement of Learning Divine and Human*, in *Works*, ed. James Spedding, Robert Leslie Ellis, and Douglas Denon Heath (London: Longman and Co., 1857), 3:263.
7. Bacon, *Works*, 8:334. For Bacon's probable authorship, see *Works*, pp. 325, 342, and Desmond Bland, ed., *Gesta Grayorum*, English Reprints Series (Liverpool: Liverpool University, 1968). D. G. James, *The Dream of Prospero* (Oxford: Clarendon Press, 1967), pp. 70–71, also speaks of *Gesta Grayorum* in relationship to *The Tempest*.
8. On the use of supernatural machinery in epic, see Thomas Greene, *The Descent from Heaven: A Study in Epic Continuity* (New Haven: Yale University Press, 1963). In discussing Ariosto, Greene remarks that "in most true romances, an episode like a conventional celestial descent is anachronistic . . . romance characteristically presents only the conclusion of the intervention . . . one may witness a miracle . . . but one never glimpses [its] origin or starting place" (p. 112).

9. According to Ficino ("Marsilio Ficino's Commentary on Plato's *Symposium*," trans. Jayne, p. 200), Socrates, Zoroaster, Apollonius Tyaneaus, and Porphyry were all known to be friends of daemons.

10. See Kott, "The *Aeneid* and *The Tempest*," p. 430. Recalling also the tradition that Mercury "disperses not only real clouds but the clouds which dim and darken the human mind," Kott refers us to *The Tempest*, 5.1.64–68. For the tradition that Mercury is a peacemaker, see Greene, *Descent from Heaven*, p. 308; for a picture of Mercury with Peace, see Jean Seznec, *The Survival of the Pagan Gods* (1940; English trans., New York: Pantheon Books, 1953). Often in *The Tempest*, Prospero uses Ariel to make peace. On Ariel as Mercury, see also E. M. Butler, *Ritual Magic* (Cambridge: Cambridge University Press, 1949), p. 168.

11. Kott, "The *Aeneid* and *The Tempest*," p. 430.

12. Bernardus Silvestris, *Commentary on the First Six Books of Virgil's "Aeneid,"* trans. Schreiber and Maresca, p. 26.

13. See, respectively, Gardiner, ed., *Parliamentary Debates in 1610*, pp. 67, 52; Spedding, ed., *The Letters and Life of Francis Bacon*, 4:120; Foster, ed., *Proceedings in Parliament 1610*, 2:135. Hereafter citations appear in the text.

14. *The Political Works of James I*, ed. McIlwain, p. 308; hereafter cited in the text as McIlwain.

15. Bakhtin, *Speech Genres and Other Late Essays*, p. 133.

16. See Rosalie Colie, *Paradoxia Epidemica: The Renaissance Tradition of Paradox* (Princeton, N.J.: Princeton University Press, 1966), pp. 3–6.

17. For similar perspectives on what "rude" characters can represent, see Louis Adrian Montrose, " 'Eliza, Queene of shepheardes,' and the Pastoral of Power," *ELR* 10 (1980): 153–82; and Javitch, *The Poetry and Courtliness in Renaissance England*, pp. 79–82.

18. On vituperation and blame as a technique of epideictic, see Hardison, *The Enduring Monument*, p. 87; and Vickers, *In Defence of Rhetoric*, pp. 54–62.

19. Cf. Bourdieu, *Distinction*, p. 156: " 'the field of struggles' is the system of objective relations within which positions and postures are defined relationally and which governs even those struggles aimed at transforming it."

20. Bakhtin, *Speech Genres*, pp. 65–66.

21. See Weston and Greenberg, *Subjects and Sovereigns*, pp. 10–15.

22. See Sommerville, *Politics and Ideology in England 1603–1640*, pp. 151–59, for the notion of "absolute property" as a concept that was used in 1610 and later to argue against absolute monarchy.

23. Bakhtin, *The Dialogic Imagination*, p. 76. See also Linda Hutcheon, *A Theory of Parody: The Teachings of Twentieth-Century Art Forms* (London: Methuen, 1985), pp. 69–83.

24. Greene, *The Light in Troy*, p. 46.

25. Bakhtin, *The Dialogic Imagination*, p. 76.

26. See Foster, ed., *Proceedings in Parliament 1610*, 1:132, 2:164, 182, 245; and Gardiner, ed., *Parliamentary Debates in 1610*, p. 102.

27. As Clifford Geertz, "Deep Play: Notes on the Balinese Cockfight," *Daedalus* 101 (1972): 26, explains, "Any expressive form works (when it works) by disarranging semantic contexts in such a way that properties conventionally ascribed to certain things are unconventionally ascribed to others, which are then seen actually to possess them. To call the wind a cripple, as Stevens does, to fix tone and manipulate timbre, as Schoenberg does, or, closer to our case, to picture an art critic as a dissolute bear, as Hogarth does, is to cross conceptual wires; the established conjunctions between objects and their qualities are altered and phenomena—fall weather, melodic shape, or cultural journalism—are clothed in signifiers which normally point to other referents. Similarly, to connect—and connect, and connect—the collision of roosters with the divisiveness of status is to invite a transfer of perceptions from the former to the latter, a transfer which is at once a description and a judgment."

28. See David Kunzle, "World Upside Down: The Iconography of a European Broadsheet," in Barbara A. Babcock, *The Reversible World: Forms of Symbolic Inversion in Art and Society* (Ithaca, N.Y.: Cornell University Press, 1978), p. 82.

29. See Gardiner, ed., *Parliamentary Debates in 1610*, p. 82.

30. Foster, ed., *Proceedings in Parliament 1610*, 1:278, 279, 282.

31. Cf. the variation on the Sinon episode in Sir Philip Sidney, *The Countess of Pembroke's Arcadia*, ed. Maurice Evans (New York: Penguin Books, 1977), p. 96.

32. By contrast, in *3 Henry VI*, 3.2.190, Richard says that he will "like a Sinon take another Troy." In *Titus Andronicus*, 5.3.85, Marcus instructs Lucius: "Tell us what Sinon hath bewitch'd our ears." In *Cymbeline*, 3.4.59–60, Imogen, angered at having been accused of unfaithfulness, recalls that once "Sinon's weeping / Did scandal many a holy tear."

33. See also Eleanor Prosser, "Shakespeare, Montaigne, and *The Rarer Action*," *ShS* 1 (1965): 161-64; and John B. Bender, "The Day of *The Tempest*," *ELH* 47 (1980): 250-51.

34. Croft, ed., "A Collection of Several Speeches," p. 302.

35. For discussion, see Trousdale, "Recurrence and Renaissance: Rhetorical Imitation in Ascham and Sturm," pp. 173-74.

36. See Baldwin, *William Shakspere's small Latine & lesse Greeke* 2:448-51. Baldwin also emphasizes Shakespeare's use of Ovid in Latin, not in English translation.

37. And see Weston and Greenberg, *Subjects and Sovereigns*, pp. 12-15.

38. David William, "*The Tempest* on the Stage," *Jacobean Theatre*, Stratford-upon-Avon Studies I, ed. John Russell Brown and Bernard Harris (London: Edward Arnold, 1960), p. 135. And see Wiltenburg, "The *Aeneid* in *The Tempest*," pp. 167-68.

39. The imitation and variation here turn on the words used to describe that which covers and conceals the hero—Aeneas or Prospero—and which must then be removed to reveal him. Virgil, who describes Aeneas as covered with a cloud, uses the word *amictu*, meaning "garment," as a metaphor for the effect the cloud has: it robes him. Then Shakespeare, imitating this image when he is about to have Prospero reveal himself, has Prospero remove his magician's garment; but Shakespeare does not describe it as a garment or robe or mantle or cloak. Rather, he uses the verb *discase*, a word not usually applied to disrobing, just as *garment* is usually not used in speaking of a cloud. In his *Thesaurus*, Cooper defines *amictus* as "a garment or apparayle: araiying or cloathying." And as one of his examples he cites this very line in Virgil and then translates it as follows: "Dyd caste a thick clowde about them." Shakespeare's only other use of the word *discase* occurs in *The Winter's Tale*: "discase thee . . . and change garments" (4.4.634-36).

EPILOGUE

1. Kermode, ed., *Tempest*, p. 134.

2. Robert M. Durling, *The Figure of the Poet in Renaissance Epic* (Cambridge, Mass.: Harvard University Press, 1965), p. 185; Durling compares a passage from *Gerusalemme liberata* to the passage I have cited from *Georgics* 2.42-44. For the comparison of Douglas to the diffident Virgil, see Douglas, trans., *Virgil's "Aeneid*," ed. Coldwell, 1:144.

INDEX

Absolutism, discourse of: duty of the subject, 112, 117–18, 128; king as colonizer, 55; king as father, 46, 48, 99; king as god, 46, 48, 52, 99, 109; king as head, 46, 48, 99; king as husband, 99; king as law, 51–52; king as *primum mobile*, 52, 109; king as *primum movens*, 109, 128; king as *primus motor*, 109; king as *principale agens*, 52, 109, 128; law of nature, 49. See also Colonization, discourse of; Constitutionalism, discourse of; Epideictic; Neoplatonism; Parliament, 1610; Parliament, members of; Prerogative, royal

Aeneid: Anchises, 25, 36, 78, 83–85, 197; arrival in Italy, 30–31; Augustus, 82–83; Avernus, 89; Carthage, arrival at, 24–25, 26; Carthage, building of, 100–101; Carthage cave episode, 25, 79–81, 103; Celaeno, 75–77; Dido's banquet, 131; Elysium, 25, 70, 78–79, 88–92; golden bough, 88–91; hell, 25, 76; labyrinth, 71; Laocoön, 22–23, 24; *o dea certe*, 21, 24, 95; Priam, 123–24; reunion of Trojans, 130; Sibyl, 25, 76–77, 78, 107; Sinon, 123–24, 125; tempest, 19–20, 24; Troy, 25, 70, 86–92, 106, 107; Turnus, 34, 36, 123

Aeneid passages cited: 1.53, 19; 1.149, 123; 1.208–9, 94; 1.257, 108; 1.328, 21; 1.328–33, 95; 1.377, 19; 1.411–12, 130; 1.595–96, 130; 1.610–12, 130; 1.643–56, 90; 1.657–722, 80; 1.688, 80; 1.753–55, 131; 2.203–8, 22–23; 3.226, 75; 3.242–43, 75; 3.253, 77; 4.165, 80; 4.166–70, 80; 4.169–70, 80; 4.172, 79; 4.238–58, 109; 4.244, 109; 4.307–8, 101; 4.323, 101; 4.361, 101; 4.160f., 82; 5.588–93, 165n. 14; 6.105, 107; 6.136–38, 88; 6.191–205, 88; 6.201, 89; 6.205–9, 91; 6.257–63, 92; 6.283–84, 89; 6.567–69, 76; 6.606, 76; 6.624, 77; 6.759, 107; 6.792–93, 83; 6.852–53, 84; 6.860–901, 83; 6.867–71, 84; 6.882, 84. See also Augustus; Colonization, discourse of; Imitation; James I; Parliament, 1610; *The Tempest*; Virgil

Allegory, 26–32; and imitation, 29; as neoplatonic, 28; and Sturm, 26. See also Bernardus Silvestris; Spenser

Allen, D. C., 169n. 40

Allen, Judson Boyce, 149n. 21

Ariosto, Ludovico: on Augustus, 34, 54–55; and Este line, 33; and imitation of Boiardo, 5; and imitation of Virgil, 70; and *Orlando furioso*, 5; and romance, 70

Aristotle: on praise, 105; and unity of action, 71

Augustus: as Aeneas, 34–35; as celebrated by Virgil, 33–34, 55, 65, 68, 82–83; as criticized by Virgil, 34–36; as criticized by Dryden, 151n. 12; as peace-bringer, 54. See also Ariosto; James I

Bacon, Sir Francis, 51–53
Bakhtin, M. M.: and addressivity, 144nn. 11, 13, 14; and parody, 114
Baldwin, T. W.: on Celaeno, 75; on Juno, 82; on Medea, 127; on Shakespeare's knowledge of Virgil, 17
Barroll, J. Leeds, 166n. 19
Bauhin, Johann, 90

Beaumont, Sir Thomas, 50
Bernardus Silvestris: on elm, 90; on Elysian Fields, 78; on golden bough, 90; on Mercury, 109; on Virgil as allegorist, 28, 31
Blackwood, Adam, 50
Bloom, Harold, 5
Boccaccio: and imitation, 11; on Virgil glorifying Augustus, 34
Bono, Barbara, 3
Bourdieu, Pierre, 67, 166n. 21, 176n. 19
Bowra, C. M., 175n. 5
Bradshaw, Brendan, 162n. 81
Brown, Alexander, 160n. 69
Bruno, Giordano, 171n. 10, 172n. 17
Burke, Kenneth, x, 74
Butler, Edmund, 61

Caesar, Sir Julius, 117
Calendar of State Papers, Ireland, 59
Camden, William, 163n. 90
Caxton, 103
Cecil, Robert, Earl of Salisbury: on clemency, 126; on Great Contract, 47; on James and finance, 8, 97; on impositions, 47, 115; and Ireland, 62, 63; on justice, 124; on king as *primum mobile*, 52. See also Parliament, 1610
Chamberlain, John, 47
Chapman, George, 38
Chicester, Sir Arthur, 62–64; 161n. 78
Chronicle of Ireland, 59–62
Cicero, 24, 175n. 5
Cinthio, Giraldi: on killing of Turnus, 36; on unity of action, 72
Cleopatra, 35
Coldwell, David, 136–37
Colie, Rosalie, 172n. 16
Colonization, discourse of: Aeneas, ix; cannibal, 163n. 90; Carthage, x, 101–2; and critique of absolutism, 55, 58, 64–65; glory, 62; law, 56; liberty of the subject, 61, 63; *meum et tuum*, 56, 63; property, 56, 62, 63; right to dispute, 61; rule of law, 57; slavery, 57; Sythians, 163n. 90.

See also Absolutism, discourse of; Constitutionalism, discourse of; Ireland, colonization of; Virginia, colonization of
Commons, House of: silence and fear in, 119–20, 124–25. *See also* Colonization, discourse of; Consitutionalism, discourse of; Parliament, 1610; Parliament, members of; Petition of Right, 1610; Petition of Temporal Grievances; Prerogative, royal
Constitutionalism, discourse of: bondage, 46; complaint, 118, 120; consent, 50, 100, 113; contract, 99–100; dispute, 50, 118, 129; grievance, 48; law of nature, 49; law of reason, 50, 128; liberty of the subject, 48, 113; Magna Carta, 113; *meum et tuum*, 93; property, 48, 50, 113; reciprocity, 93, 94; 99–100, 112; restraint, 48, 118; rule of law, 51, 128; slavery, 46, 50, 113, 118. *See also* Absolutism, discourse of; Colonization, discourse of; Epideictic; Neoplatonism; Parliament, 1610; Parliament, members of
Cooper, Thomas: on *amictus*, 178n. 39; on *incumbo*, 147n. 14; on *praecipio*, 175n. 5; on *prospero*, 105
Croft, Pauline: on news of Parliament, 47, 156n. 48; on Prince Henry, 39, 171n. 14
Cuddy, Neil, 155n. 42

Dale, Thomas, 57
Davies, Sir John, x, 65, 66, 102
DiCesare, Mario A., 174n. 35
Douglas, Gavin: and imitation of Virgil, 136–37; and Landino, 30–31; and translation of Virgil, 30
Dryden, John, 151nn. 8, 12
Durling, Robert, 136

Edmondes, Sir Thomas, 113
Edward III, King of England, 115

Egerton, Thomas, Lord Ellesmere, 121
Elizabeth, Princess of England: and betrothal festivities, 43; and marriage negotiations, 41–42
Elizabeth I, Queen of England: celebrated by Spenser, 33; fiscal situation of, 44–45; and impositions, 115; and Ireland, 62
Epic: and epideictic, 6–7. See also Romance
Epideictic: and blame, 7–10, 111–22; and heroic poetry, 6–7; and persuasion, 9, 105; and praise, 7
Erskine-Hill, Howard, 150n. 2

Ficino, Marsilio: on golden bough, 90; on Mercury, 109
Flaherty, David H., 161n. 72
Fletcher, Angus, 69
Foster, Elizabeth Read, 171n. 12
Fulgentius, 28
Fuller, Nicolas, 119, 120

Geertz, Clifford, 177n. 27
Gerarde, John, 90
Gesta Grayorum, 108
Giamatti, Bartlett, 165n. 12
Gray, Robert, 56
Gray's Inn, 108
Greene, Thomas: on imitation, 5–6, 16–17, 143n. 6, 147n. 12; on parody, 114; on romance, 175n. 8; on Virgil imitating Homer, 32–33
Gunpowder Plot, 45
Gurr, Andrew, 48–49

Hakewill, William, 47
Harington, Sir John: on Ariosto imitating Boiardo, 5; on imitation, 4–5; "The Life of Ariosto," 4; and romance, 68
Hedley, Thomas, 112–13, 128
Helgerson, Richard, 163n. 85
Henry, Prince of Wales: as chastity, 96; as conqueror, 7, 96; cost of supporting, 39, 96–97; as dedicatee,

38; education of, 38; as figure of love, 7; investiture of, 38, 39; and *Londons Love*, 38; and marriage negotiations, 41–43; and *Masque of Queenes*, 16; and *Oberon*, 7; as patron of Virginia colony, 102; representation of, 38–40; as spendthrift, 39; as unifier, 39. See also James I
Henry IV, King of France, 41
Henry VII, King of England, 37
Hermes Trismegisthus, 108
Heroic poetry: and Aeneas, 27; and epideictic, 6–7; and romance, 69
Hobbes, Thomas, 34
Holinshed, Raphael, 59
Holles, Sir John, 152n. 26
Homer: and Achilles, 36, 123; and representation of private and public, 106; and Sturm, 13, 15; and Virgil, 13, 15, 19, 36
Hooker, John, alias Vowell, 59–62
Hoskyns, John, 50, 100, 128, 158n. 64
Howard, Henry, Earl of Surrey, 30
Hulme, Peter, 3, 169n. 41

Imitation: and allegory, 26–32; concealing in, 5, 20; conflation in, 24, 73, 75–77, 78–79, 88–92, 104, 106–7; as defiguration, 28–29; discontinuity in, 24, 26, 29, 73; of narrative kernels, 24–25; parody as, 114; revealing in, 5, 20; reversal in, 24–25, 73, 79, 88–92; and source, xi; and system in *The Tempest*, x, 4; translation as, 21; varying in, 23, 26. See also *Aeneid*; Ariosto; Greene; Harington; Jonson; Petrarch; Riffaterre; Seneca; Sturm; Tasso; *The Tempest*; Trousdale; Virgil
Ireland, colonization of; in Armagh, 63; as Carthage, 60, 66; and cess, 61, 63; Chicester on, 62–64; in *Chronicle of Ireland*, 59; Davies on, x, 65, 66, 102; and Elizabeth, 62; Hooker on, 59–62; and impositions, 61; James I and, 59; in Munster, 61;

and Parliament (1568), 61; and
Salisbury, 62; and H. Sidney, 50,
60, 61; and J. Stanyhurst, 60, 61; R.
Stanyhurst on, 59, 65; Stow on, 62;
and Tyrone, 63-64; in Ulster, 59,
62; and Waterford, 61. *See also*
Butler; Camden; Colonization, discourse of; Riche

James I, King of England: as Aeneas,
ix; as Augustus, ix, 7-8, 97, 125;
and Book of Bounty, 157n. 59; dissolves parliament, 53; and education
of Henry, 38; and financing, 44-45;
forbids dispute, 53; and *Hymenaei*,
82; and investiture of Henry, 39;
and Ireland, 62-63; and marriage
of children, 41; and masque, 67-68;
and patriarchy, 99-100; as peacebringer, 54; as philosopher, 108;
preface to *Works*, 7-8; as Sejanus,
54; as Tiberius, 54; and Union of
England and Scotland, 44, 45;
speeches of, 46, 47, 51-53, 55, 62,
99, 109, 112, 117-18, 120, 121,
124. *See also* Absolutism, discourse
of; Parliament, 1610; Prerogative,
royal
Jonson, Ben: and epideictic, 7;
Haddington Masque, ix; and Henry,
7, 38; *Hymenaei*, 82; on imitation,
11, 16; marginal glosses of, 17;
Masque of Queenes, 16; *Oberon*, 7,
8, 38; on unity in *Aeneid*, 71; Virgil
as authority for, 82

Kermode, Frank, 18, 90, 91, 136,
147n. 10, 172n. 19
Knapp, Charles, 147n. 14
Kott, Jan, 3, 26, 168n. 34, 175n. 10

Landino, Cristoforo: and allegory of
Aeneid, 1-6, 28, 29-30; on Avernus, 89; *Camaldolese Disputations*,
29; on Celaeno, 75; cited by Douglas, 30-31; on elm, 89; on Elysian
Fields, 78; in England, 30-31; on
the fury as avarice, 76; on golden
bough, 90; on journey of Aeneas,
171n. 10; on Stygian Swamp,
169n. 42; on Venus, 95-96
Lewknor, Samuel, 125
Londons Love, 38
Lords, House of, 49, 54. *See also*
Egerton; Parliament, 1610
Ludus Scacchiae: Chesse-play, 103

Macrobius, 170n. 7
Marcus, Leah, 145n. 19
Mark Antony, 35
Martin, Henry, 50, 111-12, 128
Mary I, Queen of England, 115
Merchant, W. Moelwyn, 159n. 69
Miola, Robert, 3, 142n. 3
Montague, Sir Henry, 49
Montague, James, Bishop of Winchester, 7
More, Sir Thomas: on chess, 103;
Utopia, 103

Neoplatonism: as absolutist, 72-73,
93; and allegory of *Aeneid*, 28; as
constitutionalist, 72-73, 93; and
hearing, 95; and moral defect, 86;
and service, 93, 97-98; and sight,
95; soul as mistress in, 97; and
wonder, 97. *See also* Bernardus Silvestris; Bruno; Ficino; Landino;
Macrobius
New Life of Virginia, 57
Norbrook, David, 170n. 3
Nosworthy, J. M., 3, 26

Olbrechts-Tyteca, L., 9
Orgel, Stephen, 3
Ovid: Medea in, 116, 127-29;
Metamorphoses, 136, 168n. 40
Owen, Sir Roger, x, 125

Panofsky, Erwin, 174n. 33
Parker, Patricia, 69
Parkinson, John: *Theatrum Botanicum*, 90
Parliament, 1606-7, 46. *See also*
Union of England and Scotland
Parliament, 1610: and Bates's Case,

45; and debate, 47–48; dissolved, 53; Great Contract, 46, 47, 51, 104; and Prince Henry, 39; impositions, 45, 47, 49, 51, 113, 115, 128; and James' request for financing, 44; as news, 47; speeches printed from, 47; and Troy, x; Union of England and Scotland, 44, 45, 46. *See also* Absolutism, discourse of; Cecil; Colonization, discourse of; Commons, House of; Constitutionalism, discourse of; Henry, Prince of Wales; James I; Lords, House of; Parliament, members of; Petition of Right, 1610; Petition of Temporal Grievances; Prerogative, royal
Parliament, members of. *See* Bacon; Beaumont; Blackwood; Caesar; Edmondes; Fuller; Hakewill; Hedley; Holles; Hoskyns; Lewknor; Martin; Montague, H.; Owen; Wentworth; Whitelocke
Parody, 114–15
Parry, Graham, 38, 153n. 29
Patterson, Annabel, 153n. 28
Patterson, Lee, 147n. 9
Perelman, Chaim, 9
Petition of Right, 1610, 50, 53, 118, 121
Petition of Right, 1628, 50
Petition of Temporal Grievances, 50–51, 115, 116, 118
Petrarch: on imitation, 4, 11, 12; and knowledge of classics, 16; letters of, 17
Phaer, Thomas: on *Aeneid*, 27; in *Chronicle of Ireland*, 59–60; and Douglas, 30; on golden bough, 91; and R. Stanyhurst, 102; translation by, 30, 89
Pitcher, John, 3, 173n. 31
Plotinus, 172n. 17
Pope, Alexander, 34
Prerogative, royal: Bates's Case, 45; Chicester on, 47; debate on, 44; and Queen Elizabeth, 44; and impositions, 45, 51; as indisputable, 117–18, 128; and necessary powers, 112; right to dispute, 50. *See also* James I; Parliament, 1610
Putnum, Michael, 36
Puttenham, George: on decorum, 9–10, 121; on praise, 105; on voice, 110

Quinn, Kenneth, 151n. 5

Raleigh, Sir Walter, 41–42, 153n. 28
Riche, Barnabe, 163n. 90
Riffaterre, Michael, 5, 143n. 6
Romance: and Ariosto, 70, 71; and Cinthio, 72; and epic, 68–72; and epic machinery, 109; as heroic poetry, 69; imitation in, 69; and Sidney, 68, 92; and Spenser, 68, 69, 92; and Tasso, 68–72; *The Tempest* as, 68–72; and Trissino, 72; and unity of action, 71; and wandering, 69–71; and wonder, 70, 74, 97
Russell, Conrad, 155n. 42

Salisbury, Earl of. *See* Cecil
Sandys, Sir Edwin, 57
Savoy, Duke of, 41
Saxl, Fritz, 174n. 33
Schmidgall, Gary, 3
Sejanus, 54
Seneca: on imitation, 12, 16; on *praecipere*, 175n. 5
Sessions, William, 170n. 8
Shakespeare, William: *All's Well That Ends Well*, 134; *As You Like It*, 134; *The Comedy of Errors*, 134; *Cymbeline*, 68, 177n. 32; *2 Henry IV*, 135; *Henry V*, 135, 136; *3 Henry VI*, 177n. 32; *King Lear*, 4; *Love's Labour's Lost*, 3; *A Midsummer Night's Dream*, 3, 134; *Pericles*, 68, 135; *Titus Andronicus*, 177n. 32; *Troilus and Cressida*, 135; *The Winter's Tale*, 68, 178n. 39. *See also The Tempest*
Sidney, Sir Henry, 59, 60, 61
Sidney, Sir Philip: on Aeneas, 27; *Defence of Poesie*, 27; and education

of princes, 92; and heroic poetry, 68; and plot of *King Lear*, 4
Silvestris, Bernardus. *See* Bernardus Silvestris
Smith, G. R., 157n. 62
Smith, Sir Thomas, 57
Sommerville, J. P., 99–100
Spenser, Sir Edmund: and allegory, 27, 70; and education of princes, 92; and Queen Elizabeth, 33; *The Faerie Queene*, 74; and Letter to Raleigh, 68; and Una's wandering, 69
Stanyhurst, James, 60, 61
Stanyhurst, Richard: on *Aeneid*, 27; and *Chronicle of Ireland*, 59–60; and Phaer, 59–60, 102; on plantation, 65
Still, Colin, 3, 74
Stow, John: *Abridgment*, 62; on plantation, 62
Strachey, William: as Aeneas, 65; and *Lawes Divine, Morall and Martiall*, 57; *A True Reportory of the Wrack*, ix
Sturm, Johannes: on Cicero, 24; on concealing, 14–16; on defiguration, 14, 28–29; on figuration, 14; on Homer and Virgil, 15–18, 73; *A Ritch Storehouse or Treasure*, 13; on techniques of imitation, 13–16, 26; on varying, 14–15, 18, 23, 101

Tasso, Torquato: on Aeneas, 27; celebrating Alfonso II, 33; on heroic poetry, 68, 69, 70; imitating Virgil, 136; on public and private, 33
The Tempest: and *Aeneid* (1–6), x, 4, 17, 24–25, 31–32; Ariel and Caliban, 110–22; betrothal masque, 67, 78–85; caricatures in, 117; cave of Prospero, 103; chess, 103–4; Claribel, 40–43; conspiracy in, 25, 86–92; discasement, 129–31; education of Ferdinand, 92–104; epilogue, 134–37; glistering apparel episode, 67, 85–92; harpy banquet, 67, 74–78; and Henry, 40; and James, 37; Juno, 81–83; line tree, 89–91; log-carrying, 97–103; magic in, 108–9, 126–29; as masque, 67–68; mercy in, 122–26; Miranda and Ferdinand, 77–83, 94–105; Miranda and Prospero, 99–100, 106–7; neoplatonism in, 72–73; political discourse in, 53–54; Prospero, 105–9; as romance, 68–72; reunion in, 129–31; revels speech, 83–85; Setebos, 114; and Shakespeare's knowledge of *Aeneid*, 17; swimming in, 21–23; Sycorax, 115, 116, 127; tempest in, 19–20; Widow Dido, 17–18. *See also* Absolutism, discourse of; Allegory; Colonization, discourse of; Constitutionalism, discourse of; Imitation
Theocritus, 13, 15
Tiberius, 54
Trissino, 72
Trousdale, Marion, 142n. 3
A True Declaration of the Estate of the Colonie in Virginia, 56
Trumbull, William, 113
Tyrone, 64

Union of England and Scotland: discourse of, 46; and James, 44, 45

Vickers, Brian, 105
Virgil: *Eclogues* 136; *Georgics*, 136; as imitator of Homer, 13, 15, 19, 36; as Platonist, 28. *See also Aeneid*; Imitation; Sturm; *The Tempest*
Virginia, colonization of: Council of Virginia, 66; and Dale, 57; discipline, 102; and form of government, 57; and Gray, 56; and Prince Henry, 102; and James, 57; and martial law, 57; *A New Life of Virginea*, 57; and Rome, 66; and Sandys, 57; and Smythe, 57; and Strachey, 57; *A True Declaration*, 56; Virginia Company, 57. *See also* Colonization, discourse of

Waswo, Richard, 65, 102
Webbe, William: *Discourse of English Poetrie*, 27
Wentworth, Thomas, 118, 122

Whitelocke, James, 47, 50, 113, 114
William, David, 129
Williamson, J. W., 145n. 19
Wiltenburg, Robert, 3, 142n. 2

www.ingramcontent.com/pod-product-compliance
Lightning Source LLC
Chambersburg PA
CBHW020947230426
43666CB00005B/214